PENGUIN BOOKS

STRANGER TO THE GAME

Bob Gibson lives in Omaha, Nebraska. Lonnie Wheeler is the co-author of *I Had a Hammer* and most recently of *Hard Stuff: The Autobiography of Mayor Coleman Young*. He lives in New Richmond, Ohio.

# STRANGER TO THE GAME

## BOB GIBSON

### AND LONNIE WHEELER

PENGUIN BOOKS

PENGUIN BOOKS
Published by the Penguin Group
Penguin Books USA Inc., 375 Hudson Street,
New York, New York 10014, U.S.A.
Penguin Books Ltd, 27 Wrights Lane, London W8 5TZ, England
Penguin Books Australia Ltd, Ringwood, Victoria, Australia
Penguin Books Canada Ltd, 10 Alcorn Avenue,
Toronto, Ontario, Canada M4V 3B2
Penguin Books (N.Z.) Ltd, 182–190 Wairau Road,
Auckland 10, New Zealand

Penguin Books Ltd, Registered Offices: Harmondsworth, Middlesex, England

First published in the United States of America by Viking Penguin,
a division of Penguin Books USA Inc., 1994
Published in Penguin Books 1996

1  3  5  7  9  10  8  6  4  2

THE LIBRARY OF CONGRESS HAS CATALOGUED THE HARDCOVER AS FOLLOWS:
Gibson, Bob.
Stranger to the game/Bob Gibson and Lonnie Wheeler.
p.   cm.
ISBN 0-670-84794-1 (hc.)
ISBN 0 14 01.7528 8 (pbk.)
1. Gibson, Bob.   2. Baseball players—United States—Biography.
I. Wheeler, Lonnie.   II. Title.
GV865.G5A3   1993
796.357′092—dc20
[B]   94–11049

Printed in the United States of America
Set in Century Old Style

*To my son, Robert Christopher Gibson.*
*May your life be as rewarding as mine,*
*and, I hope, a little easier.*

# ACKNOWLEDGMENTS

The authors have numerous people to thank for their generous assistance in pulling this book together. Among them:

Former Cardinals (and Bob Gibson's valued friends) Curt Flood, Tim McCarver, Joe Torre, Mike Shannon, Bill White, Reggie Smith, Orlando Cepeda, Dal Maxvill, Dick Allen, Bob Uecker, Joe Hoerner, and Nelson Briles;

Former ballplayers Hank Aaron, Willie Horton, Johnny Bench, Jim Ray Hart, Ed Charles, Doug Flynn, Earl Williams, and Richie Ashburn.

Broadcasters Harry Caray and Jack Buck, sportswriter Bob Broeg, and trainer Gene Gieselmann;

Friends and relatives Fred Gibson, Anita Gibson, Barbara Jean Stevens, and Chuck Newby;

Former Omaha Tech High School coach Neal Mosser;

Historians Kevin Grace and Tom Van Hyning;

And *Omaha World Herald* librarian Jean Donohoe.

Bob Gibson would like to extend a special thanks to a couple of buddies who have stood by him over the years, Rodney Wead and Norman Hahn.

Literary agent David Black and editor Nan Graham made the book happen, and Bob Schron's original research was the foundation upon which it was developed.

Finally, Wendy Gibson was warmly supportive throughout the project—and mashed some mean potatoes, as well.

*The man was going to war when he pitched. When he pitched,
I'd say to myself, "You'd better have your shit together today,
Reg, because it's gonna be a war."*
—REGGIE SMITH,
*former teammate of Bob Gibson*

# INTRODUCTION

The thing is, Bob Gibson was washed up by the time Reggie Smith joined him on the Cardinals in 1974. That might seem like a cold thing to say about a prideful man and Hall of Fame pitcher whose autobiography I'm coauthoring here, but plainspoken truth is something the guy has never had a problem with (he is regarded, in fact, as one of its foremost practitioners); and besides, his own knees said it first. The right one was blown out in 1973, but both of them were practically shot by then anyway and Gibson pitched the last few years on guts and brains. Smith should have seen him before that, when the guts and brains had legs—long, strong, basketball legs that seemed, as he kicked and whirled and cata-pulted off the rubber, to make up about three-fourths (his arms were also about three-fourths, totaling a pitcher and a half) of maybe the best ath-lete who ever squinted at a catcher's gnarled fingers. Anybody who cares anything about baseball or has an interest in what the game used to be all about or what it's like when a great athlete takes it to the limit should have seen Bob Gibson in his prime.

Actually, Smith, who was with the Red Sox at the time, caught a good glimpse of Gibson in the 1967 World Series (which the Cardinals won), and anybody who knew Gibson from the World Series—any World Series—knew him well because that was when he revealed himself. What a thing he was in the World Series. Everyone would be making a fuss about all the pressure of the World Series and here, with two fingers gripped across the seams of the ball held behind his back, was a fellow who had grown up playing on black ghetto teams that would pile into borrowed trucks and get out at little soybean towns in Iowa, where, about the fifth inning or so, his big brother, the coach, would stand out in the middle of the diamond mad as hell about whatever way his boys were being cheated this time and offer to take on the whole place. There were tough choices on those days: to win and face the town or lose and face the brother. Knowing Josh Gibson as they did, Bob and his buddies took their chances with the town every time. The World Series? For Gibson, it was heaven, Iowa without knuckles, a day at the ballpark devoted to nothing but the pure pursuit of being the best. It was a frosty mug of his favorite thing—winning—in its most concentrated state. He devoured it. In the most studious book written on the World Series, baseball historian Joe Reichler rated Gibson as the best World Series pitcher there ever was.

Under the heading of "Best Pitcher There Ever Was," Gibson also ranks at the top of the subcategory "In a Single Season." The season was 1968, and if Gibson didn't own baseball that year, he at least had it rented for the summer. National League batters, presuming to stand before him and hit, came and went at his unpitying discretion, as attested by the 1.12 earned run average that has not been matched in modern history. In the Year of the Pitcher he was the Pitcher of the Year, the pitcher of all years. The next-best ERA in the National League was 1.99 (by Bob Bolin of San Francisco), and despite the abnormal pitching statistics that characterized the 1968 season, the fact is that no other ERA champion has ever led a league by such a vast percentage. No other pitcher has ever put shivering fastballs and cutthroat sliders on the outside corner with such methodical, unbroken, devastating consistency. So thorough was Gibson's mastery of the game (two earned runs in *eight weeks*) that the St. Louis relievers, baseball's equivalent of Maytag repairmen, were reduced to playing board games in the bullpen. "Unhittable" is not a tenable word in the context of major-league baseball, but in this case it suffices. Doug Rader, a former third baseman for the Houston Astros and major-league manager, was once asked to name the five toughest pitchers he ever encountered, and to start off he said, "That's easy. Bob Gibson in 1968." The other four: "Bob Gibson in 1969, Bob Gibson in 1970, Bob Gibson in 1971, and Bob Gibson in 1972. No one else was even close."

Hitters, of course, are neither a unified caucus nor an objective band of men, and some of them from Gibson's day will single out Sandy Koufax or Don Drysdale or Juan Marichal or Jim Maloney or possibly some otherwise pedestrian pitcher as the most troubling in their experience. The same list of suspects comes up in discussions about the fastest fastball, etc. Regarding Gibson, however, they are fervently and eloquently unanimous about one specific thing: In the pitching fraternity, he was the alpha and omega of competitors. If Gibson's speed was memorable—and it was—his fierceness was legendary. If his overall athletic skills were remarkable—and they were (nine straight Gold Glove awards, five stolen bases in 1969, a .303 batting average in 1970, a team-record twenty-four career home runs)—his noncompliance with pain was inspiring. If his records and achievements are historic—they were sufficient to get him elected to the Hall of Fame on the first ballot despite a career-long public relations problem—his baseball immortality obtains rather from the impression he left on the game. That impression was created by the chilling expression cloaking his face when he turned for the sign; by the rear ends he reddened when batters failed to show proper respect for his inalienable right to a part of the plate; by the night he pitched to three batters on a broken leg; by the will to win that came through palpably in every grunt and grimace and game situation; by the stories he deposited in baseball's bounty of oral history.

There's scarcely a National Leaguer from Gibson's time who doesn't have an anecdote or more about him. Most of them have to do with various aspects of intimidation—guys he knocked down or somehow scared the hell out of. The stories stack up as Gibson's monument and they dramatically commemorate his place in the game, but they also serve a more subtle and possibly larger purpose. Having already become lore in just twenty years, they are testimonies of a different kind of player in a different kind of time. The game has changed that much since Gibson played.

It is no longer the kind of sport that extends the athlete's competitive limits, no longer the kind of pastime that begets legends and characters. At this point, the likes of Bob Gibson must be celebrated or lost.

The poignancy of his tale arises from the realization that we are on the brink of losing him. Baseball has replaced its locks to keep out estranged family members such as Gibson, whose only connection to the contemporary game is in our memories. It's a shame, because a man like Gibson has much more than war stories to offer. He represents baseball when it was better, and more like him would make it better again. What baseball is missing, exactly, is guys who play hurt and go the distance and scheme and pester and bully—anything to get an edge; anything to *win*—and perhaps hate each other (some of the best hitters and pitchers used to hate each other on *principle* if not for personal reasons) and, although this one might be pushing the envelope of plausibility, negotiate their own one-year contracts. What it's missing is Bob Gibson.

It's flagrantly ironic that so many other old Cardinals, in particular from the world championship team of 1964, have gained prodigiously in baseball prominence since retiring as players. The Cardinals were baseball's best and brightest, and while eschewing Gibson—as well as Curt Flood and Lou Brock—the game, in a manner not pertinent to any other club, has embraced the multiple talents of Bill White, Tim McCarver, Bob Uecker, Roger Craig, Mike Shannon, and Dal Maxvill, among others. Good and plugged-in friends of Gibson's such as White, McCarver, Shannon, and Joe Torre, the current St. Louis manager, would like to return his rare qualities to baseball, but it seems that the obstacles, while vague and largely unidentified, are almost institutional or, short of that, pervasive. Gibson, of course, is not the type to passively tolerate such an affront. One of the skills on which he prided himself as a ballplayer was agitating, and it is one, unlike foot speed, that he has retained undiminished. He applies it now to the forces that keep him out of the game he gave himself over to.

This, however, does not make Gibson a disagreeable man on all fronts; far from it. The point is extremely germane because Gibson's peevishness—and he will admit that he put on a forbidding game face as a pitcher—is at or near the center of his frustrations. It is a matter of reputation, and Gibson's, aside from the pitching credentials, is not good. In this context, the critics grossly misunderstand him. He was unfriendly (some would opt for *mean*) as a pitcher because he thought it made him a *better* pitcher; but the same demeanor does not make him a better father (to his ten-year-old son, Christopher) or husband (to his second wife, Wendy) or carpenter or businessman, and it would not make him a better baseball executive if the opportunity ever, belatedly, presented itself. And so his petulant side has been, for the most part, retired alongside uniform number 45.

Nobody makes more demands upon a person than his collaborator, and this one will testify that there is simply no legitimacy to the chronic opinion that Bob Gibson is difficult, that he is unapproachable. On the contrary, I found Gibson to be the standard for agreeable, against which most other public figures have quite a ways to go. When I visited Omaha to conduct research and interviews for this book, he put me up in his house, cooked dinner, drove me around, invited *other people* over for me to talk to (this, trust me, goes well beyond the industry norms), dug up his old pictures and even *had them copied* so that I could take them along. After I was back home, he called, without prompting, as he remembered stories he hadn't told me. He is so approachable to his friends that they walk through his front door without knocking. His kitchen table is a community center. This is not to suggest that Gibson has turned into Mister Rogers, or that he has lost any of his characteristic directness. (When I called one Saturday afternoon in January, during the NFL playoffs, he said, "Aren't you watching the game?" I said, "I'm trying to write your autobiography. I can't be watching football games." He said, "Well, if you're not going to watch, at least know what's going on so you don't call me with three minutes left in the half.") But there is no offense intended in his indelicate manner, and none taken by those who really know him. After a while, in fact, his frankness takes on the hue of an attribute.

Unfortunately, though, baseball doesn't see it that way. It seems bent on becoming a kinder, gentler game, and would apparently prefer not to see Bob Gibson at all except in the old World Series clips, which preserve him ready, focused, and loose-jointed, his cap pulled purposefully over his face, glove resting impatiently on his left hip, sweat rolling onto his wrists from under his suffocating red sweatshirt, then his arms pumping into accelerated motion, the left leg jamming into the slope of the mound and the right rushing over it in an urgent, arms-flailing tumble toward first base as the pitch, white-hot and sizzling with intensity, singes the outside corner at the knees.

In the politically correct, number-crunched, no-salt-added modern facsimile of baseball, there is no place for an old pitcher to whom the game, any game, was war. And so, for the October hero of the St. Louis Cardinals, the battle drags wearily on.

L.W.

February 1994

# STRANGER TO THE GAME

# CHAPTER I

In the summer of 1968, I mastered my craft.

I attribute it mainly to evolution—mine and baseball's. I was thirty-two years old at the time and in my prime, having started late as a pitcher by reason of a youth devoted to other duties on the diamond, not to mention basketball. When I started winning in 1961 (not coincidentally, the year my favorite manager, Johnny Keane, replaced my least favorite manager, Solly Hemus) and getting the breaking ball over the plate, I won more and more each year until Roberto Clemente fractured my leg with a line drive in July of 1967. But I put away three victories against the Red Sox that fall in the World Series, which the Cardinals won, and picked up from there in 1968, by which time I was doing with the ball pretty much as I wished.

This is not to say that I was a perfect pitcher, because I made mistakes (although not as many as other years) and a perfect pitcher is an impossible concept, anyway, as long as major-league hitters remain capable, as many are (damn them), of hitting perfect pitches. But in 1968, we of the pitching profession came as close to perfect as we've ever come in modern history and probably ever will. It wasn't only me. There was Detroit's Denny McLain with thirty-one victories in the other league, where Carl

Yastrzemski won the batting title at .301. Don Drysdale of the Dodgers pitched 58⅔ scoreless innings in a row, a record that I would have broken but for a wild pitch in Los Angeles that might have been scored differently in a city that didn't have a conflict of interest. And my earned run average, 1.12, was the lowest since Babe Ruth invented the home run, so to speak.

That was in 1919, after which baseball became a different game. The owners, rolling their mustaches over the public response to Ruth, pumped up the ball so that the Babe and the rest of the hitters could knock it over the fences with less resistance. From that moment on, the pattern in base-ball has generally been that when changes are made in the rules or param-eters of the game, they are made for the benefit of the hitters. I've often thought that pitchers should have some legal recourse against this shame-less form of collusion by the owners—that we should be able to sue the bastards for messing with our earning power.

Inevitably, by virtue of our inherent preeminence (we are an egotistical breed by nature), pitchers have been able, over time, to reestablish the fundamental order of things. Sandy Koufax helped this process along in the mid-sixties, and by 1968, vitalized by the breakthrough of black and Latin pitchers, our ranks included such artists as Juan Marichal of the Giants, Luis Tiant of the Indians, and Ferguson Jenkins of the Cubs (to go along with Drysdale, McLain, the Giants' Gaylord Perry, and the Mets' Tom Seaver). We all threw hard and threw sliders and hit the corners and moved the batters off the plate to make certain they understood who was setting the agenda. There is no other way to explain the Year of the Pitcher, as it is called, except to acknowledge that we had raised the indus-try standards. Pitchers are more capable of this than hitters for the simple reason that the pitcher initiates the exchange between the two. A pitcher has inventiveness, strategy, and a wide range of physiological alternatives at his disposal to complicate things for the batter, who has no workable op-tion but to hit the ball in the form that it is delivered to him. The pitcher acts and the batter reacts, and consequently, evolution favors the former. The 1968 season was hard evidence of this; our success was obviously not occasioned by a lack of competent hitters, whose number included Clemente and Hank Aaron and Willie Mays and Pete Rose and Willie McCovey and Richie (later "Dick") Allen and Ernie Banks and Billy Williams and Willie Stargell and Orlando Cepeda and two Alous (Felipe and Matty) in the National League alone. We had simply become damn good at what we did.

In the eyes of the baseball establishment, we had, in fact, become too good. My earned run average was Exhibit A in the case it constructed against the pitcher, and in that respect, peculiar as it seems, my effect on the game was similar to Ruth's. On account of first him and then me, half a century later, the balance between pitcher and hitter was artificially manipulated in favor of the latter.

When done in Ruth's day this was, by universal consent, a good thing for the game, which had been sullied by the Black Sox scandal in 1919. I suppose there are those who believe that the changes of 1969 were also positive. By lowering the pitcher's mound and condensing the strike zone, baseball certainly introduced more offense into the game. But it wasn't content to stop there. The strike zone seems to shrink a little more each year, its upper limit now being the navel; and the most radical, unnatural modification of all lies in the manner that pitchers have been restricted east-west. They are no longer permitted to miss inside by any significant or purposeful amount. Leagues and umpires now levy suspensions and heavy fines for this sort of indiscretion, and the batters, taking their cue from the authorities, are swelled with enough righteous indignation to rush the mound vengefully if a pitch merely strays too close for their comfort.

The effect of this important nuance had been enormous, in my estimation. To a degree equal to or greater than their impact on hitting in the major leagues, the pitching constraints have simultaneously—and more significantly—undermined the basic competitiveness of the game. The major-league baseball I knew and loved was a battle between the pitcher and the hitter. Hank Aaron, for instance, despised pitchers nearly as much as I despised hitters. I wouldn't even say hello to hitters on the other teams, because I didn't want one of them to get the idea that I liked him or something, or that, since I'd given him the time of day once, I might not buzz one under his chin. Hitters were the enemy, and the inside pitch was my warhead. My mission was to win, and the only man who could keep me from completing that mission was the son of a bitch in the batter's box.

It didn't matter who it was. I was completely indiscriminate in my attitude toward hitters, because there wasn't one of them who wasn't trying to beat me. Bill White, for instance, was one of my best friends on the Cardinals for a long time, and still is, but he was also the damnedest pull hitter I ever saw. He'd stand up there stiff as new blue jeans and pull everything that came within flailing distance. He'd pull a fast one; he'd pull a slow one; he'd pull his own teeth if he were ahead in the count. I'd watch him reach over the plate with those big robot arms of his and pull fastballs that could have been pitchouts. As a pitcher, I considered that a form of cheating, at worst, and at best overconfidence. I advised Bill that if he were ever traded away and came to bat against me, he should *not* try to pull a pitch on the outside corner. Well, in 1966 the Cardinals sent him to the Phillies; and the first time he batted against me I threw a fastball four or five inches outside and *damn* if that sucker didn't lean in and whip it foul down the first-base line. The next pitch found its way to his elbow. Bill couldn't believe it. He looked at me and yelled, "You're crazy, Gibson!" I shouted something back, then he went down to first base and we got on with the ballgame. When his elbow stopped hurting, Bill understood that I had to do what I'd told him I was going to do.

There was a general understanding, in fact, between pitchers and hitters, the basis of it being that each had certain entitlements. The hitters were entitled to establish their own hitting zone and to take advantage of the pitchers' mistakes, and the pitchers were entitled to keep the hitters within those parameters—to keep them honest, more or less, and prevent them from taking liberties that exceeded the implicit contract. Despite the impression given off by the incriminating folklore that has accumulated over the years, I was certainly not the only pitcher to interpret the guidelines in such a way.

*The first time I batted against Don Drysdale, he struck me out on three pitches the first two times up. After that, I was determined not to strike out the third time. Then he got two strikes on me and I thought, okay, you've got to do something here. So I choked up and punched the ball, hit a line drive to right. The ball was caught and I was oh for three, but the fourth time I came up he wheeled*

*me out of there. I got up, dusted myself off, looked out at the*
*mound and said, "You're right. I was cheating." I had violated*
*the code, and we both knew it. I had no argument with him.*
　　　　　　　　　　　—MIKE SHANNON
　　　　　　　　　　　*former Cardinal*

It seemed that somebody was invariably being knocked down when the Cardinals played the Dodgers, and neither team thought any less of the other for it. I particularly admired the Dodgers' pitchers, because guys like Drysdale and Stan Williams and Koufax raised the level of competition by claiming their territory and daring you to take it from them. Koufax was the nicest of the bunch, but he could not have achieved the success he did without asserting himself on the mound now and then. In 1965, he shut us out three times in a row and we desperately needed to find a way to get to him. Lou Brock finally discovered that he could beat Koufax by bunting on him. Twice in a row, Brock bunted for a base hit, stole a base or two and scored. It was a major breakthrough for us, and everybody knew that the next move was Koufax's—that he somehow had to stop Brock. I knew how *I* would do it, but Koufax was not an aggressive man by nature and I wasn't sure if he had it in him to take control of the situation. He had been bunted into a corner, however, and before it went any further he did what he had to do. He came in on Brock the next time and fractured his shoulder. Nobody charged the mound. Brock went down to first base and wouldn't even rub it until he came into the dugout after the inning.

One of the very first times I faced the Dodgers, I had to take a comparable stand with Duke Snider. Snider was an excellent left-handed pull hitter, and I pitched him away even though the Los Angeles Coliseum had a short left field. When he saw what I was doing, he reached out and poked one over that friendly left-field fence. That was fair enough, but the next time I was still pitching him outside and I noticed he was edging out that way, daring me by venturing close to the plate. So I threw the next one tight to brush him back. He was still expecting the pitch away, and leaned into it. The ball broke his elbow. As far as I was concerned, though, he had named the tune and there was no need to apologize. I saw Snider later, and he kind of laughed and said he had really caught it good that time. He understood.

It was for that sort of thing that the media often referred to me with words like angry and menacing and glowering. But all those words missed the point. My thing was winning. I didn't see how being pleasant or amiable had anything to do with winning, so I wasn't pleasant on the mound and I wasn't amiable off it. Pitching inside, on the other hand, had a lot to do with winning, so I pitched inside. For that reason, I certainly wasn't what you would call batter-friendly. But even so, in spite of what a lot of people seemed to think and say—and still do—I never hit batters for the sake of hitting them. That would have had nothing to do with winning, either. You don't frighten big-league hitters. The idea of pitching inside is not to strike fear into their hearts, but to make them think about and re- spect the inside pitch. Then, while they're mindful of the inside pitch, you throw outside to get the job done. In my day, pitching tight was a funda- mental element of strategy. It was a matter of doing what was necessary to get the batter out; and if that made me mean, then what the hell, I guess I was mean.

By that definition, a lot of pitchers in my day were mean, and some, like Drysdale and Williams, were meaner than I was. I seemed to be *consid-ered* the meanest, however, and I believe there were some specific reasons for that. One was my color. I don't believe I would have been nearly as threatening to white people if, like Drysdale and Williams, I had been their color. Another was that I was impatient. When I was on the mound, I didn't believe in screwing around; I wanted only to get the ball and throw it and win the game and go home. Also, my arm usually hurt, and my gri- mace might have been mistaken for a glare. On top of that, I didn't wear my glasses when I pitched and I couldn't *see* very well. I had to squint to get the signs from McCarver, and that might have been a little unnerving to the guy standing sixty feet away. Of course, my antipathy for the batter might have shown through a little bit, too. The fact is, I didn't feel very charitable toward him and his intentions at the plate.

*I wouldn't say that Gibson was unfriendly when he pitched. Hate-*
*ful is more like it. Drysdale was the same way. He didn't talk*

*much to other players, either. Late in Drysdale's career, he walked up and shot the breeze with me for a minute or so before a game one day, and I thought, "Hey, this son of a bitch must be ready to retire." Sure enough, he announced his retirement the next week.*

*My first personal contact with Gibson came in the 1965 all-star game. I knew Gibson was an asshole. I can say that now because he's one of my best friends in the world, but on the field he tried to intimidate you. Hitters like to be relaxed at the plate, and what helps them relax is that they have a little idea of what's in the head of the pitcher. When the pitcher doesn't let you in, you really don't know. Gibby wouldn't let anybody in. He wouldn't even talk to his teammates at the all-star game.*

*In the 1965 game in Minnesota, I was catching and he came in to pitch the last inning. We had a 6–5 lead, and the first man up was Tony Oliva. It goes strike one, strike two, and I know what I want him to do next. Oliva's a great low fastball hitter, so I want him to come up with the ball. I think, should I just signal that, or should I go out and tell him so I won't second-guess myself? I went out and said, "Bob, a good fastball up and in. Not down and in, up and in." He just looked at me as if I wasn't there. I turned around and went behind the plate and called fastball. He threw it down and in. Double to left center. I said, Well, fuck it, I did what I had to do. He then proceeded to strike out the next three guys. One of them was Killebrew, who killed fastballs and had already homered against Maloney, who threw as hard as anybody in baseball. Gibson threw him nothing but fastballs. The last out was Joe Pepitone, and I'll never forget it. He threw Pepitone two fastballs, and Gibson's fastball sailed so much that after the second one, Pepitone turned to me and said, "Throw me that high slider again." I said, "Okay." Gibson throws another fastball and strikes him out on three pitches.*

*After the game, he and I are the last two in the shower. I turn to him and say, "Great pitching." He's just soaping himself down like I'm not even in the damn shower. Wouldn't say a word. That's just the way he was.*

> *When I was traded to the Cardinals four years later, he was the
> first one to welcome me.*
> —JOE TORRE
> *Cardinal manager and former Gibson teammate*

These days, there is a more neighborly air between the pitcher and the
hitter. Modern trends have made them allies in many important respects.
Many share an agent. They play golf together and consort in business affairs, subscribing to the same source of career advice. Meanwhile, they
are well aware that their confrontations on the field will be closely moni-
tored by the umpires, and consequently one has no reason to regard the
other, his professional cohort, as an immediate threat to his livelihood.
The real gamesmanship in which they participate is conducted largely off
the field, in strategy sessions at the agent's office. The rules promote this
sort of congeniality. They ensure that major-league baseball does not become personally adversarial to the point of being fierce. The rancor between the pitcher and the hitter, which characterized the game in my time
and Ruth's and Cobb's and Musial's, has been legislated out in favor of a
kinder, gentler game in which there is more cheap offense for the paying
customer.

If I were the paying customer, however, while I might take momentary
delight in a wealthy third baseman drifting into a fastball away for a
350-foot home run, I would much prefer a pitched battle at sixty feet six
inches. This might be my bias as a pitcher coming through, but I believe
I'm speaking instead as a baseball person—in the interest of the game—
when I say that I take offense at the concept of more offense, coming, as
it has, at the expense of traditional, hard-nosed sportsmanship. I'm proud
to have been part of a great game, but these days I hardly recognize it.

All of these developments have put considerable distance between me
and the institution to which I have devoted my best years. Over the past
decade or so, I've often heard broadcasters say that a guy like Bob Gibson
wouldn't be able to make a living in baseball today. I disagree with the
premise—as a pitcher compelled to win by whatever means were available, I'd like to think I would find a way to do so under the present or any
conditions—but I acknowledge, all the same, that baseball, through its

rule changes, gentrification, and sterilization, has done what it can to exterminate domineering, battle-dressed players (especially pitchers) like the kind I admired and attempted to be. More pertinent to me is the painful irony of what the broadcasters say. The fact is that I *can't* make a living in baseball today. Believe me, I've tried.

I've held a few media jobs that ended abruptly for one reason or another, usually of my doing. I've coached a couple of times under Torre, but it's been quite a while now, and I'm restless. The Cardinals won't have anything to do with me despite my close relationship with the manager. I had a position lined up with Bill White and the National League, but it was sidetracked by at least one of the clubs. Baseball writer Murray Chass pointed out recently in *The New York Times* that I hadn't held a major-league job in nine years and that "as poor as the quality of pitching has become, this is one former pitcher who could add knowledge and attitude to any staff." The phone never rang afterwards. I attempt to come up with specific reasons for this state of affairs, and I have a few theories, which I'll get into later, but basically it boils down to the fact that baseball, by all indications, wants nothing to do with the likes of me—nothing to do, that is, with a glowering black man who wouldn't make small talk or apologize for pitching inside.

Nowadays, I'm much more accommodating than I was as a player—I don't have to go out and *pitch* anymore—but I still don't make apologies for the way I did my job on the mound, and if I could still pitch, I'd still pitch inside. In fact, that's what I'm doing here, in a manner of speaking. I advise you not to lean too close to the book.

# CHAPTER II

We all noticed a change in my oldest brothers, Josh and Richard, when they returned from the war. They never talked about what had happened; I only knew, from their moods and their attitudes and from what I'd heard about the experiences of other black soldiers, that the service had been profoundly disillusioning. Josh, the oldest, was stationed in India, where many of the locals actually believed that black people had tails. He would be walking down the street and Indians would sneak in behind him trying to get a good look. Richard was with the Air Corps in Italy, and something there apparently disturbed him deeply. He became angry and withdrawn. At one point after they were back home, Josh and Richard fell into a long, impassioned argument, presumably about the past, and their relationship was never the same afterwards.

Richard kept to himself and before long moved to New York. Meanwhile, Josh (whose real name was Leroy, although nobody called him that) completed his work for an undergraduate degree in history, got a job in a meatpacking plant, and settled down with the rest of the family in Omaha, which was to my good fortune because he had always been the central figure in my life—father, coach, teacher, and role model. I could add "pain in the ass," but, while essentially true, that would be grossly ungrateful for all that Josh did—not only for me, but for all the boys in the ghetto. We were all, one way or another, a reflection of Josh.

I can never remember a time when Josh didn't have adult responsibilities. He was fifteen years older than me and became the man of the family after my father, Pack Gibson, died from what we called quick consumption (a form of tuberculosis) in 1935, a few months before I was born as the seventh and final Gibson. From what I'm told, Mother and the other kids were a wreck, and some of the older ones—Beulah and Richard and maybe even Josh himself—were so distraught that they wouldn't even eat. My mother placed a gray wreath on the front door, and to this day my sister Barbara Jean won't buy a Christmas wreath because it reminds her of our father dying. But Josh put his mourning aside and stepped right in to keep us going.

Fortunately, he didn't have to earn a lot of money to replace my father's income, because my father didn't have much of an income. My mother, Victoria, worked at Omaha Lace Laundry and cleaned houses and hospitals in her spare time, but my father, who was considerably older, wasn't so lucky. He couldn't find steady work as a cabinetmaker, despite the considerable skill he'd brought to Nebraska from Louisiana (which he had fled to get away from a miserable stepmother), and often covered the rent by doing carpentry work for the landlord. When they first moved north, he and my mother had both held jobs at hotels in Lincoln, but those positions dried up during the Depression and my father caught on with construction crews for the Works Progress Administration in Omaha. That kept him going only temporarily, however, and afterwards he was employed off and on by the city as a janitor. All the while—particularly during the down times—he donated his services to Morningstar Baptist Church, where he was a trustee. Among other projects, he built a pulpit that's still in the church's basement, with his initials carved into it. (Having been named Pack Robert Gibson in my father's honor, my initials were also P.G.—originally. But while I revere the legacy of my father, I couldn't stand his first name and had it changed to Robert as soon as I was on my own.)

My mother's brother, Napoleon Brown—we called him Uncle Son—

lived with us after my father died, and helped manage the family. I thoroughly enjoyed the fried chicken he brought home every Saturday night (during the week we ate mostly rice, pinto beans, and the vegetables we grew in the garden), but even so I always thought of Mother as my provider and Josh as my protector. When at the age of three I became deathly sick with asthma or pneumonia—my family seems to disagree on the particulars—Josh was the one who wrapped me in a quilt, carried me to the hospital, and promised to buy me a baseball glove if I got well. According to what a nurse told my mother, as they were about to wheel me into some dark room for treatment, I looked up at the nurse and asked, "Are you going to kill me?" When she said no, I said, "Good. Please don't kill me because my brother Josh told me that if I don't die, he'll buy me a baseball glove." It was a while before I could use the glove, however, because I was weakened by childhood diseases I only faintly remember, including a bone problem called rickets, for which my mother laid me out in the sun in a buggy to strengthen my marrow (despite the efforts of Barbara Jean, who tried her best to pull me out of the buggy so she could play with it).

After Josh earned his degree from Creighton University, he searched all over the city for a job as a teacher and coach. When he was unable to find one, it aggravated the disillusionment he had obtained during the war and prompted him to do several things: He became very angry; he abandoned whatever faith he still had in the American dream; and he organized the neighborhood kids into athletic teams at a recreation center on Lake Street.

By then, we were living at the Logan Fontenelle projects, having moved there after several bad experiences in rented houses on Maple and Hamilton streets on the north side of the city, including one on Hamilton that was infested with rats after the foundation caved in from snow. We nailed tin cans over holes in the floor to keep the rats out, but they ate through the cans and one of them bit me in the ear while I was sleeping. Another house of ours on Hamilton was haunted, according to Barbara Jean, who said she saw a ghostly image standing next to her once in the bathroom. Another time, as she was getting ready for bed, a strange voice called her name. She told our brother Fred about it, and Fred ordered her to fetch him the baseball bat. She said, "What if it's Jesus? You gonna hit him if it's Jesus?" Fred said, "Yep." That's the way Fred was.

These days, people think of housing projects as the urban dregs, representing all that is vulgar and depraved about ghetto life, but to us in 1942, Logan Fontenelle was heaven in Nebraska. It was, at worst, a gilded ghetto. The units were brick, they were new, they were centrally heated—we were accustomed to the house being frigid until we got the fire going in the morning—and best of all, there were ball fields and running tracks just a few steps from our doors. Actually, the track was a sidewalk that rimmed the grassy plaza in the center of the major black section of housing, but to us it was a perfect layout for relay races, long sprints—we had both a 440 circuit and a 220—and barrel-jumping on roller skates. It was no coincidence that, year after year, the best sprinters in Nebraska came out of Logan Fontenelle. In many urban neighborhoods, you had to be mean to survive, but in ours, you had to be *fast*. Speed was the thing that separated the men from the boys at Logan Fontenelle. I could move well enough to hold my own, but even so, I was no match for guys like Leon Chambers, who was about the quickest I ever saw. Mind you, this is coming from a man who played with Lou Brock and watched Gale Sayers grow up. Leon Chambers was the prototype for Gale Sayers. If only he had finished high school, there's no telling what he might have accomplished as an athlete.

The sidewalk was convenient for stretching our legs, but when we really wanted to blow off steam we took to the large field separating the black and white sections of the projects. The field—the famous field—was the place for baseball, football, and interracial fighting. I quarterbacked our little project football team (handing off at opportune moments to Leon Chambers, as you might imagine), but my friends and I had to step aside for the big games on Thanksgiving Day, when the older boys and young men from Logan Fontenelle would take on a team from the black community on the south side of town in the annual Cold Bowl. It was rough-and-tumble, no-holds-barred tackle football with everything but pads. Josh, Richard, and Fred all played for our side, and everybody in the projects turned out to watch. The game generally culminated in a full-scale fistfight.

There was also a basketball court adjacent to the field, and since basketball was my best and most natural sport, my brothers permitted me to
play with them. The five Gibson boys—Josh, Richard, Fred, David, and
I—would often challenge all comers. With Josh throwing his weight
around under the basket and me dishing off and shooting behind my
brothers' screens, we were rarely, if ever, beaten. When the courts were
covered with snow or the basketballs were too cold to bounce, we moved
the games to Josh's gymnasium or the smaller one at the project recreation center, which was located on the edge of the white housing section.

Actually, there were two rec centers in the projects—both of them separate from Josh's on Lake Street, which later became the local YMCA.
One, which was for arts and crafts and academic tutoring, was where the
girls and college-bound boys hung out. My friend Rodney Wead dragged
me there quite a bit. But my hangout was the rec center at Twenty-second
and Clark run by Marty Thomas, which, in addition to basketball, offered
table tennis and a wild gymnasium game we called box hockey. Occasionally, when the sun was down and the balls were quiet, Marty would bring
in crawdads that he had caught and cook up stew for about a half dozen
of us. Some of our best nights revolved around Marty's crawdad stew and
a Joe Louis fight on the radio.

Marty attracted enough boys to the center to operate a fast-pitch softball league, and Josh tapped into the same talent pool for basketball and
later baseball teams that he organized. We didn't think much of it at the
time, but in retrospect it seems curious that our group of jocks included
white boys like Dick Mackie and Glenn Sullivan, who lived on the other
side of the projects. Both of those guys were superb athletes, and I suspect now that Marty and Josh recruited them into our crowd on the premise that they would get to compete alongside some of the best young
ballplayers in Omaha. Not only did Mackie and Sullivan play on our teams,
but they also fought at our side when the black kids of Logan Fontenelle
rumbled with the white kids on the big field. (I suspect that my strong
feelings about discrimination result in part from the fact that our neighborhood and school were always integrated, with a mixture of black,
white, Jewish, and even Chinese and Indian. Nearly everybody I know
from the neighborhood feels the same way I do in this respect.)

I've heard it said that Josh's misfortune in finding a teaching job turned out to be the best break the boys of North Omaha ever had. But while it's true that occupational frustrations drove him in our direction, it was also obvious that his involvement with me and my friends ran deeper than that. In equal measure, Josh thrived on athletic competition and was completely devoted to kids—especially to me, for whom he felt a personal responsibility. I was ten years old when he returned from the war, and Josh noticed right away that I had begun to fall in with the wrong crowd. Along with the paternal, protective role he had always taken on around me, Josh was the sort of fellow who didn't drink or smoke (when I was twelve or so, I got hold of some tobacco, rolled it into a little pipe I had bought, and hid it in the closet, but Josh found the pipe, popped me in the back of the head, kicked me in the pants, and that was that), and he possessed an almost religious fervor about sports and education. He was headstrong and demanding and rough, but in many ways Josh was the ideal role model. He was also a hell of a coach.

I've always assumed that my interest in sports had a lot to do with Josh being a coach, but as I reflect upon it, I suspect now that Josh's interest in coaching had a lot to do with me being an athlete. For both of us, the commitment is probably traceable to a conversation we had when I was eleven. One day late that summer, Josh sat me down in front of our house for a hard lecture on being a professional man. Traditionally, professionalism was and is a matter of education, but at that moment something new was opening up for black people. It was 1947, and Jackie Robinson had just joined the Brooklyn Dodgers. Suddenly, there was the unexpected possibility of a black man being a professional athlete. Josh explained to me that I had to make a commitment one way or the other, and since I never had much enthusiasm for studying in books, I decided on the spot to be a ballplayer. I didn't know if the sport would be baseball or basketball, but I would play one of them professionally.

I expect, though, that Josh knew which it would be. Until that time, black kids in most cities had generally played softball—as we did for Marty Thomas—rather than baseball. But when Jackie Robinson made the big leagues, we rounded up hardballs, moved the bases back, and began firing overhanded. Josh took a particular interest in the pitching part, and as soon as we made the transition to baseball he took me over to Kellom Elementary, the integrated neighborhood school that I attended, built a pitcher's mound in a corner of the play field, and marked off home plate sixty feet six inches away. He had me throwing there practically every day from March until the first snow.

When we played ballgames, though, Josh usually had me as the catcher or shortstop. I guess he figured it would be a long time before black pitchers would make much of a dent in the big leagues—besides which, I was pretty damn wild back then. There was only one catcher, Rudy Skillman, who could hang onto my fastballs, and it really wasn't worth the trouble because we had two fellows, John Halcomb and Wendell Booth, who could throw strikes and take care of business on the mound.

There was a huge amount of talent on Josh's teams, and it wasn't long before we were proudly representing the new North Side YMCA, which opened on the same site as the rec center with John Butler as director and Josh as program director. Among the teams Josh coached was an adult basketball team, the Y Travellers, which he and my brother Fred played on. The Travellers made the rounds of Nebraska and Iowa playing local all-star teams, and few were their equal. Josh was ruthless when it came to winning—an attitude that I suspect had something to do with his war experience and his inability to find a job commensurate with his qualifications—and when the lead opened up and he really wanted to humiliate the opponent, he would put in his skinny thirteen-year-old brother, the water boy. I was more than happy to shoot it up and not at all self-conscious about the uniform that was several sizes too big for me.

From that time until I signed a professional contract and left home, it seemed that I spent every summer crowded into the back of some big old moving van or another that Josh had rented for the occasion. The youth team I played for—the Monarchs (probably named for the Kansas City Monarchs of the Negro Leagues)—traveled just as much as the Travellers. Josh carried us to places we would never have seen if it hadn't been for baseball—places, in fact, that few people have ever seen, little towns in Nebraska and Missouri and especially Iowa, where I have basically fond memories of the likes of Glenwood, Hamburg, Avoca, Exira, Onawa,

Logan, Harlan, Missouri Valley, Shenandoah, Red Oak, Griswold, and Woodbine. It was a world we couldn't see from our front stoops at Logan Fontenelle, and if it seemed strange at times—like the day in Iowa when a young girl asked to rub my skin to see if the color would come off—it was seldom unpleasant. We were as much a curiosity to the country folk as the country life was to us.

> I can't remember better times than the ones our youth team would have playing in the outer reaches of Nebraska and Iowa and Missouri. What we were experiencing—for a group of young black kids from the inner city—was an entirely new universe. We hadn't known anything but what we saw in the city—the sidewalks and factories—or heard much of anything but the noise of the street-cars. Now here we were, traveling country roads in the back of a truck, screaming, laughing, and best of all, playing ball. I won't say we were the most welcome visitors in that part of the country, and when the people saw a group of young black kids get out and begin playing ball, there was some abuse. But the best part of it was that once the games started, everything disappeared. I think each community grew to respect each other more, even if they didn't always care for one another.
>
> Whatever we felt about each other, Josh saw to it that we commanded respect. I remember one day in Maryville, Missouri, when, after the game, they lined us up on the curb of the town square for cold watermelons. We're tearing into those watermelons and they're standing back taking pictures of us. We didn't know what was really going on, but Josh sure did. He ordered us to stop and ask for a fork. We'd never in our lives used a fork to eat watermelon, but that was Josh's rule for the road. If somebody offers you watermelon, ask for a fork. That worked fine for everybody except Bob. He thought it was demeaning to be served watermelon in the first place and wouldn't touch any if they brought it out on a silver platter.
>
> —RODNEY WEAD
> Gibson's boyhood friend

Some of those towns were serious about baseball, and as a result our talents were not unappreciated. One of our infielders, Jerry Parks, and I were noticed in Woodbine by a local coach named Red Brummer, who asked us to join the farmboys on his Woodbine Whiz Kids. When we weren't touring with the Monarchs, we hooked up with the Whiz Kids and won a few weekend tournaments. The Monarchs also had the honor of playing the first game in Woodbine's new Midget League park, which was the best in the area. We accepted that as a tribute to our baseball skills.

Not surprisingly, there were times when the locals would stack the deck against us. Josh was always alert to this and had no patience for it whatsoever. He was hell on umpires and anybody else who wouldn't give his team a fair shake. In Griswold, there was an umpire with a speech impediment who couldn't bring himself to rule one in our favor and would often change his call in midstammer when he realized who was playing. He'd yell, "B-b-b-b-STEERIKE!" The guys on the bench would be holding their sides in laughter—Haskell Lee, who later became a minister, has talked about that umpire for years—but Josh would be furious. In another town, he once argued so persistently with the umpire that the ump finally asked him if he would like to take the mask and do it himself. So Josh took the mask, put it on, and squatted behind home plate. With that, the ump threw him out of the game. Other times, if he thought he had a sympathetic crowd, he would pace in front of the stands and say, "Did you see that? Can you believe that?" We were amused by Josh's antics most of the time, but it wasn't so funny when my brother tried to fight the entire park. If he thought we were being treated badly, and especially if the fans were taking part in the abuse, he would walk out to the pitcher's mound and invite the home folks to meet him there. There were a few times when we thought Josh was going to get us killed.

There were also times when I wondered if Josh was going to kill me himself. He was much harder on me than he was on the rednecks from Iowa—no doubt because I had committed myself to becoming a pro ballplayer and Josh wasn't going to let me default on that commitment. The other guys on my team would watch silently after practice when Josh would order me back on the field and hit me vicious ground balls until the sun set. After I took one of his best shots in the eye one day, I ran home crying to my mother. She told me that I didn't have to play for Josh anymore, but of course I wasn't about to quit. Josh might let up for a day or two now and then to get Mother off his back, but after that it was always more of the same.

As much as I hated him sometimes, it was impossible not to admire and believe in Josh, because he led by example. He required no more from any of us than he gave himself and, most important, he was no hypocrite. Josh would have loved to have the opportunity, as I had, to pursue a career in professional sports, and in fact he probably had the talent to pull it off. He was bullishly strong, surprisingly agile, and Lord knows he never backed down from a challenge. But since that avenue was closed to him—the color barriers were not broken in time to help Josh—he did as he told me I would otherwise have to do: He got an education. And don't think the boys on the team didn't notice. I recall one day when Josh was late for baseball practice, and Josh was *never* late for practice. Somebody asked where he was, and I said he was at school. He was attending Creighton, studying for his master's degree. The guys couldn't believe it. After a while, here comes Josh—this snarling, two-hundred-pound, kick-ass coach—carrying a stack of schoolbooks. It made quite an impression.

As a coach, Josh could be questioned—not to his face, of course—about the techniques and strategies he taught, but I never played for a coach or manager, in any sport or at any level, who taught me more about winning than Josh did. At that stage of his life, Josh did not have the temperament to accommodate losing. He was hell-bent to win, and pity the man or team or injury or excuse that got in his way. Most of the kids who played for Josh developed the same attitude. Our ability to win far exceeded our ability to hit and throw and field. The Y Monarchs played to win, and we won.

In 1951, when I was fifteen, we became the first black team ever to win a Nebraska state championship. It was an American Legion tournament, although few if any of the teams were sponsored by American Legion posts as they are now. The legion supervised the league and found business sponsors for the teams, all of which, except for ours, had full matching sets of uniforms. There were no merchants willing to buy a whole set of uniforms for a black team, however, so Josh paid some out of his pocket and the Y paid some and local establishments would kick in for about a player each. We took the field with one kid wearing the name of a funeral home on his back, the next a neighborhood tavern, and on down the line. But when the games started, we were sharp. Halcomb and Booth did most of the pitching for the Monarchs, I did the rest (between stints at shortstop and center field and catcher) and hit cleanup, Jerry Parks played the heck out of short and second base, and Rodney Wead gave us a big target at first. The finals were in Hastings, Nebraska, and strangely, I don't remember the triumphant details. I only remember how sick and depressed I felt in those years whenever we lost, which wasn't often. I didn't share all the bitter experiences of Josh's past, but I definitely took on his attitude.

The Nebraska championship qualified us for a regional tournament in Kansas City, Missouri. For reasons that most likely were part economic and part racial, we holed up at a community center in St. Joseph, about fifty miles away, and slept on pool tables. While there, we managed to get in some practice on a field that had a little dirt between the rocks, and as Josh was smashing ground balls at me in the manner that he and I so loved, one of them bounced up and put a gash over my eye. I still have the scar. Josh had little sympathy for me, but he did have a Band-Aid, which he stuck on the cut while ordering me back to my position.

We were eliminated early in the Kansas City tournament, but when we arrived home I learned that I was an American Legion all-city selection as a utility player—a distinction that did absolutely nothing for me the next spring at Omaha Technical High School. Blacks didn't play baseball at Tech, despite the fact that we comprised approximately half of the student body. According to school policy, the spring sport for black athletes was track. This was largely the doing of the baseball coach, Ken Kennedy, who apparently hadn't heard of Jackie Robinson, and the track coach, Dutch White, who knew a good thing when he had one.

Kennedy also coached football, where a few blacks were permitted, and he had cut me as a freshman because I stood less than five feet tall and weighed about ninety pounds. Usually, Kennedy picked his squad by lining up the players on the sideline and having them roll up their pants legs. He kept the guys with scars, figuring they were the toughest. But I was eliminated before I even got to show him my shins. I told Kennedy that I had been playing football all my life with many of the guys he was keeping and could outrun, outthrow, and outkick most of them. He told me to eat some potatoes and come back later. Not a chance. By the time I was a senior, I had shot up to about six feet, 175, and Kennedy caught a glimpse of me tossing and booting around the football one day with my friends. He came up to me and said he'd get me a uniform, and I essentially told him what to do with his uniform.

When, in my teenage innocence, I tried out for the baseball team as a junior, I reasoned naïvely that my all-city status ought to count for something—that, and the fact that the Monarchs had pounded the crap out of the summer team that most of the varsity guys played for. But Kennedy informed me he couldn't accommodate me on the team because I had reported a day late, and it wasn't until years later—in fact, during my induction party at the Hall of Fame, when another Tech coach gave me the real poop—that I found out about the school policy.

Like all of the other blacks who were shut out of baseball, I turned to Dutch White's track team, which was the best in the state. I wasn't quite fast enough to sprint for Tech—although I suspect I could have run any race I wanted for any other school in Nebraska—but I manned a leg on the sprint relay team that claimed the city title, won a few broad jumps, and set the Omaha indoor high-jump record at five-eleven.

Finally, in my senior year—by which time I'd already been offered a contract by the Kansas City Monarchs—we got a new baseball coach, Tom Murphy, and I was allowed to participate. I pitched some and played the outfield. Jerry Parks also made the team as a shortstop, and together we broke the color line on Omaha Tech's baseball team. Socially, it was no big deal, since we commonly played with white guys in the neighborhood and in the small towns of Iowa and Nebraska, and the ballplaying benefits proved to be mutual. There was no state championship in high school baseball, but in the Intercity tournament (so called because the league included two schools from Council Bluffs, Iowa, across the Missouri River from Omaha) I was called on to pitch the semifinal game against Omaha North. I threw strikes that day and North managed only a scratch single in the sixth. That put us in the finals, also against North, and we beat them again for the championship. As a result, I made all-city as an all-purpose

player. It was more meaningful to me, however, that as a switch-hitter I finished second among the city's batting leaders with an average of .368.

Since pitching was only secondary to me at the time—and all I could really do on the mound was throw hard—I assumed that my future lay
somewhere in the outfield, perhaps, or maybe third base or even catcher.
Or basketball. Basketball was easily my best sport, and the one for which
I received the most recognition in high school.

Tech's basketball coach was an energetic young guy named Neal
Mosser who, much like Josh, made everything else secondary to winning.
He was my kind of coach, and his kind of player was one who could play.
On that basis, I was in. So were Jerry Parks and several of my friends from
the projects, including the white boys who played with us at the rec
center—Dick Mackie, an excellent left-handed shooter, and Glenn
Sullivan, another lefty who shot even better than Mackie. I started at
guard as a junior and, feeding Mackie and Sullivan, averaged only six
points a game for a team that was ranked second in the city and third in
the state. Our season came to an abrupt end early in the state tournament,
however, when we were upset by Fremont.

I was certain that my senior year was going to be our year. Sullivan was
gone, but we had so much talent returning that Mackie started only occasionally. Among my friends from the projects, Jerry Parks was a cracker-
jack point guard and Artie Sanders played a nifty game at center. I was one
of the smallest guys on the team, but since I could jump I played small forward, from which spot I could rebound and score and maneuver. Although
we didn't win the Intercity League—things being as they were, Tech had
a lot of difficulty on the road—we clobbered the teams that were at the
top, Creighton Prep and Abraham Lincoln, and considered ourselves easily the equal of any team in the state.

Our chance to prove that came at the state tournament in Lincoln, and
Mosser had us ready. He put his heart into his job and as a result was an
extremely excitable coach, well known for screaming at referees and
jumping up and down in front of the bench. One time, he was so upset during a game that he threw himself chest-down onto the floor. Like Josh, his
conduct stemmed, in large part, from the fact that our team often got
screwed. Mosser knew that he offended a lot of people by starting so

many black players, but he didn't give a damn. When we were called to take our places in the Nebraska University gym to play our state semifinal game against Fremont, he courageously sent five black players onto the floor. That had never happened before, and there was stone silence in the arena as we were announced. I'll never forget that eerie feeling.

The evening grew increasingly peculiar as it wore on. Fremont was a scrappy team but very small and not particularly gifted. Its strategy was to stall with the ball, which made sense. Nothing else made sense that night, however. As slow as the action was, somehow the referees managed to foul out four of our starters in the first half. I was the only one remaining to start the second half, and I was gone a couple of minutes later. When it was over, we had lost by a point, 40–39. I cried in the locker room afterwards, unable to cope with the reality that we had been cheated and there wasn't a thing we could do about it. I believe it was the last time I ever shed tears over a ballgame.

I gained a small measure of consolation when I was a unanimous choice for the all-city team, having averaged seventeen points and involved myself quite a bit with the rebounding and ball handling. I still have the clipping from the *Omaha World Herald* when it announced the all-city team, saying, "The most spectacular [of the all-city players] is Gibson. He's the boy with springs in his toes and basketball magic in his fingertips." Strangely—Omaha politics being what they were—I made all-state in the Lincoln paper but not in the *World Herald*.

After the season, I played some AAU basketball for Offutt Air Force Base, just outside Omaha, and the Kitlow Institute, a correspondence school in the southwest Nebraska town of Alma where I averaged twenty-five points. My objective was to make a name for myself and catch the attention of Branch McCracken, the coach of Indiana University's national championship team. Coach Mosser wrote McCracken on my behalf, and then I waited. Finally the reply arrived: "Your request for an athletic scholarship for Robert Gibson has been denied because we already have filled our quota of Negroes." The quota was apparently one per class—or perhaps two on the whole team, it was hard to tell. The Hoosiers already had a black fellow a year ahead of me from New Jersey named Wally Choice, who turned out to be their leading scorer as a senior, and in my class—in my place, as I saw it—there was a guard from Indianapolis, Hallie Bryant, who started as an upperclassman and later played for the Harlem Globetrotters. They were good ballplayers, but that didn't change my opinion about the situation. I remember watching Bryant play on television over the next few years and thinking to myself, "They got the wrong Negro."

When they played in Omaha, the Negro League teams used to park their old multicolored Greyhounds on the street in front of my friend Rodney Wead's house, which of course wasn't far from mine. Rodney would rush me over there, and we would gawk at the guys as they stepped off the bus to walk to the rooming house a block and a half away (the street in front of it was too narrow to park on) or to find some supper or occasionally to practice at the same field we used on Twenty-second Street. The players were all alike to me, but Rodney read up on them and would get carried away when he spotted Sam Jethroe or Luke Easter or Ernie Banks. He followed them around and got their autographs and somehow managed to be the batboy when Easter's team played in Omaha or across the river in Council Bluffs.

It might have been because of Jackie Robinson that I wasn't especially interested in the Negro Leagues. Jackie had played with the Kansas City Monarchs, but as soon as he made the big leagues, the Negro Leagues seemed to me to be a moot point. Besides that, I wasn't especially interested in watching someone else play ball. Whereas a guy like Rodney had to keep his mind busy, I had to keep my hands busy.

That was part of the reason why I seemed like a mama's boy. (Actually, many of my friends were mama's boys, too, as attested by the fact that, in the ghetto tradition of "playing the dozens," we called each other by our mother's names. I was Victoria, Rodney was Daisy, and so on.) Mother was good with her hands, and by copying her I learned to mend my own clothes and cook and fix things around the house. Because I had been so ill when I was young, I also slept with my mother for several years and became her pet, more or less. She had much more patience with me than my brothers and sisters did, and they all tired of hearing her tell them to "leave my baby alone."

*Robert was always into something or bothering somebody. Josh had been a big track star in high school and he had a box full of medals. One day, Robert was trying to get a ride on another kid's bicycle and ended up trading the kid all of Josh's medals. Another time, he was playing with Richard's model airplanes and set them on fire by lighting a match to a tray of glue. Robert and his friends used to make go-carts out of wheels and orange crates, and once, when he didn't have any wheels handy, he took them off a buggy I played with—the same one Mother had laid him in for sun treatments when he was smaller. He also used my roller skates to make a scooter.*

*Robert was always getting into some kind of trouble. When he was about three, he followed the rest of us to school and then couldn't find his way home. Mother finally called the police. After that, she had to chain him up in the yard to prevent him from running off. Nothing could stop him, though. Once he ran off and fell into Carter's Lake and had to be pulled out. Robert just wouldn't sit still. Josh and Uncle Son used to offer him dimes if he would stay in one place for five minutes, but he couldn't do it. Apparently, he was the same way in school. He was always bringing home notes from the teachers about throwing paper wads or pulling some poor girl's hair. Mother would find the notes hidden in Robert's shoe. He was a pest, is what he was. If you sat still, Robert was going to bother you. We would all get so mad. We'd say to Mother, "Why don't you give him a whipping?" She'd say, "I don't have to. Every one of you has beat him already." He would always go to her for sympathy. I can remember him still sitting on Mother's lap and crying when he was twelve years old.*

*—Barbara Jean Gibson Stevens*

That's not to say that Mother wouldn't spank me. She packed a wallop, and she packed it often. When I was thirteen, she was still spanking me, but I figured I was too old for it by then and one time I just laughed. I said, "You can't hurt me." With that, she grabbed my head and pushed it through the Sheetrock.

I suppose I gave her ample reason to discipline me from time to time. Like all little brothers, I liked to hang around with my big brothers. Josh would never lead me astray, but Fred wasn't quite so fatherly and his buddies were even less concerned about the example they set. They weren't big-time troublemakers but delighted in profitable mischief. For example, street vendors used to make their way through the projects selling ice cream, milk, and tamales. Stealing from the ice-cream guy was a tricky proposition because he could tell something was missing by the amount of steam coming up from the dry ice; so we would stick our treats under the truck until he drove off. The tamale vendor was nearly blind, but that didn't make him an easy mark—he could still feel things pretty accurately. He sold three tamales for a dime, and our hustle was to fool him with a penny. There were silver pennies back then, but he could distinguish them from dimes by feeling the edges, so we would crimp the edge of a penny with a pair of pliers to make it feel like a dime and walk off chomping on three tamales. We didn't bother with the milk guy—although, now that I think about it, we could have used some milk to go with the doughnuts we stole. On Lake Street, not far from the projects, there was a bakery that sat on a steep incline. The baker worked in the basement, which, because of the hill, had a window just off from and a little below the sidewalk. Fred and his friends would stand a few steps up the hill, then dangle me by the ankles upside down over the window of the doughnut shop. When the baker took a sheet of doughnuts out of the oven, he would place it on a rack right in front of the window. My job was to reach in and take the sheet off the rack when he turned away, then hand it to Fred or somebody. The doughnuts were great, but the best part was seeing the look on the baker's face when he discovered them missing. Around the fourth tray or so, he'd stop and look around and scratch his head. I don't think he ever figured it out.

For all of our petty crime, we never got into any serious trouble with the police—primarily because we could always hear their cars coming from a couple of blocks away. The police cars all had the same sort of standard transmission, and we recognized the sound of the cops downshifting when they took off. On top of that, their unmarked cars all had license plates beginning with 420.

Ironically, Fred did get arrested several times in later years when he was doing nothing more than walking home from work late at night. Every time, he'd say to the officers, "You know I've been working," and every time, they threw him in jail anyway. I was never harassed by the cops in that manner, but I did spend part of a day in jail when I was about seven years old. My friends and I were making a clubhouse and knew where there was a keg of rusty old nails in an abandoned barn at the end of an alley. We managed to get ourselves spotted taking the nails. Most of us ran off, but one boy, Donald Moore, was picked up and told on everybody else. I had sprinted straight home and jumped in bed, which is what I always did when I was scared, and while I was under the covers there was a knock at the door. The policeman took me in and locked me up for a couple of hours.

Donald Moore, in fact, made my life miserable more than once. He was a little older and meaner than Rodney and me and used to chase us both home from school. He would give us a head start and tell us that he would beat us up if he caught us. He never caught us, but it got to be tiresome after a while and I happened to mention it to Barbara Jean, who's about three years older than me. Barbara Jean told us to run past a certain location the next day, and when Donald came by the same way she stepped forward and beat the crap out of him. Donald never bothered me after that.

There was an even tougher kid, though, named Tony King, who was the neighborhood bully. He threatened me a lot and one day got me cornered by the pool table in the recreation center. I had no choice but to fight him, and to my surprise I came out of it unscathed. I was so scared that I pounded the guy into the floor. I never had to fight after that. (Years later, Tony King was found dead in an alley in Chicago.)

Fighting was fairly routine around the projects, and if I didn't participate in many fights, I was seldom far from one. Fred and his cronies often found themselves in the mood for a scrape, and when the urge hit them they simply walked over to a redneck bar at Twentieth and Charles, the opposite side of the neighborhood. I'd always be right behind them, but when they went inside I stayed out. All they had to do was order a beer, and fists were flying. Now and then, somebody would come crashing through a window and land at my feet. It always amazed me that by the next day, Fred's crowd and the rednecks would be walking to and from school together as if nothing had happened. It seemed like it was their *duty* to beat on each other from time to time—to at least give off the appearance of mutual hate—and once the duty had been fulfilled, things could get back to normal for a while.

The worst and scariest fight I ever saw was at a football game between Creighton Prep and Boys Town High. That was always one of the biggest games of the year and people came from all over town to watch. It was a mean-spirited rivalry because Creighton Prep was a well-heeled private Jesuit school and Boys Town had a lot of homeless and black kids. When I was thirteen or so, I was watching the game from outside a fence on a hill beyond one of the end zones. A lot of people were milling around, including a couple of ex-marines who were apparently spoiling for a fight. Making sure they had an audience of black guys, one of the marines announced, "I can beat the shit out of any nigger I've ever seen." Naturally, a circle of people quickly gathered, and I saw a guy named Raymond Manuel, who happened to be standing right next to me, take a handkerchief out of his pocket and wrap it around his hand. Without saying a word, he stepped through the crowd, walked up to the marine, and with one punch knocked the guy out cold. The marine never saw the fight that ensued. Before long, the whole stadium was involved, inside and outside the fence. It was black against white, and it was ugly. There were people hanging from the fence, hooked by their shirts to the wrought-iron spikes at the top.

At another high school game, Omaha South, an integrated team, was upsetting a mostly white team in the third quarter when what seemed like the entire student body of the white school came over to the other side and provoked a major melee that left me cold and frightened. There were fistfights all through the bleachers and spilling down onto the sidelines. The game was called when the police arrived in force.

I give Josh credit for the fact that the violence of the neighborhood never really touched me or many of his athletes. Years later, after I had achieved some success in baseball, I made periodic visits to the state penitentiary and nearly always saw somebody I knew from school or the projects. Generally, though, they weren't Josh's kids. His athletes weren't choirboys, but for the most part we vented our aggressiveness—and there was plenty of it to go around—on those who would try to beat us or cheat us.

There are other neighborhoods in America that have produced impressive lists of athletes, and maybe some have been more prolific than the north side of Omaha. Oakland and Los Angeles and Cincinnati and Mobile have turned out numerous major-leaguers, for instance; but I have a hard time believing that any community as small and isolated as the Logan Fontenelle housing projects can match us for quantity and quality and diversity of athletes. I was the first of Josh's protégés to hit the big time, but not long after I made it in baseball, Bob Boozer turned up with the Cincinnati Royals of the NBA. Around that time, Gale Sayers set pro football on its ear by zigzagging down the field for the Chicago Bears; some still think he's the greatest running back ever. Few people realize that Gale's brother, Roger, was a world-class runner. Then came Marlin Briscoe, who with the Denver Broncos was one of the first black quarterbacks in the NFL; Ron Boone, who set a consecutive-games record while playing for several teams in the American Basketball Association and NBA; and Nebraska's Heisman Trophy winner, Johnny Rodgers—all disciples of Josh Gibson and alumni of the North Side YMCA.

As a kid, my universe revolved around the Y and the rec center. Aside from fighting on the big field, footracing around the sidewalk, and hanging out by the clubs and shops of Twenty-fourth Street, there wasn't much in the way of diversions in my neighborhood. Only one family in the projects had a television, and the rest of us watched cartoons and cowboy movies through their window. Some of us shined shoes downtown, but there weren't enough shoes to go around. So we were content to spend entire days in the gym.

The project rec center was more convenient for us than the Y, and I took full advantage of that fact. It closed from five to seven in the evening, but Marty Thomas knew that I loved basketball and he would let me in during those hours to shoot around by myself. I'd invent all sorts of crazy, impossible shots, then pull them out in the next Tech game.

I also got plenty of practice—and plenty of elbows from Josh—on the concrete floor of the Y (which also had a low ceiling that forced me to develop a flat jump shot). The only difficulty in utilizing the Y was finding a safe way to negotiate the ten blocks between there and the projects. The unwritten rule was never to cross over to the white side of the neighborhood, so we walked straight down Twenty-second Street to Lake, steering two blocks clear of the roughest corner in town at Twenty-fourth and Lake. The danger resided in the fact that our mothers usually gave us a few pennies for something to eat, and everybody knew it. Our strategy was to lie low and swing by the bakery for orange juice and day-old doughnuts. We generally managed to avoid trouble, and the only real scare I received along the route occurred when I was walking alone at about five o'clock one morning, on my way to meet up with the rest of the team for an out-of-town baseball game. On Twenty-second Street, a few blocks from the Y, a car full of rednecks pulled up alongside me. I tried not to pay any attention, but one of the guys inside rolled down the window and said, "Hey, we need some good old black poontang. You know where we can get some?" I kept walking and said, "Follow me." My plan was to lead them straight to the Y, where a small army of my friends would be waiting to kick their asses. Unfortunately, the good old boys got bored and turned off before we reached the party.

We could usually find Josh at the Y, where, if he wasn't conducting a practice of some sort, he was doling out lectures in his deep, gruff voice, imparting homespun lessons in growing up while nervously weaving rubber bands between his meaty fingers. As a coach, Josh was part social worker, which, in fact, he officially became much later, specializing in counseling single mothers. (Rodney Wead also—not coincidentally—gravitated toward the field of social work and remains in it to this day.) Among the social services Josh performed for me was setting me up, more or less, with my first wife. He had married his secretary, who happened to have an attractive niece named Charline who visited often at the Y. I was in my element there, which was fortunate because I was not generally comfortable in the company of girls and my encounters with them often didn't develop as I'd hoped.

Probably my first serious flirtation occurred when I was about twelve. There was a particular girl from school who I thought was pretty special, and I managed to meet up with her once at the back door of her house. She was standing with her heel against the wall, as girls do, and we were getting along nicely until suddenly she broke wind. I couldn't believe it. I guess I had imagined that girls didn't do that sort of thing. Anyway, with no further adieu I took off running home because I couldn't wait to tell my friends. There was no way I could date the girl after that. I wouldn't have been able to look at her without laughing.

Things went a little smoother with Charline, whom I met the summer after high school and started going steady with almost immediately. We had no immediate plans, however, because I had no idea what I'd be doing over the next few years. I bided my time playing for a city league baseball team sponsored by the Chicago Bar, all the while depressed over being rejected by Indiana and second-guessing myself over passing up the offer from the Kansas City Monarchs. I was also being tempted by the St. Louis Cardinals, who had a Triple-A farm team in Omaha and whose local scout, Runt Marr, had been in contact with me for several years. Professional scouts were fairly commonplace around Omaha because, in addition to the Cardinals, the city hosted the College World Series every year, and I'd talked informally with representatives from several teams, including the Dodgers and Yankees. Marr seemed to be the scout most genuinely interested, however, and the only one who offered me a contract—such as it was—after high school. I wanted to accept it, but Josh said no. He still supported the idea of being a professional athlete, but since the immediate prospects were slim, he also insisted that I go to college. The problem was, I couldn't pay for it, and the colleges weren't beating a path to my door with scholarships. It was incumbent upon Josh to make something happen.

A few weeks before school was to start, I was shooting baskets at the Y when Duce Belford walked in. He was the athletic director and baseball coach at Creighton University, which was located only a few blocks from the projects, but he was there mainly to talk to me about the Blue

Jays' basketball program. It was coached by a fellow named Subby Salerno, and I didn't know much about it because nobody I knew had anything to do with Creighton basketball; the team consisted mostly of workmanlike white boys from the private schools. Josh was a little more familiar with Creighton since he had earned his bachelor's and master's degrees there, and he was acquainted with Belford well enough to put in a good word for his kid brother—which explained why the athletic director approached me instead of the basketball coach. I don't know if Belford accepted Josh's word at face value or whether he or Salerno had seen me play, but that didn't matter. Nor did it matter that I wasn't Catholic. What mattered was that he was offering me a full athletic scholarship—a chance to get an education and play college basketball at the same time.

I shook hands with Belford, thanked Josh, and kissed my mother.

# CHAPTER III

I could have walked to Creighton if we hadn't moved. But Mother had married an unfriendly man named Paul Bolden while I was in high school, and the family—that is, Mother and Mr. Bolden and David and I—moved to a forsaken country address just out of the city on the south side. I was probably grouchy on general principles, having been snatched from my neighborhood and friends, and Mr. Bolden's personality (or lack of it) being what it was, we had no chance at getting along. Our relationship exploded into a fight one day, and I ended up knocking him backwards through a door and into a chair in the other room, just like a cartoon. He didn't see the humor, however, and stomped off saying he was going to get his gun and come back to kill me. Mother held on to me and said not to worry, he wouldn't hurt me. I didn't know how she could be so sure until I noticed his pistol in her apron.

Barbara Jean was separated from her husband at the time, and I moved into her house for a while to get away from Mr. Bolden. But I wanted to be closer to Creighton and to Charline—the operative word there is Charline—so my brother Fred and his wife, Anita, let me share a room in their attic with Anita's brother, Grant. He was about my age and extremely crass. We got along great together. I'm sure we were a large annoyance to Fred and Anita, making rude noises and doing completely irresponsible things like throwing their baby across the living room to each other. But Fred wasn't much different from us at heart, and there was never a better sport than Anita, so they patiently tolerated me—even attending my basketball games—until I could see my way clear to moving back in with Mother and Mr. Bolden (which I eventually did). To pitch in a little, I kept my job at a nearby filling station and took another one carrying mail during Christmas break. I couldn't stand being chased all day by dogs, however, and one afternoon I left all my letters in the pickup box and went home. (Dogs gave me a hell of a time in those days. When I walked to high school, there was a big one that would hide behind a house at the top of a hill when he saw me coming and then race down the yard barking and snarling. He did it every day, and every day I'd jump and run out into the street. One day I decided I'd had enough. I put on a pair of gloves when I left home and watched for that dog when I approached the house. Sure enough, he was hiding, and when I got close he started charging down the hill. But this time I didn't run. I stood my ground, turned, and waited for him. When he saw that I wasn't scared, he hit the brakes and skidded down the hill on all fours, coming to a stop right in front of me, whereupon I pulled back my fist and punched him square in the nose. The dog never bothered me again.)

Since a career with the postal service seemed to be out of the question and I didn't show much enthusiasm for academics, it was a good thing I could play ball. The only trouble I had with playing ball was playing enough of it. After freshman basketball games, for instance, I found I could duck out of the Creighton gym—this was before the Blue Jays started using Ak-Sar-Ben (which is "Nebraska" spelled backwards) Arena—while the varsity was getting drilled and play another neighborhood league game or two at Kellom Elementary before I had to report to my all-night job at the filling station. In between I found time to see Charline, who was still in high school. I slept in class. My first class was history, and about five minutes into it every morning my five-pound history book would hit the floor—*Boom!* Everybody would turn and look, and I'd go back to sleep.

With all of the more appealing distractions before me, the academic part of the college experience was fairly low on my priority list until I came to understand about eligibility. I was in imminent danger of losing mine before I even had a chance at the varsity. When I finally caught on to the relationship between academics and basketball, I raised my grades to Cs and Bs (majoring in sociology) and started at guard as a sophomore.

I was the first black to attend Creighton on a basketball scholarship, although a neighborhood friend of mine, Clarence Jones, had played a little freshman ball. There were obviously racial aspects to the situation, but one of the main problems I had was finding teammates who could catch my passes. Our center, for instance, was a big fellow from Omaha named Lyle O'Dell. Lyle could rebound a little and he worked hard, but he wasn't the least bit familiar with the kind of basketball I had learned at the rec center, and I finally told him, "Lyle, if I have the ball, expect a pass. No matter what you see or think, expect a pass." Even with that warning, I was still bouncing passes off Lyle's face and head.

It helped, though, that I was preceded by and played a year with a little guard named Eddie Cole. By the time he left Creighton, which was my sophomore year, he was the school's all-time leading scorer. Eddie Cole could shoot from anywhere on the floor and he handled the ball like Bob Cousy. He didn't play with a street style, but he had some tricks that I hadn't seen before. In turn, I think he appreciated having another creative player on the team, and he wasn't reluctant to share the ball. He had twenty points and I had nineteen in my first game, when we beat Buena Vista 66–51, and we both lit up Drake for thirty-one in his last game, a 94–87 victory. But we won only three times in between and finished 5–14, which was pretty typical for Creighton.

I hated the losing but enjoyed everything else about my sophomore season except Tulsa. On the train ride to the Tulsa game, which was the fourth of the season, Belford informed me that I wouldn't be able to stay with the rest of the guys. Until then, the color factor really hadn't kicked in because I knew most of my teammates from the Intercity League in high school. One of them, in fact, was my buddy from Tech and the projects, Glenn Sullivan. Given all of that, the idea of not being able to stay where they stayed just didn't compute. I'm sure that if Belford had told me about the situation before we left Omaha, I would have stayed home. But as it was, I couldn't think of anything else to do but cry. When we arrived in Tulsa, we went to a restaurant where they served me in the kitchen. Sullivan walked back there with me, but I wasn't going to eat in the damn kitchen and told Glenn I'd wait until I got to the other side of town, which was where I was supposed to go when the other guys checked into their hotel. Sullivan came with me to my rooming house and offered to spend the night there, but I sent him back over to the rest of the team so I could brood and curse in private. I would have liked to make Tulsa pay for its bigotry, but my eighteen points and Cole's twenty weren't enough to keep us from being beaten 69–54.

That was the only time in my college career that I had a problem with accommodations in either basketball or baseball, for which we traveled very little. My junior year, our major basketball trip took us north and east, where we were in over our heads against the likes of Marquette, Holy Cross, and Seton Hall. Since I was our leading rebounder, I often lined up at center, which resulted in a situation where I wasn't big enough to stop the other team's big man and he wasn't fast enough to stop me. At Marquette, I scored twenty-eight and the Warriors' big man, Terry Rand, poured in twenty-nine as we lost handily. At Holy Cross, I scored twenty and the Crusaders' big man, Tommy Heinsohn, worked me for twenty-two points and twenty rebounds as we were pounded 97–60. As far as I know, Heinsohn was the only NBA player I faced at Creighton, and he made an impression. The first time I tried to take the ball to the hoop against him, he jammed it down my throat. I respected him more the next time, and as I drove to the basket the same way and we both went up in the air, I reversed to the other side for a layup. Since they won by thirty-seven, he wouldn't remember that play; since we lost by thirty-seven, I do.

That year, Tommy Thomsen had replaced Subby Salerno as our coach. Thomsen was more of a strategist, and since we were light on talent he installed a patient, patterned offense. I didn't like it much, but I had no legitimate beef. My twenty-two points a game were more than twice as many as the next guy's—which neither Thomsen nor my teammates especially cared for—and our record of 15–6 was the school's best in more than a decade. I ended up making third-team Jesuit all-American, which doesn't sound like much until you consider that the first team included Heinsohn, Bill Russell, and K. C. Jones—three-fifths of the great Celtic dynasty of the sixties. (A fourth member of those Celtics, Sam Jones, is the player whom my friend Rodney Wead says I most resembled. But I don't agree with much of anything Rodney says. Neal Mosser, my high school coach, suggests instead that my style was on the order of Elgin Baylor's, and I'll gladly endorse that comparison.)

My senior year was less memorable, mainly because I had established something of a reputation by then. The papers wrote about me quite a bit, using terms like "whirling dervish," and apparently my teammates had a sense of being upstaged. Admittedly, it was awkward for them, because Creighton had always been the stamping ground for fair-haired local boys from well-known Catholic families. One of our forwards, for instance, was a lawyer's son from Creighton Prep named Dan Simon who had made all-state in high school, which was more than I did. College was a different game, however, and I can understand that it wasn't easy for a guy like him to play in the shadow of a guy like me. After a while, though, the situation developed into a virtual conspiracy that was detrimental to the team in all respects. Nobody would pass me the ball, and as a result I was reluctant to give it up when I got it. On one occasion, I pulled down a rebound, dribbled the ball down the floor, and made about a forty-footer. Thomsen yanked me out of the game for taking a low-percentage shot, and I explained to him that I wasn't in the mood to pass the ball to teammates who would not return the favor.

The season did not reflect well upon the team, which never played up to the level we had attained the year before, or upon me. Apparently I failed to distinguish myself as a professional prospect, despite making honorable mention all-American and passing Eddie Cole as the school's career scoring leader—a record that stood until Paul Silas, who would go on to become an NBA star, broke it six years later. (Silas, who led the country in rebounding in 1963, was working out at the Creighton gym one afternoon that winter when I stopped by and engaged him in a little one-on-one. He later told Bob Broeg of the *St. Louis Post-Dispatch* that I had worn him out on the boards, a compliment that I accepted as a polite exaggeration.) The only NBA team to contact me was the Minneapolis Lakers, who never made an offer. I was sorely disappointed, because I still believed strongly that basketball was my best sport and the one least likely to discriminate against me. I'm certain that it was mostly for basketball, not baseball—at least not *college* baseball—that I eventually became the first member of the Creighton sports hall of fame.

Anyway, having failed to secure my future in basketball, I felt it was vital to have a big senior year in baseball. By the spring of 1957 we had a new coach—Bill Fitch, who later made his name in basketball as coach of the Celtics. (A few years after I had retired from baseball, I ran into Fitch at some sort of banquet and he said to me, "Hey, I've found another Bob Gibson. His name is Larry Bird." Unfortunately, I don't think he was talking about basketball talent; he was referring to competitiveness.) Even then, Fitch was primarily a basketball coach, and his appointment indicated the relatively low priority Creighton placed on baseball.

I wish I could say that while I was playing baseball for Creighton we laid the groundwork for the program that has become a national power in recent years. With the College World Series being held in Omaha, it's natural that the school would emphasize baseball, and nowadays it does, but that wasn't the case when I was a Blue Jay. We stayed close to home, and Creighton baseball was so inconsequential that the athletic department kept no records of it until the late sixties. Given the school's indifference about baseball, the players likewise approached it casually. Before a game I would frequently wander over in my baseball uniform to the track, if there was a meet going on, and take a few cracks at the high-jump bar. (I cleared six feet in spikes.) Baseball was, at best, my second sport, and I really didn't have a niche in it. At various times in my college career I played catcher, third base, outfield, and occasionally pitcher, demonstrating a notable wildness in the latter capacity.

My most serious baseball during those years came during the summers, when I took to the small towns and played semipro for $350 a month. To keep things on the up-and-up, I was given a summer job along with a spot on the local ball team. At Estherville, Iowa, for instance, I batted .381 in the Sac County League and drove a trash truck for the Ford dealership, hauling boxes out to the edge of a cliff and dumping them into the landfill. Another year I split my time between Crofton, Nebraska, of the Tri County League, and the Basin League outpost of Chamberlain, South Dakota.

There was very little during these years to make me approach the game any differently than I had when I was playing out of Josh's moving truck. As I entered my senior season, however, I recognized the importance of taking it up a notch. At the age of twenty-one I was about to marry Charline and I didn't want to even contemplate a life and livelihood outside of sports. Bearing down as a result, I led the Nebraska College Conference (which Creighton won) with a .333 average that I attribute in large part to switch-hitting. The ability to bat left-handed gave me a useful advantage on cold days—of which there were many—when, instead of suffering at the plate with raw, stinging hands, I frequently beat out bunts. I also hit a few home runs, stole fifteen bases in twenty games, and caught most of what was hit my way.

> *I went to Dana College in a little town north of Omaha, and we played baseball on a huge field that was actually a cow pasture. We shared the field with the football team, and their scoreboard was way out in left center. When we played Creighton at our place once, a guy on our team hit a ball about a mile in that direction and went into his home run trot. The next thing I knew, somebody was throwing him his glove and our guys were running out onto the field. I found out that Hoopster—that's what I call Gibson— who was playing center field, had run behind the scoreboard into the street to catch the ball. It was the most amazing thing I ever saw—or didn't see.* —RODNEY WEAD

My pitching was occasional and erratic. I finished with a 6–2 record my senior year, and once as a junior had a no-hitter going through five innings, at which point Duce Belford took me out of the game to allegedly save my arm (although I still wonder: from what?). He told me I'd have plenty of time to pitch no-hitters. I suspect, also, that a lack of faith might have had something to do with his decision to pull me. I was admittedly wild back then, but I submit, if I may, that my wildness as a young pitcher has been somewhat overstated. I was consistently wild, but not ridiculously wild. In other words, I missed the plate often, but not by much. At least, that's how I remember it. It's quite possible that I *seemed* wilder than I was because of the possibilities of a ninety-five-mile-an-hour fastball; I can sympathize with the fact that even a moderate lack of control is not taken lightly at that speed.

I can't dismiss the likelihood, also, that my color might have had something to do with the perception of wildness. Because pitcher is the most commanding and cerebral position on the field, it is the one—like quarterback in football—that the sport and society is least willing to hand over to a black man. This was especially true in the 1950s, when black players were still novel commodities in mainstream baseball. If a black pitcher managed to get the job done on the mound, credit was given to his physical skills much more readily than to his mental attributes, to his power rather than to his finesse. A black pitcher met the stereotype if he was wild, and only if. It should be added that the stereotype may also have received some small assistance from the brotherhood of umpires, who were entirely white and in some cases not altogether indifferent to the color schemes.

At any rate, I was not so wild as to write myself off as a pitcher. In fact, I determined around my senior year that since black outfielders were relatively plentiful, my best chance to make it in the pros might occur as a pitcher. There was very little to suggest, however, that my hopes were realistic. The fact is, at that point of my life I really didn't have a clue about what might be in store—as a pitcher or an athlete or a young adult. All I could do was play ball and wait for a break.

Sure enough, things started breaking in the spring—but not in a way I had imagined. The Harlem Globetrotters came to town to play a touring team of college all-stars, and since their custom was to add a local player to the all-star team at each of the stops, they asked me to suit up for the game. Actually, Coach Thomsen had recommended me to Abe Saperstein of the Globetrotters, but Saperstein told him that I didn't have the national reputation necessary for selection and wasn't going to pick me until Thomsen pressed his point and won out. For me, the whole affair wasn't particularly convenient in the respect that I was married on a Sunday, the Globetrotter game was on Monday, and I had a baseball game Tuesday.

But I was accustomed to fitting basketball games into the cracks of my schedule and looked forward to being on the floor with the likes of Meadowlark Lemon, to say nothing of highly publicized all-stars such as Lenny Rosenbluth of North Carolina and Chet Forte of Columbia.

As the game progressed, however, it appeared that I might not make it onto the floor. The all-stars were giving the Globetrotters a stiff challenge for a change—the college guys had won only about two of twenty games in the series—and the coaches were reluctant to put in a little-known local kid. Late in the third quarter I still hadn't played, and as the Globetrotters took over the lead with a full-court press and began to pull away, the fans at Ak-Sar-Ben began chanting for the all-stars to put me in the game. When I finally checked in, I was fresh and frisky. I scored the first time down on the floor on a twisting layup, which the crowd very much appreciated, and that pumped me up even more. Immediately, I began chasing the ball all over the gym and coming up with it. My next three shots were on the mark, and suddenly we were back in the lead.

All of this annoyed the Globetrotters extremely. On one occasion, I drove the ball into the lane and flashed past one of their big men, Andy Johnson. The next time down, Johnson had a message for me. He delivered it with his elbow, which sent me sprawling, and included words to this effect: "This is my territory, son. Come in here again, and it's your ass." His remarks turned out to be the best pitching advice I ever received. Eventually, I came to regard the outside corner of home plate in exactly the same way that Andy Johnson felt about the lane.

I stayed in the game the rest of the way and finished with ten points, five rebounds, and several steals in just over a quarter. Chet Forte, who later gained renown as a sports and news producer for ABC-TV, was our big scorer (Lenny Rosenbluth managed only three points), but I was given most of the credit for the rare victory. The *Omaha World Herald* reported the next day that I "pestered the famous Trotters to no end ... The All-Star coaches credit Bob with the best spot performance by a one-nighter in the eight-year history of the Globetrotters–All-Stars series."

Beating the Globetrotters got their attention, and after the game their representative, Parnell Woods, asked me if I could join the team—the Trotters, that is, not the stars—for the rest of the tour. It was the right question but the wrong time. I hadn't intended to spend my honeymoon spinning a basketball on the end of my finger, and told him I would have to wait at least until school was out—Charline was attending college also, at the University of Omaha—before I could make such a major decision.

In the meantime, I was scheduled to pitch in the baseball game the next day, but my encounter with Andy Johnson had left me with a sprained right wrist, which meant that my roll was over. I came back down to earth when I asked a scout from the Yankees for thirty thousand dollars and he replied that I wasn't good enough to play Class D ball. The guy from the Dodgers felt the same way. He said, "You're not naïve enough to think you can play major-league ball, are you?" The Phillies were interested in me as a catcher, but not for the kind of money I was determined to get. Around that time, the Braves were signing guys like Bob Taylor and John DeMerit (don't feel bad if you haven't heard of them; that's the point) and Tony Cloninger for a hundred thousand dollars, and the Reds paid sixty-five thousand for Jay Hook, the latter two being pitchers. But it would be another couple of years before Richie Allen essentially broke the color line for big-time bonuses by getting sixty thousand from the Phillies. In 1957, by unanimous consent of the teams that knew I existed, I would be lucky to bring the price of an Oldsmobile. The White Sox and the Athletics also happened by, offering change out of their pockets.

Since the Cardinals were the only organization that had shown a continuing interest in me, Josh and I met with Runt Marr, who took us to see Bill Bergesch, the general manager of their American Association affiliate in Omaha. Bergesch was aware of me through Josh's team—he donated equipment to it every now and then—and was prepared to offer me a contract, but was in no position to throw money at me. He explained that the Cardinals would have to place me on their big-league roster if they paid me more than four thousand dollars. That was understood to be out of the question, so, convinced that I couldn't get an adequate deal from baseball, I renewed my talks with the Globetrotters. Abe Saperstein had originally tried to sign me for five hundred dollars a month, but seeing that I had an option he raised his offer to seven thousand for the season. With that information I called Bergesch back, and after speaking again with Saperstein we reached a compromise that satisfied all parties. I would sign with the Cardinals for a bonus of a thousand dollars, play out the season for another three thousand, then join the Globetrotters at a thousand a month for four months of the baseball off-season. The total was eight thousand dollars, but the real value of the deal was that it kept me alive in both sports. I still wasn't ready to pick one.

I had never seen the Omaha Cardinals play, and I knew even less about their manager, Johnny Keane. That made us even. He didn't know what to expect from me, either, which was to my advantage because it meant that he had no prejudices concerning the way I played my respective positions. He had no prejudices concerning my color, either, and on the morning I reported he asked me, first thing, to warm up and then throw some pitches to a few of the Omaha batters. Owing, I suppose, to fear and my fastball, none of them hit one out of the cage. Keane chuckled and told me I was a pitcher. He never saw me play the outfield.

Johnny Keane spent twenty-one years managing in the minor leagues, which suggests, quite accurately, that he was a patient man. He was, in fact, the closest thing to a saint that I came across in baseball. Keane had actually studied for the priesthood before succumbing to the temptations of baseball, a decision that proved to be more beneficial for baseball than for him. As a Texas League shortstop, he was beaned in the head and nearly died from the blow. He came out of it, as most do, with his perspective adjusted. He never became a priest, but as a manager to nervous greenhorns like me, he was part father.

I was one of those who drew out all of the patience a minor-league manager could muster. The first time I pitched for Omaha, I kept walking batters and letting up for soft strikes until three runs had scored with only one out. Keane had no choice but to rescue me on the mound, which he did by taking the ball and saying, "That's pretty good for the first time. We'll get back to you later."

He kept his word, purposefully selecting a situation that was fraught with trouble. There were runners on second and third, and I ushered both of them home with wild pitches. With that, Keane reckoned that I would be going nowhere until I was able to confront my jitters. He presented my next opportunity in the ninth inning of the second game of a double-header, with the score tied 2–2. I walked three batters and, having no place to put the next, struck him out instead and got us into the tenth, when we scored a run to win. I was better from then on.

That's not to suggest, however, that I had found precise control all of a sudden, although I still maintain that the stories of my wildness are somewhat apocryphal. Rodney Wead likes to tell people that he and Bob Boozer and other friends of ours went to one of my games shortly after I'd signed, and my first pitch went over the umpire's head and banged against the screen. That might be approximately true, but there was more to it than met the eye. I had been getting cuffed around pretty good—mostly when I let up to throw a strike—and my brother Fred had suggested that I do something to get the batters' attention and keep them from digging in. So I fired one against the backstop. Keane, for one, must not have been terribly worried about my control (although he joked that I could throw a ball through the side of a barn if only I could hit it), because he counseled me to stop worrying about the strike zone and throw hard. He also advised me that what I thought was my curveball was actually a slider. He would ask for a curve, I'd throw one, and he'd say, "That's a slider. Throw me your curve."

While I'm quick to defend my control, I make no excuses for my curveball. It never was any damn good, and I became a better pitcher once I understood that basic fact, which took a while. In the interim, I was paddled out of Omaha and sent along to the Cardinals' Sally League team in Columbus, Georgia, for a little maturation.

The reassignment was not without merit, because a black fellow could grow up very quickly in Columbus, Georgia. It was a world to which I was unaccustomed, and I'm not referring to minor-league baseball. I'd had a sample of that in Omaha, although the conditions there were deceptively good: I was living in my hometown, playing for an enlightened manager in front of a friendly audience. My roommate in Omaha, a young outfielder named Curt Flood whom the Cardinals had obtained from the Cincinnati organization, was one of the brightest, funniest, most worthwhile individuals I've known to this day. The team as a whole was essentially free of racial undercurrents, with the possible exception of a guy named Boyd

Lynker who was not long for the organization. We were showering at the same time one very hot afternoon when Lynker said to me, perhaps innocently, "Hoot, if the sun keeps beating on us like this, I'll be as black as you." I pushed him up against the wall and told him that if he ever said something like that again, I'd kill him. I may have overstated the case, but the problem never recurred.

Things weren't quite so simple in Columbus. Although it had been a full ten years since Jackie Robinson broke into the National League, baseball in the South wasn't fully integrated yet. As late as 1952, the Tri-State League had banned David Mobley, a black who was on the roster of the team in Rock Hill, South Carolina. The only black player in the long history of the Southern League was a guy named Nat Peeples who batted one time for the Atlanta Crackers in 1954. The color line in the Sally League, where Columbus played, had not been crossed until Hank Aaron and four others did it memorably in 1953. They were greeted by death threats, black cats thrown onto the fields, and screaming fans with mops on their heads. It helped that Aaron led the league in everything but autographs.

In many southern towns, it was still illegal in 1957 for blacks and whites to even play checkers together, much less baseball. Columbus was a long way from the promised land of integration, and as a result I restricted myself to the black side of town during the few weeks of my Georgia sentence. Fortunately, there was another black player on the club, a catcher named Al Davis. We lived at the YMCA and took our meals in the neighborhood. Actually, if not celebrities, we were conspicuous curiosities in the black section of town. I specifically recall, for instance, being eyeballed as I sat in the barber's chair. One fellow, in particular, would watch me through the window of the barbershop and then follow me all over town. I supposed he might have gotten the wrong idea from the fact that I lived among men at the YMCA, and I made sure to stay several steps ahead of him.

I was exposed in Columbus to several layers of society I hadn't before experienced. The people at the ballpark represented another. I was especially intrigued by one of the many nicknames they used in connection with me and Al Davis: Gator Bait. I laughed when I heard it, but years later

I happened to ask a doctor friend if he knew what the term meant and he explained that one of the redneck traditions down in the lowlands was to tie a black kid to the end of a rope and drag him through the swamp in order to lure and trap alligators. When the gators drew close, they would jerk the kid out of the water. No sense in wasting good bait, I suppose.

Taking care to steer clear of the bigots in the grandstand and also of the tobacco juice spit all over the dugout by our manager, Skeeter Newsome, I finished out the season with a 4–3 record as a starting pitcher for the Columbus Foxes. We just missed qualifying for the league championship series, which didn't upset me too much because it meant that I could skedaddle out of Georgia and join up with the Globetrotters.

The Globetrotters actually had two teams, one that traveled the East and another that covered the West, and it was arranged for me to meet up as soon as possible with the East team, which was headlined by the legendary Meadowlark Lemon. After four years with the Jesuits, I was immediately struck by the level and diversity of talent that had been assembled on the Globetrotters. Our ranks of gifted players—many of them of NBA ability—included fellows named Tex Harrison, Carl Green, Goose Tatum (who had also played Negro League baseball with the Indianapolis Clowns), and Leon Hilliard, the designated dribbler. The greatest Globetrotter dribbler, Marcus Haynes, had just retired from the team and another famous one, Curly Neal, had not joined it yet.

Meadowlark was my roommate in the beginning, and I came to know him as a sincere, serious guy—much different from the image of a clown he portrayed so brilliantly on the court. He was not religious, however, and I was surprised when I heard later that Meadowlark had become a minister. I'm sure he was equally surprised that I became a pitcher, because—at least according to what he once told a reporter—he had me pegged for the upper echelon of the NBA. I think maybe Meadowlark was carried away by the sight of a college player who could run and dunk like me, because there weren't many of us in those days. Bob Cousy was about the only big-time player who passed behind his back, and fancy dribbling was considered the sole province of the Globetrotters. Basketball was played so straight in those days that my brother Josh was once taken out of a high school game for shooting one-handed.

I did a lot of creative ball-handling for the Globetrotters, and as the shortest guy on the team, I was the one who broke out of the warm-up circle—where we spun the ball on our fingers and bounced it off each other's backsides—and started the dunking parade. I got a charge out of dunking and attracted some attention with my two-handed backward jam, but often we played twice in a day and by the second game I was too damn tired to carry off anything stylistic. I nearly ended up in the hospital one night when I crashed to the floor while trying the two-handed backward jam after playing a game earlier in the day and then riding two hundred miles on the bus.

The aspect of my Globetrotter experience I most enjoyed was playing the second and third quarters. Our clowning routines were scheduled for the first and fourth periods, when Meadowlark tossed buckets of confetti (made to look like water) at the crowd and we dribbled between the legs of Red Klotz and the Washington Generals. The tricky stuff came natural to me and I looked forward to it, in a sense, because it allowed me to show off the moves I used to practice alone at the Logan Fontenelle rec center, but I was too competitive by nature to be content, basketball-wise, with goofing around. My time was the middle of the game, when we set aside the silly stuff and cleaned the Generals' clocks. If the Globetrotters had played more serious basketball, I probably would have been more serious about staying with them.

It would have helped, also, if I could have remained with Meadowlark's group, but after a few months in the East I was sent over to the West team. One of the reasons I missed Meadowlark so much was that on the West squad I roomed with Sam the bus driver, who snored so loud I couldn't get to sleep. I would try to hurry into the room and get to sleep before he did, but nothing seemed to work. I couldn't bring myself to try the only good suggestion I heard. One of my teammates told me that when he'd had the same problem with a roommate, he'd walked over one night and kissed the guy on the lips. After that, his roommate stayed awake all night watching him. But as much as I wanted to sleep, I wasn't kissing Sam on the lips or anywhere else.

Aside from Sam and a portable floor we played on in Seattle—it was so springy that I was looking down into the basket when I dunked—there was little memorable about the western swing. By then, I was ready to get some rest for the next baseball season, which is exactly what the Cardinal general manager, Bing Devine, wanted me to do. When my Globetrotter tour was over, he tried to persuade me to give it up and stick to baseball exclusively. I told him I'd be happy to do that if I could somehow replace the money Abe Saperstein paid me. Devine asked me how much I made with the Globetrotters, and when I told him four thousand dollars he said, "If I gave you the four thousand, would you quit?" It was the best deal I ever made. For the first time, I was headed in one and only one direction.

Not only was I down to one sport, but one position in that sport. Unless I failed, I would be a big-league pitcher. The prospect of failing was not one that I would or could entertain, however—especially in light of the fact that, in September of 1957, our first child had been born, a spunky, bright-eyed daughter we named Renee.

The irony of the situation—of resolving all my career uncertainties in favor of baseball—was that I was still a much better basketball player. Even in the context of baseball, it seemed peculiar that I wasn't playing the outfield or third base or some position where I could spend my energy on the field every day and switch-hit like I'd been doing for most of my life. As I reflect on it now, I think I could have batted between .280 and .300 as an everyday player, with twenty to twenty-five home runs a year and thirty to forty stolen bases. On the other hand, there was no way in 1957 that I could have predicted comparable numbers for myself as a pitcher. I didn't know what it *took* to be a winning pitcher in the big leagues—or even in the minor leagues.

Whatever it took, the Cardinals apparently thought I had a little of it, because they invited me to their big-league camp at St. Petersburg in 1958. I rode the train to Florida, sitting solemnly in a seat assigned to black passengers as we rolled through the South. That didn't stop three yahoos from trying to rough me up, assuming, I guess, that I needed to be taught a lesson for having the gall to ride on their train instead of the Greyhound bus. Relieved to finally pull into St. Petersburg and say good-bye to Jim Crow's railroad, I walked across the street from the train station to the Bainbridge Hotel, where the Cardinals stayed. There, I got my first sampling of big-league life. When I went up to the desk to register, the clerk advised me that there would be a room waiting for me in a private home on the other side of town. Then he pointed to a door at the end of the hall in the back of the hotel and said that there would be a cab waiting for me on the other side of the door. Curt Flood and a veteran pitcher named Sam Jones and three or four other black players were already at the house when I pulled up in the taxi.

If nothing else, we ate better than the rest of the players and didn't have any coaches banging on our doors at curfew. A few among us made the club that year, including Sad Sam, who, in the only waking moments in which he wasn't chewing on a toothpick, led the league in both strikeouts and walks; and my friend Flood, who started in center field most of the season between Wally Moon and Del Ennis. Although I hadn't yet mastered the control and movement of my pitches, there was plenty of opportunity on the Cardinals for somebody my age with my arm. Fred Hutchinson, a former pitcher, was the St. Louis manager, and the pitching staff, which was ordinary beyond Jones (who, whatever else he might have been, was *never* ordinary), benefited from the presence of shrewd guys like Sal Maglie and Billy Muffett. Maglie, on the verge of retiring an old body that he had milked for every last pitch, took an interest in me for whatever reason. I guess my fastball was sort of conspicuous.

> *The first time I saw Gibby, I knew he had the ability to be something unique. It was before a game the Cardinals were to play against the Reds at Al Lopez Field in Tampa, and I was watching him warm up from the press box. His velocity was very intense, and to get a better look I quickly moved down to the field. I walked over to one of the Cardinals' scouts, Joe Mathis, and said, "My God, Joe, his ball not only is incredibly fast, but I've never seen a ball move as much as that." He was raw, no doubt, but it was truly an outstanding thing to see him go on from that moment to become probably the greatest competitor to ever pitch.*
>
> —BOB BROEG,
> *baseball historian and former*
> St. Louis Post-Dispatch *sports editor*

I was not yet ready for the big leagues, but at least I had seen the last of Columbus, Georgia. After two weeks in St. Petersburg the Cardinals re-assigned me to the minor-league training center at Daytona Beach, and when the season opened they mercifully placed me back home in Omaha. I didn't turn the American Association on its ear, but my 3–4 record included a couple of shutouts that prompted a promotion to the Cardinals' other and higher Triple-A club, Rochester of the International League.

The plan was for me to ease in at Rochester by pitching out of the bull-pen, but I caught a break early. One of our starting pitchers, Lyn Lovenguth, had trouble in the first inning one night, and when the manager, Cot Deal, came out to the mound to remove him, Lovenguth argued long and hard. When he received no satisfaction that way, he stormed into the clubhouse, changed his clothes, packed his bag, and went home. Just like that, I was in the rotation. With regrets to Lovenguth, it was a good situation for me. Deal was actually a terrific guy, and black players were nothing new or objectionable to either Rochester or the International League. There were no impediments for me except hitters who ripped my mediocre curveball. My fastball, however, was voted the fastest in the league at the end of the season, which I completed with a 5–5 record and 2.45 earned run average. I also came within one out of a no-hitter. I was making so much progress as a pitcher, in fact, that I wasn't terribly upset when the Cardinals, worried that I would take a fastball in the right arm while batting left-handed, directed me to stop switch-hitting.

Facing my first winter without basketball, I consented to work on my pitching in the Dominican Republic. I was with the Santo Domingo team for a month or so, then was unexpectedly sold to Puerto Rico. I assumed I was headed for San Juan, but when I got there I found out I was sup-posed to report to Ponce. So I told the cabdriver to take me to Ponce—I figured it was the next town or something—and he started winding through the hills and mountains, driving so fast it made me sick. About six hours later, he stopped the car and said, "Here." I said, "Bullshit." As I re-call, I stuck around for a day or two, and that was it. I had a wife in college and a baby back in Omaha, and that was where I was going. I ended up playing some basketball that winter, after all. They were glad to have me back in the Kellom Elementary league.

# CHAPTER IV

Sal Maglie, the old warhorse pitcher, was released before the 1959 season started, but on his way out he apparently put in a good word for me with one of his sportswriter friends from New York, where he had previously played for the Giants. On Maglie's advice, a writer from a magazine—all these years, I'd remembered it as being *Sports Illustrated*, but in trying to verify that I haven't been able to—showed up in St. Petersburg one afternoon, and we had a cordial conversation while a photographer shot pictures of me with one of my teammates, a black first baseman named George Crowe. I didn't know what to expect in the way of an article, if anything, but I felt reasonably good about the interview. When the magazine came out, there was a forgettable short story accompanied by a photograph with an unforgettable caption that said something like: "I don't do no thinkin' about pitchin'. I just hum dat pea." Charline wrote the magazine (whichever it was) a very sharp letter in response, explaining, in effect, that I hadn't studied Uncle Remus dialect at Creighton. Certain that the article and caption were in *Sports Illustrated*, I never bought another issue until I broke down in 1993—thirty-four years later (by which time I'd begun to have doubts about where the piece appeared)—when *SI* put me and Denny McLain on the cover of a 1968 nostalgia edition.

I had a good chance to make it with the Cardinals in 1959—ostensibly—and then again I really didn't. On the encouraging side, I was learning a slider to go along with my fastball (and to give me a better option than my curveball), and the team was in a rebuilding phase. After breaking Dizzy Dean's Cardinal strikeout record for a season, Sam Jones had been traded to the San Francisco Giants for a first baseman and outfielder named Bill White. That left a mostly unproven starting rotation of Lindy McDaniel, Ernie Broglio, Larry Jackson, and Vinegar Bend Mizell, and I was a leading candidate (allegedly) for a job that would be split between starting and long relief.

The bad news was that my performance would be judged by the Cardinals' overmatched new player-manager, a utility infielder named Solly Hemus, who, at thirty-six, was two years younger than our universally popular superstar, Stan Musial. Hemus must have been the only manager ever to have a problem handling Stan the Man, who didn't hit well that year—in part because Hemus had him and our other power hitter, Ken Boyer, bunting and hitting behind the runner, a strategy best restricted to utility infielders like Hemus—and found himself on the bench, of all places. Then Hemus moved him from left field to first base, which sent Bill White to the outfield, where he floundered. Under better circumstances, White might have gotten some help in the outfield from Curt Flood, who was the best center fielder I ever saw, but Flood was in no position to help anybody after Hemus told him he'd never make it as a big leaguer and replaced him with Gino Cimoli.

Hemus's treatment of black players was the result of one of the following, and I won't try to speculate which: Either he disliked us deeply or he genuinely believed that the way to motivate us was with insults. The result was the same regardless. He would goad us, ridicule us, bench us—anything he could think of to make us feel inept. He told me, like he told Flood, that I would never make it in the majors, and went so far as to suggest that I take a shot at basketball instead. He was apparently convinced that I didn't have a thought in my head when I was on the mound, and was not in the least reluctant to insult my intelligence. When the pitchers would meet before a series to review the hitters on the other team, Hemus would say things like, "You don't have to listen to this, Gibson. You just try to get the ball over the plate."

As far as I was concerned, Hemus's true colors came out one day when we played a doubleheader against the Pirates. He started himself in the second game, and in the first inning the Pittsburgh pitcher, a black righthander named Bennie Daniels, hit him in the leg. The team had not been hitting, and I can understand that Hemus wanted to light a fire under us, but that was no excuse for calling Daniels a "black bastard." Daniels didn't think so either, and the fight that ensued emptied both benches. The next time up, Hemus doubled to the opposite field, and in the sixth inning Daniels knocked him down again. This time, Henus flung the bat at him and they wrestled on the mound. We had a team meeting after the game, and in it Hemus referred to Daniels as a "nigger." Either it didn't occur to him or he didn't care that guys like me and Flood and White and Crowe—not to mention Musial and Boyer and Alex Grammas and other white players—would be personally and profoundly offended. It was hard to believe our manager could be so thickheaded, and it was even harder to play for a guy who unapologetically regarded black players as niggers.

Needless to say, I didn't stay in touch with Hemus after we parted professional company, and I didn't give him a lot of thought. But we bumped into each other at the hundred-year Cardinal reunion in 1992 and he approached me to say that despite what I and Flood thought, he was not a racist. I reminded him of the Bennie Daniels incident and he said that it wasn't a matter of racism; rather, he was a master motivator doing what he could to fire up the ballclub. My response was, bullshit.

I made the team in 1959, but Hemus had me convinced that I wasn't any damn good and consequently I wasn't. My first appearance came in the fifth game of the season against the Dodgers. We were trailing 3–0 when I relieved Larry Jackson, and the first batter I faced was a thirty-year-old infielder named Jim Baxes who was in his first and only season in the big leagues. He took me deep. John Roseboro, the Dodgers' catcher, did the same thing the next inning and we lost, 5–0, as Don Drysdale—a pitcher I would often be linked with in the years ahead—completed his shutout. The next night I got banged around in another defeat by the

Dodgers. Two nights after that, I relieved Phil Clark with two outs and two
runners on in the eighth inning against the Giants, and Orlando Cepeda
tagged me for a double. Then I sat for a week and the Cardinals sent me
back to Omaha.

> *We were at the stage of our careers where we still questioned our-*
> *selves. Looking at Bob, for example—here was one of the all-time*
> *greats, with so much talent, and in the Cardinal organization it*
> *seemed that things too often were made too hard for someone like*
> *him to succeed. It seemed we were looking at brick walls all the*
> *time. We'd make strides, and then we'd be sent back to Omaha.*
> *Up and down, up and down. All along, I thought there was more*
> *involved than purely professional judgment. I thought there were*
> *personal prejudices that entered into it. I was very suspicious of*
> *that.*                                    —CURT FLOOD

I would have been happier in Omaha if Johnny Keane had still been
there, but he was busy in St. Louis trying to talk some sense into Solly
Hemus. Under the new manager, Joe Schultz, I nonetheless pitched better
than I had with the Cardinals, going 9–9 with a couple of shutouts and returning to St. Louis in late July. The Cardinals were in sixth place at the
time (there were eight teams in the National League) and headed down.
With nothing to lose, Hemus started me for the first time on July 30
against the Reds and Jim O'Toole, a young lefthander whom I had known
briefly during my semipro days in Chamberlain, South Dakota. Actually,
O'Toole and I had competed for the same spot on the Chamberlain team
and I had won it. He had beaten me to the big leagues, though, having broken through late in 1958.

Maybe seeing another Basin League face put us both at ease that night.
For whatever reason, we pitched like veterans for a couple of hours, espe-
cially after I wriggled out of a two-on, one-out jam in the first by retiring
Frank Robinson and Jerry Lynch. Boyer doubled and Joe Cunningham
singled him home in the second, and I took a 1–0 lead into the ninth.
Lynch led off the ninth with a single, but Ed Bailey forced him and Willie

Jones fouled out. I was one out away from a shutout, but then I walked Frank Thomas, a dangerous right-handed hitter. At that point, I was half-expecting Hemus to yank me out of the game. McDaniel was beginning to establish himself as an excellent closer—although the term had not yet been invented—and there was no telling what Hemus would do anyway. Once, a black pitcher named Frank Barnes was working on a no-hitter in the fifth when he walked a batter and Hemus relieved him on the spot, never to start him again. But he let me continue against the Reds, even when I walked Don Newcombe (who was pinch-hitting despite being a pitcher) to fill the bases. The next batter was Johnny Temple, a good-hitting second baseman, and with the count two and oh he lined a ball to short center that Flood caught on the run. It wouldn't be the last time that Flood saved a game for me, or a shutout.

Hemus made me the fifth starter after that, but even then I never knew where I stood with him. I pitched and sat and pitched and sat. One night the first batter of the game hit a fly ball to White, who was playing out of position in center field. He misjudged the ball, which was not surprising for a first baseman, and I suppose it rattled me a little bit. I walked the next batter, and with that Hemus came storming out of the dugout. When he reached the mound he told me I was out of the game. I said, "Why in the hell are you taking me out after two batters?" He said, "Get somefucking-body out, and I'll leave you in!" I thought seriously of punching him as we stood there, but decided against it and walked off.

Late in the season I broke a personal losing streak by beating the Cubs with a six-hitter and striking out ten, but apparently Hemus was unimpressed. For whatever reason—he didn't really need one—I stayed on the bench until the last day of the season, when I got the victory in long relief against the Giants to finish the season 3–5 with a 3.33 earned run average, second best on the team behind Larry Jackson's 3.30.

The Cardinals would have liked me to try winter ball again after the season, but our second daughter, Annette, had been born and I didn't want to be that far away for that long. Besides, I had a better offer. Willie Mays had invited me to barnstorm with his team of black all-stars. They toured the South (there's always a catch) playing against a team of white all-stars selected by Mickey Mantle and sharing in the gate receipts. A guy like me could make as much money in a month of barnstorming as he made the whole regular season.

Although I didn't fraternize much during the season, I was familiar with most of the players and had met several of them at Don Newcombe's wedding, where I tasted champagne for the first time. White and Jones, the two guys traded for each other before the 1959 season, were on the tour, as were Newcombe, Frank Barnes, an American League catcher named Earl Battey, and one of Mays's former Negro League teammates, Piper Davis.

I had gotten to know Mays through Bill White, who had played with him in San Francisco. When we were on the coast during my rookie season and had a day off once, White took me out to Mays's house for a casual dinner. I had pitched against the Giants a few times in relief, throwing hard and wild, but Mays didn't really know me up close—especially with my glasses on. When he opened the door, he looked at me, then he looked at White and said, "Who the hell is that?" Bill said, "That's Gibson." When Mays gets excited, his voice goes up a couple of octaves, and this time he became a soprano. "Gibson!" he screamed. "Gibson wears glasses?! Why don't you wear 'em when you pitch, for God's sake? Shit, man, you're gonna kill somebody!"

We did kill Mantle's team, over and over, on a circuit that took us to Baton Rouge and Houston and Laredo and a stop or two in Mexico. The black squad traveled in a caravan of cars, staying and eating along the way in black neighborhoods. It wasn't always easy to get what we needed and occasionally we resorted to gimmicks, such as sending somebody into a white restaurant wearing a chauffeur's cap. Sam Jones could sometimes pass for white if he wore a hat and didn't say much. So he'd pull a stocking cap over his ears and pretend to be a deaf-mute, ordering hamburgers with sign language.

No matter how much I did it, I could never get accustomed to traveling in the South. Nor could I ever forget my first experience there, as a teenager, when our family drove to Louisiana for the funeral of a relative. I vividly recall that we stopped at a filling station in Texarkana, Arkansas, and

I asked the attendant where the bathroom was, but his accent was so thick I couldn't make out the answer. I couldn't keep from laughing, and the whole time my mother was nudging me in the side, trying to get me to stop. When he left she told me I was supposed to go around to the back of the building. There was a filthy, stinking room back there with no lighting or sink, and I decided to just pee in the bushes instead. Ten years later, I still dreaded pulling into gas stations and watching Charline and our daughters walk into Colored Only bathrooms. When that was the only alternative, I sometimes told the attendant to forget about the damn gas. When we finally filled up the tank, I drove until I could drive no more, then we slept in the car because the motels wouldn't take us.

St. Petersburg itself was no better, the difference being that the men who made up the Cardinals, with the exception of the manager and rare others, represented a more enlightened society than the South. We were segregated by the law of the land, but by the spirit of the Cardinals—the players, that is—we were together. It was largely because of that attitude that we were able to reverse the segregation that prevailed in our part of Florida during spring training.

Down in Vero Beach, the Dodgers all stayed together at their training complex, but the other Florida teams were divided into black hotels and white hotels in keeping with the Jim Crow traditions of the South. Many of the black players in the big leagues were from that part of the country and had become resigned to segregation, so there was no serious movement to correct the situation during the 1950s. By 1960, however, the mood had begun to change. Black players had become superstars in large numbers, a fact that served to underscore the ignorance inherent in banning us from places where white people and players could go.

On the Cardinals, the issue came to the fore over an incident involving the St. Petersburg Yacht Club, which every year hosted a breakfast for members of the Cardinals and Yankees, who also trained there. Players were invited individually, on different days, and we noticed that the list of Cardinal players—which was supplied by the Cardinals—included Doug Clemens, a rookie outfielder who had never swung a bat in the major leagues, but didn't include Bill White or Curt Flood or Bob Gibson or

George Crowe or Frank Barnes or Marshall Bridges. White, in particular, took exception to this. He has been raised in a basically white community in Ohio, was college-educated, and by nature took shit from nobody. He was polite, dignified, and unyielding on this point, having been hardened by playing minor-league ball in Burlington, North Carolina, where he sometimes carried a bat in order to get through the hostile crowds that stood between him and the team bus. Local people threw stones at the bus as it drove off.

White made a point to mention the Yacht Club invitation list to Joe Reichler, a baseball writer for the Associated Press out of St. Louis. Reichler wrote a story that was printed by the black paper in St. Louis, which was sufficiently offended to call for a public boycott of Anheuser-Busch, the brewery that owned and still owns the Cardinals. When the news got around, black players on other teams training in Florida began to speak out about the Jim Crow laws, under which not only the hotels but also the restaurants and movie theaters and swimming pools were segregated. White was our unofficial spokesman in St. Petersburg, aided by a black doctor named Ralph Wimbisch who was a friend of the black players and a well-known advocate of civil rights issues in the area. As the pressure increased, August Busch, owner of the brewery and the Cardinals, took up the cause and threatened to move the Cardinals out of Florida if conditions didn't change. About that time, White was quietly asked to a Yacht Club breakfast at some ungodly predawn hour. He said no, thank you.

Meanwhile, a local businessman arranged to buy two of the best motels in St. Petersburg and make them available to the Cardinal players and their families. Several of the white players had traditionally stayed with their families in beachfront cottages during spring training, but when Musial and Boyer gave up their private accommodations to move in with the rest of the team—blacks included—the Cardinals had successfully broken down the local custom. The Cardinal motel became a tourist attraction. People would drive by to see the white and black families swimming together or holding one of our famous team barbecues, with Howie Pollet making the salad and Boyer, Larry Jackson, and Harry Walker (who gave me a great recipe for barbecue sauce) grilling up the steaks and hamburgers.

*I didn't want to go to the Cardinals when I first heard that I had been traded there, because they trained in a city where intense segregation was the rule. There was the infamous story of when Jackie Robinson played in St. Petersburg in 1947 and the Cardinals and the fans razzed him mercilessly; even threw a black cat onto the field. When we were able to integrate our motels, it proved to be a major thing, I believe, not only for the team—I think the unity on our ballclub was a direct result of the entire integration process—but for the city of St. Petersburg as well. To get it accomplished, there were a lot of unsung heroes. Stan Musial and Ken Boyer gave up their personal comforts to move in with the black players, and that lent a large measure of credibility to what we were doing. I also appreciated the considerable efforts of Bing Devine and Arthur Fleischman of the Cardinal front office, because as long as the ballclub accepted segregation, there would be no change. It took a lot of people to pull off what we did, and in the end I think most of us came away with a new respect for the South. It was our own little civil rights movement.*

—BILL WHITE

The camaraderie on the Cardinals was practically revolutionary in the way it cut across racial lines. Musial, for starters, never met a feller (as he would say) he couldn't get along with, and that included Solly Hemus. I suppose that if Stan had made things hard for Hemus, which would have been easy to do, he could have done the club a favor, but Musial never concerned himself with that sort of thing. While he stuck mainly to his hitting and his harmonica, Boyer was the real leader of the team. It was a role Kenny took on naturally. When we traveled, for example, Boyer was the one who rallied everybody together for dinner or a movie or whatever, which went a long way toward establishing the distinctive character of our ballclub. Close friendships were struck up between black and white players like George Crowe and Alex Grammas, or—and this was completely out of the blue—me and Tim McCarver.

I first met McCarver when I spent a few weeks at the major-league camp in 1959. He was younger by six years, but on a much faster track.

McCarver had been practically a legend back home in Memphis, but he was still a teenager and had never been anywhere else to speak of. It was not surprising that he shared the social attitude of his southern homeland. In fact, I expected this of him, and he didn't disappoint me. I happened to be watching him one time that first spring when a black kid jumped the fence during one of our practices and tried to run off with a foul ball. McCarver went after the kid and called him a "little nigger." When I heard that, I got right up in McCarver's face and told him what I thought of his language, his mother, his hometown, his catching ability, and anything else I could think of.

We got along a little better after that, but there was still an air of racial tension between us. After a ballgame in Bradenton one really hot day in the spring of 1960, McCarver got on the bus eating an ice-cream cone. I was eyeing him as he sat down and then I nodded at Flood, who was sitting next to me, and said, "Hey, Tim, can I have a bite of that ice-cream cone?" McCarver didn't know what to do. He looked at me, then he looked at Flood, then he looked back at me, and finally he mumbled, "I'll, er, I'll save you some." Flood and I just exploded in laughter. By then, though, McCarver was already changing, and he ultimately did a 180-degree turnabout in his racial attitude. I have to give him a hell of a lot of credit for that. It was the first time I ever saw a white man change before my eyes.

*I think it's pretty obvious how I was affected in relating to Bob. My prejudices were related directly to my early environment— Memphis, Tennessee, where I was brought up through the age of seventeen years old. Memphis, of course, was a place where some of the most acrimonious protests were held against integration. When I was signed by the Cardinals in the late fifties, I had never played against a black man, much less with one. I heard prejudices spoken around me all the time when I was a kid. It was a substantial thing to overcome all of that. I hadn't formed any opinions of my own. Thank God I was out of there at age seventeen.* —TIM MCCARVER

As well as we got along with the white players, the black players on the Cardinals had been through a lot together and there were still things that we liked to do by ourselves—such as play basketball. We had some guys who could play basketball. One time a group of faculty from a black junior college in St. Petersburg challenged us to a game. They had been playing together as a team and thought they were pretty good, but they had no idea what they were getting into. In addition to me—and I was by no means the hotshot on this team—we had Dick Ricketts, a pitcher who was six feet seven and had been a first-team all-American (along with Bill Russell and Tom Gola) at Duquesne; his brother, Dave, a catcher who was just about as good as Dick; George Crowe, who had played with a famous touring basketball team called the Renaissance Five; and Bill White, who was our hatchet man. (White was as strong as they come, but to this day I've never seen another human being as completely stiff. I called him Robotman. After he was traded to the Phillies, I used to stand in the dugout with my arms out, rocking like a robot, while he was out on first base trying to keep a straight face.) With the talent we had, even White looked good on the basketball floor. We kicked the crud out of those teachers. I expect that, with a little practice, we could have done the same thing to most of the major college teams in the country.

At that point, nothing had changed my mind about being a better basketball than baseball player. Nothing had changed Solly Hemus's mind, either, but at least he kept me with the big club to start the 1960 season—for a while. He also put White at first base and Flood more or less (with emphasis on the "less") in center field, where everybody in St. Louis and the National League knew they belonged. The pieces were slowly starting to come together. Ernie Broglio, with one of the best curveballs in the game, was poised for a big year, and Lindy McDaniel had made a home for himself in the bullpen. Musial wasn't the player he once was, but Boyer had become a full-scale star at third base. It seemed like I was about the only one who wasn't keeping up with the program.

Part of the problem was that I was still messing around with the curveball, which, coming out of my hand, did not resemble Broglio's. A few years ago, I was reminded of my curveball troubles—and why I eventually junked it, for all practical purposes—when I saw Ted Williams at an old-timers' game in Boston. During the cocktail party after the game, he came over to talk and I said, "You know, I faced you once in Arizona." Before going north to start the 1960 season, we stopped in Arizona to play an exhibition game with the Red Sox. "That's right," he said. "I hit a ball past your ear." I couldn't believe he remembered. Naturally, I would remember it, even though it was nearly thirty years before, because he was *Ted Williams*; but I was practically a rookie at the time and it was spring training, for crying out loud. "Yeah," I said. "I got fastball strike one, fastball strike two, and then you hit the curveball." That's where our memories parted. "No," he corrected me. "I took the fastball for a strike and you threw the curve on the second pitch." I guess that's why he was Ted Williams.

Predictably, I didn't see much action early in the 1960 season. I had pitched only nine innings when the Cardinals sent me back down to Rochester. Dick Ricketts and I had a thing working where he would go up and I would go down, then I would go up and he would go down. There was also a complication named Ray Sadecki, whom the Cardinals had signed as a nineteen-year-old bonus baby. He and Julian Javier, a fast, talented second baseman, joined the team at the same time and moved right into prominent roles. As I slinked back to Rochester, it was obvious that the team in St. Louis was taking shape without me.

It was the middle of June when I rejoined the Cardinals for good. Or for bad, as the case was. With Hemus lurking over my shoulder, I felt like I had to strike everybody out to get another chance. The result was that I walked nearly everybody instead—forty-eight in eighty-seven innings— and if I wasn't walking them I was in danger of it, which meant that I laid in the fastball and got creamed. The high point of my season was bringing us to within three games of the Pirates by beating them in an August start. The low point was everything else, which added up to a 3–6 record and a 5.61 earned run average for a team that improved to third place. I was so messed up that my best hope lay in the fact that Hemus, as much as he seemed to dislike me, might not really *know* me. He kept calling me Bridges, confusing me with Marshall Bridges, who was several years older than me, skinnier, and pitched left-handed. But he *was* black. Solly got that much right.

My discouragement reached the point late in the season that I was seriously thinking about taking Hemus's advice and turning to basketball. One day, when I was grumbling words to that effect, one of our coaches, Harry Walker, heard me and came over to lay some benevolence on me. Ironically, Harry the Hat, a Mississippian, was one of the Cardinals who gave Jackie Robinson such a rough time in 1947, and he had a reputation back then as one of the most bigoted players in baseball. But, like McCarver, he had changed his attitude completely after playing with and getting to know black players. And in my deep depression of 1960, he gave me some of the best career advice I ever received. It wasn't much, but it hit the right chord. He said, "Hang in there, kid. He [Hemus] will be gone long before you will."

That was enough to get me through winter ball, anyway. I kept imagining Johnny Keane managing the Cardinals, or Cot Deal, or even Harry Walker, and the thoughts made Christmas in South America—I *hated* spending Christmas in another country—more tolerable. The Cardinals had requested again that I get some winter-league seasoning, and remembering my experience in Puerto Rico two years before, I opted this time for Venezuela, where my teammates on the Oriente team of Caracas included a couple of future big-league managers, Jim Frey (who was my roommate in a German hostel where we stayed) and Joe Altobelli. It was basically a friendly environment, with the exception of the college campus where we played our games. The college students in Caracas were ferociously radical (many of them sympathized with the Communists, who had undertaken a terrorist campaign to oust President Romulo Betancourt because of his support for the U.S. blockade of Cuba) and fought constantly with the local militia. We had to cross a bridge to get to the campus, and every now and then there would be a tank blocking the bridge as we arrived and a line of soldiers telling us, "No game today." We could hear shots being fired on the campus in the distance.

Local politics was not my concern, however, and I pitched a shutout in my first start the day I arrived in Venezuela. Actually, Frey and Altobelli—especially Altobelli—proved to be better managers than hitters, and for lack of offense I finished 7–10 despite leading the league with 134 strikeouts and a 2.05 ERA. When the regular season ended, I was picked up by the Valencia franchise for the Interamerican Series, an annual round-robin tournament to determine the overall winter-leagues champion. The series was held in Caracas and, as usual, a bunch of big-time hitters were there, starting with Roberto Clemente and Orlando Cepeda of San Juan. Keeping my curveball out of the strike zone and slipping in sliders, I defeated San Juan twice, with a three-hitter and a five-hit shutout. The second one tied us with Rapinos, also of Venezuela, for the best record in the tournament, which meant that we had to settle the championship in a one-game playoff. Jose Bracho pitched the title game for us and when our catcher, Dick Windle, hit a home run to win it, we brought home Venezuela's first Interamerican championship after fourteen years of trying.

For the first time in my four-year career as a pro, I had contributed substantially to a winning cause. I also took home an extra sixteen hundred dollars for my winner's share of the pot, which, as it turned out, was the only money I tucked away the whole winter. I'd been earning a thousand a month plus expenses in Venezuela, all the while sending home the thousand and living off the expense money. When I got back to Omaha, I discovered that Charline had devoted all of my paychecks to shopping, which she did enthusiastically and with professional dedication.

The disappearance of my winter money put me in a foul mood, as did the prospect of reporting soon to Solly Hemus. When interviewed before spring training by newspaper reporters, I spoke the truth about my relationship with the manager, which was that I never knew what was in store. Almost as if he were trying to prove what I had said—either that, or to put me in my place—Hemus relegated me to the bullpen at the beginning of the 1961 season, despite my winter performance and a spring in which I posted an ERA of 1.29.

I got a few starts after pitching five innings of two-hit relief against the Braves in the second game of the season. One of the starts was the game in Los Angeles when I fractured Duke Snider's elbow; but I still wasn't intimidating anybody. If anything, I was being intimidated by my own manager, who continued to shuttle me between the bullpen and the rotation, belittling me all the while. I shut out the Cubs in May, but that didn't seem to count for much. After a game that Sadecki won, I was showering when

Hemus walked in and bellowed, "See, Gibson, that's the way you're supposed to pitch—not just throwing the ball, like you do!"

I was 2–6, struggling and miserable as usual, when the fireworks suddenly exploded over Busch Stadium and I gained my long-awaited independence. It was Fourth of July weekend, and the Cardinals, a disappointing eight games under .500 at the time, celebrated by firing Solly Hemus. To top it off, they named Johnny Keane as his replacement. It was a red-letter day.

One of the first things Keane did as manager was walk up to me in the clubhouse, hand me the ball, and say, "You're pitching tonight, Hoot."

It was a whole new world for the black players. With the shackles off, I hit a home run and White hit three (a fourth attempt bouncing off the top of the fence in right-center) to mark the occasion as we pounded the Dodgers 9–1. I was in the rotation to stay; White would hit at least twenty homers and drive in ninety runs for the next four years; and Flood, who would have been an asset to the team if he'd batted .250, became an everyday player and embarked on a run of nine seasons in which his collective average was over .300.

While liberated by Keane, Flood also benefited from the soft wisdom of George Crowe, who was an independent, unconventional thinker (years after he retired from baseball, he excused himself from mainstream society and holed up in a cabin in the woods of upstate New York) and a father figure to both of us when we came up. Although Crowe never played regularly with the Cardinals, he was an established home-run hitter and he knew one when he saw one. He also knew that Flood, at 165 pounds, wasn't one, despite the fact that he had produced a number of home runs in the minors. So Crowe talked Curt out of being another Willie Mays and gently persuaded him to guide the ball to right field in pursuit of .300.

But while Flood's guru was Crowe, there can be no mistaking that mine was Johnny Keane.

*It was apparent to everyone that there was a major change in Gibson when Keane was appointed the Cardinal manager. Gib-*

*son was a changed man overnight. He immediately went out and beat the Dodgers and from there his career began to snowball.*

*—Cardinal announcer* JACK BUCK

*Gibson pitched with a chip on his shoulder, which, of course, was what ultimately identified him as the great pitcher he was; but that had extended into his relations with Hemus, and early in his career it threatened to be his undoing. Hemus was a manager who would take every opportunity to criticize you in front of your teammates. Johnny Keane, on the other hand, was a man of great sensibility, with a great sense of leadership—a sense of reality! Immediately there was a better sense of organization. The most important thing, however, was this: Keane didn't give a damn about color. He said, "You're my best nine men." What a powerful, supportive feeling that was. It was a brand new page, a brand new opportunity. Suddenly, Bob Gibson was getting the ball. Curt Flood and Bill White were playing every day. It was a necessary first step because we were a great team that was being mishandled. Johnny Keane gave a player a million chances to do well or poorly. It was a critical difference.*

*—*CURT FLOOD

*Obviously, the key to Gibson's career was Johnny Keane. Gibson was delighted when Hemus was fired. In fact, he called to tell me.*

*—*BILL WHITE

I was 11–6 the rest of the year, pitching like I'd never pitched at the major-league level. I led the league in walks, which was no surprise, but my ERA of 3.24 was fifth in the league and best among all right-handed starters. I shut out the Phillies in my last start—Flood homered again (despite what Crowe told him)—and with the victory the Cardinals finished with a record of 47–33 under Keane. Under Hemus, we had been 33–41.

I proved my loyalty to Johnny Keane by playing that winter in Puerto Rico, as he wished. Actually, except for my customary depression at Christmas, I sort of enjoyed Puerto Rico this time, since I was able to live in San Juan while playing for the neighboring town of Santurce. I made it a point to learn and speak Spanish when I was there, and the Puerto Ricans appreciated that. In turn, I appreciated the eighteen-karat gold you could buy dirt cheap at any of the jewelry stores lined up along the street.

Baseball-wise, it was a strange winter in one way, and typical in another. I had a losing record during the regular Puerto Rican season for Santurce, but when the postseason playoffs arrived, suddenly everything was working for me. This wasn't something that I calculated, or even that I could fully explain. But the same thing had occurred the winter before, and it would prove to be a pattern in my career. It would prove, in fact, to be the thing that distinguished my career. For whatever reason—there are several theories I could choose from—I was a different pitcher in the postseason.

Our best pitcher in the regular winter season was Juan Pizarro, an immensely talented lefthander who was a native of Santurce. To the delight of the local fans, Pizarro led the league in strikeouts, ahead of me. Our best hitter, and the league leader in home runs, was another native Puerto Rican, Orlando Cepeda, whose father had been the most famous player in the island's baseball history. Despite our talent and our popularity, though, we finished third in the league standings.

The playoffs were a different matter entirely. For some reason our manager, Vern Benson, elected to pitch me (it could have been that he was impressed by a one-hitter I threw against Ponce earlier in the season; it could have been that, since he was employed by the Cardinals, he wanted to take a look at me under pressure; it could have been that Pizarro needed rest) in the first game of the semifinal series against Caguas, which we won 10–0. We lost the next day when Pizarro gave up home runs to Frank Howard and Jim Rivera; but after another loss, I tied the series by beating Caguas again 8–1, and Pizarro came through in the clincher, 1–0, the only run coming on a homer by a hot local player named Martin Beltran.

That put us in the Puerto Rican finals against Mayagüez, the regular season champion, and set up a showdown between me and Joel Horlen of the White Sox, who all winter had been the best pitcher in the league. I came up with a three-hitter and struck out fourteen while Horlen matched me most of the way. It took a bad-bounce triple by Leo Cardenas, our

shortstop by way of Cincinnati (and a friend who lived in the same apartment building as I did in San Juan) to set up the tying run, which scored
on a balk by Horlen as he pitched to me with the bases loaded. All the
games were that close, but we swept the series when Cepeda hit a two-run
homer in the eighth inning of the fourth game for a 5–4 victory.

The Interamerican series was in San Juan this time. Since the rules permitted league champions to add a few players from other teams—which
was how I ended up pitching for Valencia the season before—we picked
up Cookie Rojas, Tony Gonzalez, and Mike de la Hoz from Arecibo. At this
stage, the competition was virtually major-league. Even so, we had little
trouble in the tournament after getting past Panama, 5–4, in the first
game, with Orlando Pena relieving me late. We picked up the pace when
Pizarro struck out fifteen to beat Bo Belinsky 10–1 the next day and
Gonzalez made one of the greatest catches I've ever seen, climbing the
fence to make a backhanded stab while getting his foot stuck in the wire
mesh. My second victory in the series came on a three-hitter against Caracas in a game in which I hit a three-run homer. I was 5–0 in the playoffs
and aiming to make it six in the final game, but had to leave in the ninth
inning with the score tied. De la Hoz won it for us with a home run in the
eleventh against Luis Tiant.

The Interamerican series acquainted me not only with postseason pressure, but with any number of players whom I would encounter in the
National League. During the 1962 winter series (following the 1961
major-league season), I was particularly interested in the young shortstop
for Mayagüez, Julio Gotay, because he was a teammate of mine on the Cardinals and was expected to be the long-awaited answer to our perennial
shortstop problem. Gotay, who was a native of Puerto Rico, was a big guy
for a shortstop, but he seemed to have all of the physical skills. We would
learn the hard way, however, that the physical skills aren't always enough.

It was not unexpected that Gotay would have difficulty communicating,
but many Spanish-speaking players had overcome that obstacle and in
Gotay's case it figured to be less of a problem because his double-play
partner at second base, Julian Javier, was from the Dominican Republic.
(Javier's name, by the way, was pronounced *Hoolian Havier*, which
prompted several of us to ask Hoolie if he liked to hit against Cincinnati's

*Hoey Hay* [Joey Jay].) It turned out that Gotay's shortcomings exceeded the language complication. He was interested in neither discipline nor fundamentals, which translated into an uncommon number of errors and foolish mistakes. On the field and off, he would do things we just couldn't believe. One day he complained that his wife back in Puerto Rico hadn't been getting the money he was sending her. We found out he had been sticking his pay envelope in the mailbox with no address or anything. We would have been amused by Gotay except for a couple of things. One was that he was handed our shortstop job in 1962, and he wasn't getting the job done. The other was that he kept spooking us with voodoo.

Most of us didn't take the voodoo seriously, but now and then things would happen to make us a little uneasy. The scariest—and funniest— incident occurred after Gotay was traded away and playing for the Astros. Javier had pulled into second base on a double or something, and as he was dusting himself off Gotay said something to him and Hoolie jumped about three feet in the air. When he did that, Gotay tagged him out, but Javier didn't care. He raced back to the dugout and sat down in the corner. We asked him, "What's going on? What did he say?" Javier just waved his arms and said, "Voodoo! Voodoo!" Mike Shannon told him, "Fuck that voodoo," but Hoolie was dead serious, shouting, "*No más! No más!*" He wouldn't tell us what Gotay had said; he just wanted out of there.

Our problem at shortstop, among other subtle deficiencies, prevented us from making a run at the pennant in 1962, but it wasn't a lost season—at least not for me, and not for Stan Musial. The great Musial had fallen under .300 for three straight seasons, but in 1962—revitalized, no doubt, by the presence of Johnny Keane and the prospect of playing thirty-six games against expansion teams—he rallied at the age of forty-one to hit .330, third in the league, including a three-homer game at the Polo Grounds. He didn't seem to have any terrific problems in left field, either, while Bill White flourished at first base with his first of three straight 100-RBI seasons.

We were the first team ever to play the New York Mets when they joined the National League that year. The '62 season was scheduled to begin on a Tuesday in St. Louis, but the opener was rained out and reset for Wednesday, a day on which several of the Mets, including Roger Craig, their starting pitcher, were stranded for thirty minutes in an elevator at the Chase Hotel. Later, we had the privilege of handing Craig his first of twenty-four defeats that season, and the Mets their first of 120, by a score of 11–4.

My first start of the season, a few days later, resembled Roger Craig's. I was roughed up for six runs in the first inning. After that our pitching coach, Howie Pollet, made me throw more pitches and simulate game conditions in the bullpen, which seemed to help. In my next start I had a no-hitter going against Houston until Roman Mejias reached me for a home run leading off the eighth. I ended up winning on a two-hitter, then beat the Colt .45s again on a five-hitter when Musial homered in the ninth. I had found a groove. Two starts later, I got my first shutout of the season, 1–0, against the Giants and Billy O'Dell.

With that, the good reviews started to file in. I most appreciated those from the coaching staff. Pollet said that, having overcome my lack of confidence and control, "Gibson is well on his way to becoming the outstanding pitcher in the league." Johnny Keane told a reporter essentially the same thing—based on the previous three weeks, anyway—and added that I certainly had the best arm in the league. I realized it was a prejudiced and very qualified endorsement, but it did a hell of a lot for me nonetheless. For three years, I'd had a manager whose only comments about me were insults. Keane's remarks—which carried more weight than Pollet's only because he was the boss—raised my profile in the eyes of me, my teammates, and the league. Musial said, around the same time, that I was the fastest pitcher over nine innings that he'd ever seen, and it was not lost on me that over twenty-one seasons at the top of the game—including sixteen in a row in which he hit over .310, which boggles my mind—he'd seen a few.

I suppose that different athletes respond differently to praise and criticism, but I much preferred the former, and it showed. In late May I pitched 22⅔ scoreless innings in a row until Johnny Callison of the Phillies broke the streak with a home run. A year before at that point of the season, I had been demoted to the bullpen, a three-time failure nine games under .500 for my career. Now I had an outside shot at the all-star game. For that, I had the manager to thank.

*Bob revered Johnny Keane, and from the start it was obvious that John could get the best out of Bob. They had some conflicts, but the real sign that their relationship was strong was the fact that, unlike Solly Hemus, John could criticize Bob and do it constructively. I remember one instance when Bob allowed a home run to Mel Queen, a pitcher (and occasional outfielder) for Cincinnati. Bob recalls it, too, and his ability to mimic is classic. We laugh about the confrontation, but it was serious then. Keane said, "You can't concentrate! Don't go out there and just throw the ball." He might say the same thing that Hemus would say to Bob, but with Keane there wasn't the edge to it. They'd get mad, but it would blow over.*
—TIM McCARVER

Instead of comparing me unfavorably to Ray Sadecki, my younger teammate, Johnny Keane would optimistically point out to me what Sandy Koufax was doing in Los Angeles. Koufax had begun his career almost exactly as I had, throwing hard as hell but wildly in his first few years and relying too heavily on his fastball. He suddenly became a great and overpowering pitcher when he learned to throw his curve for strikes. I didn't have Koufax's curve, but my slider was coming along nicely and my control was improving each season. And with that, I was gaining more confidence on the mound. I was taking on a presence, which, to me, was and is a very large part of what pitching is all about.

Although confidence takes time to build, there was a specific moment in 1962 when I decided that I was going to do things my way on the mound. It had to do with a veteran catcher on the Cardinals named Carl Sawatski. Sawatski used to dominate the game when I pitched because he knew all about the guy batting and he figured—sometimes correctly, sometimes not—that I didn't. It used to aggravate the hell out of me, but he had been around the league many times and so I took it. Then, in St. Louis one night, I was pitching to Jim Pendleton of the Colt .45s and Sawatski wanted me to throw a fastball. I wanted to throw a breaking ball and shook him off. He shook me off and I shook him off again, and back and forth we went. It happened that Sawatski was a good breaking-ball hitter, and he reasoned that, since he could hit the breaking ball, most other hitters could, too; but that wasn't necessarily the case. Pendleton had been fouling my fastball straight back to the screen, and when that happens it means the hitter is right on the pitch. I thought, whoa, I'd better change something.

Anyway, after getting nowhere with the signs, Sawatski finally came out to the mound and said, "Goddamn it, Hoot, we're gonna throw this guy a fastball." I said I didn't want to throw him a fastball. He said, "You've *got* to throw him a fastball because that's what I want you to do!" So he took his place behind the plate and I threw the fastball and Pendleton hit it up on the scoreboard. As he rounded the bases, I stood on the mound and pouted, my hands on my hips. When he saw that, Sawatski stormed back out and said, "Goddamn it, Rook [I wasn't a rookie, obviously, except in his eyes], don't you ever show me up like that again!" He was absolutely right. That was the last time I ever expressed any emotion on the field. From that day on, I never showed anybody up, and I never, ever, let a catcher or anybody else call a pitch I didn't want to throw. I said to myself: To hell with this. If I'm gonna get beat, I'm gonna get beat my way.

It worked for me, and in early July, to the surprise of many, including myself, I was named to my first National League all-star team. With that, the rehabilitation of my confidence was nearly complete.

There were actually two all-star games in 1962, the fourth and final year of the two-game format. The first was held in Washington, and I knew I wasn't going to pitch because the game was on Tuesday and I had thrown a three-hit shutout against the Mets on Sunday. But I loved the recognition—it was bound to help me as a pitcher, I figured, by establishing my credentials in the eyes of the batters—and soaked up the hoopla. I didn't know many people, however, and was hanging around with Earl Battey of the Minnesota Twins (note that I wasn't fraternizing with any *National* League players). Battey had played a year in Washington before the franchise moved to Minnesota, and he knew his way around the city a little bit. At one point, a tall gray-haired man walked up and Battey said, "Bob, I'd like you to meet our vice president." I said hi, but I didn't really understand why Battey wanted to introduce me to the vice president of the Twins. It was only later, sitting in my hotel room, that it dawned on me that I had met Lyndon Johnson, the vice president of the United States. I happened to be a great admirer of his boss, John F. Kennedy.

We won that game 3–1 behind Drysdale, Juan Marichal, Bob Purkey, and Bob Shaw, but lost the second game three weeks later at Wrigley Field in Chicago, 9–4. In two innings of pitching, I was party to one of the American League's nine runs.

In between, I had parlayed my new confidence into three straight three-hitters. No longer fearful that the manager would banish me for the slightest indiscretion, I was throwing strikes with much greater regularity, walking just over three batters a game as compared to nearly five a game for the three seasons prior. I felt so good I was ready to take on Koufax.

Koufax missed part of 1962 and won only fourteen games that year, but he was in the first of five consecutive seasons in which he would lead the league in ERA. My first crack at him came late in the season in St. Louis, long after the Cardinals had been eliminated (we would finish in sixth place, six games over .500) but while the Dodgers were involved in a hot race for the pennant with San Francisco. I welcomed the challenge and stayed with Koufax through eight scoreless innings, giving up only two hits. The man on the Dodgers who could beat you—whom you couldn't *let* beat you—was Tommy Davis, who had an incredible 153 RBIs that year for a team that didn't score many runs, and I had to face Davis in the ninth. I had been striking him out all night with sliders low and away, however, and I seemed to have the edge on him. I had noticed that as I continued to pitch him outside, Davis was gradually sneaking up toward the plate. By the ninth inning, he was practically on top of the plate, and so, out of duty, I buzzed him inside with a fastball. I don't know if he was setting me up, but he must have been looking for the fastball on his ribs, because he backed off a step, turned on that thing, and crushed it over the left-field fence. That was all Koufax needed.

I was 15–13 with a 2.85 ERA late in the season—good numbers but a far cry from the best in the league, as Keane and Pollet had projected me—when I turned away sharply from a pitch in the batting cage, of all places, caught my spikes, and fractured my ankle. That ended my year after thirty starts, half of them complete games. Shortly before, the *Sporting News* had trumpeted me as "the next great N.L. twirler"—it was nice to hear those sentiments expressed outside the organization—but that only made it more difficult to sit out the balance of the season, especially in light of the fact that we had another crack at the Dodgers. While I watched with my leg in a cast, Curt Simmons took my spot in the rotation and beat Los Angeles twice, including a 1–0 shutout on the last day of the season that prevented the Dodgers from clinching the pennant and forced a playoff with the Giants, which San Francisco won.

At that stage of my career, I was neither well schooled nor particularly conscientious about the process of rehabilitation, and as a result my ankle came around slowly. It was fortunate for the Cardinals that Bing Devine had a more productive winter than I did, trading Gotay and pitcher Don Cardwell to Pittsburgh for reliever Diomedes Olivo and the shortstop we desperately needed, former batting champion—and basketball all-American from Duke—Dick Groat. The trade was made during the winter instructional league, and to get it done Devine had to plead his case with Branch Rickey, the venerable Hall of Fame executive whom August Busch had hired as a consultant. Rickey opposed the trade, but the rest of the Cardinal brain trust—Devine, Harry Walker, and Eddie Stanky—felt so strongly about it that they circled Rickey at Al Lang Field in St. Petersburg and wouldn't allow him to move until he approved the deal. When it came through, the trade gave us a ring of stars around the horn—White, Javier, Groat, and Boyer—whom Rickey later referred to as the greatest hitting infield he had ever seen. McCarver would take over in 1963 as our regular catcher, leaving only the outfield unresolved among the regular positions. Flood was entrenched in center, but left and right were problem areas manned mostly by Charlie James, George Altman, and Musial, who would be playing his final season.

In retrospect, 1963 is a year I wish I could have back. The Cardinals were ready to win big, and I would have been, too, if only I had seen to it more diligently in the off-season. As of May 19 I had won only one game, and the Cardinals, who had started fast, were suffering from my inability to pitch at the level they had reason to expect from me after 1962. There was a lot of fearful reminiscing about Dizzy Dean's rapid dropoff when he tried to come back too fast after having his ankle broken by Earl Averill in the 1937 all-star game. It worried me, and I couldn't pitch worried.

My girls were growing up nicely all the while (I had gotten to know them much better as I was sitting home in a cast over the winter), but at the same time there were extracurricular distractions that seemed to set me back almost as much as the broken ankle. Feeling established with the Cardinals at long last, I figured it was time to move out of the George Washington Hotel, where I had been staying, and bring my family to St. Louis to settle down—which, I knew, was not a simple proposition. A couple of years before, when I was still unfamiliar to the fans of St. Louis, Harry Caray, the Cardinal announcer, had let it be known as we broke spring training that I was looking for a house, and eight or nine calls came in. Somehow, though, it apparently got lost in the translation that I was black, because every time I went to look at a place it suddenly became unavailable. After that, Bill White had arranged to buy a house in St. Louis, but he chose not to close the deal after the neighbors picketed it. This time, after a few fruitless weeks of shopping around, I gave up the fight, took an apartment on Kingshighway, and vented my anger on the mound.

Early in the season my ineffectiveness had been offset by a hot second-year pitcher, Ray Washburn, who started off 5–0; but when he hurt his arm, the onus was on me. Since worrying obviously wasn't the answer, I decided to hell with the ankle—which was the way Josh taught me, anyway. With that, I ran off six straight victories, relying on my slider and two fastballs, one that sailed and one that sank inward like a screwball. I also started hitting after I painted a pair of eyes on my bat to see the ball better, coming up with a long two-run homer to win a game late in May that moved us into third place. Javier borrowed my bat and immediately went on a tear.

We found ourselves in a first-place tie with the Giants after I beat the Phillies 5–4 in late June despite giving up four home runs. Lew Burdette, a veteran pitcher who had just come to us in a trade with the Braves, called me "Boom Boom" in honor of the onslaught, which I'm sure he wouldn't have done if we'd lost. On general principles, I called him "cocksucker."

My teammates—and my wife and children and even the St. Louis reporters—knew better than to give me a hard time or even talk to me after a loss. Losing made me testy for two or three days, impatient to get back out there and make up for last time. As soon as my mad wore off, it was time to get my game face on, which made me grumpy all over again.

Poor Curt Flood: He caught the brunt of my pitching moods since we roomed together for so long on the road. The night before a game, I'd be so uptight, I'd start shouting at the television. After a while, I'd figure Flood was about to take a punch at me, so I'd leave the room late at night just to be alone and walk around the city, wherever we were.

I was in one of my moods during a trip to San Francisco early in July, after we had fallen out of first place by losing seven or eight in a row, including a start or two of mine. We had a doubleheader scheduled against the Giants, who were still in the race—the Dodgers had taken over the lead by this time—and I was to pitch the second game. The Giants won the first game in fifteen innings, which meant that I had to beat Marichal, who had won nine in a row, to keep us from getting swept and extending our losing streak. This put me in an unusually unfriendly state of mind.

> *It was my first day in the big leagues in 1963, and in the opener of the doubleheader I'd had a good game against the Cardinals' Bobby Shantz. Between games, Mays came over to me and said, "Now, in the second game, you're going up against Bob Gibson." I only half-listened to what he was saying, figuring it didn't make much difference. So I walked up to the plate the first time and started digging a little hole with my back foot to get a firm stance, as I usually did. No sooner did I start digging that hole than I hear Willie screaming from the dugout: "Noooooo!" Well, the first pitch came in inside. No harm done, though. So I dug in again. The next thing I knew, there was a loud crack and my left shoulder was broken. I should have listened to Willie.*
>
> —JIM RAY HART

The umpire, Al Barlick, didn't say anything when I hit Jim Ray Hart in the second inning. I guess he understood that Hart had in a way hit himself. He had a closed stance, with his left foot nearly on home plate, and was simply unable to move quickly enough to avoid an inside pitch, which I was obligated to throw him as long as he cheated toward the outside corner. (Hart was on the disabled list for several weeks after I fractured his shoulder, and in his first game back Curt Simmons conked him in the head. After that, I'm sure he cringed every time he saw the Cardinals coming. A few years ago, I was playing in an old-timers' game, and when the manager noticed that the game might end before I had a chance to pitch, he rushed me out there to throw to Hart. When I ran to the mound, Hart's mouth dropped open. He thought I'd requested to pitch to him, as if we had unfinished business.) Barlick took no action, either, when I brushed back the next hitter, Ernie Bowman. But when Marichal buzzed one past my head as I batted in the top of the third, the ump smacked him with a fifty-dollar fine. We won the game, 5–0, and afterwards I explained to the press that Hart had been hitting outside pitches in the first game and I was pitching him close to keep him from lunging. I also said that Marichal would have been justified in throwing at me, which he had obviously done, if I had been throwing at Hart, but there was a big difference between throwing at a guy and brushing him back.

Although Jim Ray Hart may feel differently, to me the significant aspects of that game were that I had beaten Marichal, a master on the mound whom I regard as the best pitcher of my generation (I wouldn't have many opportunities to beat him in later years, when he began avoiding direct confrontations), and that my reputation was evidently established—with the other team and even the umpires—as a pitcher who would bring the ball inside when necessary. The brushback pitch is a lot like the spitball in the sense that its effectiveness lies largely in the awareness it places in the batter's mind.

My reputation was not to the point, however, that I made the all-star team in 1963 with numbers that fell short. But Musial made it for the twenty-first consecutive time, and so did our entire infield. In fact, when Bill Mazeroski of Pittsburgh was unable to start at second base because of an injury, Javier was inserted in his place, completing a National League infield made up entirely of Cardinals—the only time in all-star history that one team has supplied all four positions.

The second half of the season boiled down to a race between the Cardinals and Dodgers, with the Dodgers leading it most of the way. I was particularly peeved by a game in Los Angeles when Koufax beat me 1–0, just as he had the year before in St. Louis. It was the eerie similarity of the game that made me so damn mad. There was no score going into the bottom of the ninth, and once again I had to get past Tommy Davis, who was working on his second straight batting title. Smart guy that I am, I remembered that Davis had beaten me the year before when I stopped pitching him outside and came in with a fastball. I thought, "Now, he remembers that I remember that pitch inside, and so he's thinking that there's no way I'm coming inside again in this situation. Just to cross him up, I'm gonna do it again." So I threw the fastball inside again, and goddamn if he didn't hit it out again to beat me. I learned right then that the dumbest thing you can do as a pitcher is try to be too smart.

In spite of my backfiring brilliance, we made a run at the Dodgers in September. It was one of the all-time runs, in fact. For three unbelievable weeks, we kept winning and winning and winning. We won nine in a row until Bob Veale, a huge man and hard thrower of the Pirates, beat us to stop the streak, but then we took off again. After we swept the Braves, our pennant hopes were raised to the point that Bob Bauman, our trainer, dragged out a corny old recording by Spike Jones called "Pass the Biscuits, Mirandy." That had been the Cardinals' theme song, played after every victory, when they won the pennant and World Series in 1942, and was summoned back in 1946 when the team was slumping. Sure enough, the Cardinals rallied behind the singing of Spike Jones to take the pennant and the series again in '46. However, Mirandy's biscuits had not graced the St. Louis clubhouse in seventeen years and a recording of the song could not be found until Bauman contacted Spike Jones in Beverly Hills and Jones made a copy for us. If that wasn't enough to inspire us, Musial made a diving catch near the wall in the bullpen one night and followed it with a home run—another flashback to 1942 and 1946. We were winning every way imaginable.

My personal highlight during the streak was a game against the Cubs in St. Louis when I pitched a shutout and hit a three-run homer to give me three for the season and twenty RBIs—not bad for a pitcher. I had more RBIs than most of the pitching staffs in the league—a distinction, it should be noted, that failed to impress my teammates. Although it hadn't affected me too much on the mound, I'd had a muscle spasm in my side that night against the Cubs, and as a result I took it slow around the bases, which gave my good friends in the dugout (who didn't know that my side hurt) the idea that I was showboating. They shouted "Hoot! Hoot!" as I carefully made my way around, and afterwards White ragged me hard about the modest length of my home run. That was fair enough, but when Flood got into the act, I told him that I didn't even discuss long balls with a Punch-and-Judy hitter like him. I preferred to place myself in the company of a man like Musial, who the same night put us in the lead with a two-run homer onto the pavilion roof of old Busch Stadium. Earlier that day, Musial had become a grandfather. He passed out cigars to mark the occasion, and we puffed happily in the glow of our hot streak.

This time, we won ten straight, giving us nineteen victories in twenty games. Headed back to St. Louis after a triumphant road trip, we heard on the airplane that the Giants had beaten the Dodgers to pull us within three games of first. There was no wild cheering on the plane—we weren't that kind of club—but, as Flood described it, the news was met with a lot of "loud smiles." About three thousand St. Louisans greeted us at the airport.

At home, we continued to roll on, winning one game when Mike Shannon, a native of St. Louis and a twenty-four-year-old rookie with four children, hit his first major-league home run. I got my eighteenth victory of the season—matching Ernie Broglio for the team high—in my next start against Milwaukee, but my fourth home run was taken away when a fan touched a ball that was headed for the bleachers. Then Sadecki shut the Braves out, and when the Dodgers came to town in late September we trailed them by only a game.

We were in great shape for the series, considering our momentum and the fact that Curt Simmons and I had each pitched three complete games in a row, which meant that the bullpen was rested. Lindy McDaniel was unfortunately gone in '63, traded to the Cubs along with Larry Jackson for George Altman and others, but the slack had been taken up pretty well by the left-right combination of Bobby Shantz and Ron Taylor.

Whatever shape a team was in, though, it had to really do something to outpitch the Dodgers. In the first game, Podres beat us despite Musial's last home run, which tied the game in the seventh. Koufax threw a four-hitter the next night, which put us three games out of first and meant that I had to beat a lefthander named Pete Richert if we were to stay in the race even remotely.

We chased Richert early and led 5–1 going into the eighth. I had retired seventeen of eighteen batters, and the game seemed to be in hand when Maury Wills singled and Junior Gilliam bounced a bad hop over the shoulder of Javier. Then I walked Wally Moon to fill the bases and my old nemesis, Tommy Davis, singled in two runs to make it 5–3. Keane removed me in favor of Shantz, who allowed another run on a wild pitch and fly ball, but Taylor retired Moose Skowron to preserve a 5–4 lead going into the ninth.

Among the players the Dodgers had called up when the rosters were expanded in September was a left-handed hitter named Dick Nen with whom none of us was familiar—that is, until that miserable ninth inning at Busch Stadium. He had made his first major-league plate appearance earlier in the game and left no particular impression. That was why nobody in our dugout believed it when we saw the ball bouncing on the pavilion roof over the right-field grandstand. We still could have won the game in the bottom of the ninth or any of the next few innings—especially the thirteenth, when Groat led off with a triple against Ron Perranoski—but the moment was destined to be remembered as Dick Nen's. The Dodgers outlasted us that night and for the season, ultimately taking the pennant by six games and then sweeping the Yankees in the World Series.

Despite the disappointing finish, there were unmistakable signs that a new day was at hand for the Cardinals, as it was for St. Louis itself. Construction on the Gateway Arch began in 1963, and also on a new Busch Stadium along the Mississippi River to replace the old one—the former Sportsman's Park, the oldest major-league field in operation at the time— which was situated in a deteriorating inner-city residential neighborhood. There was a tangible energy in the environment surrounding the Cardinals, and with the infield we had and the pitching staff coming together as it was, there was every reason to believe we could grab the ring next time. We only wished that Musial could be with us in 1964.

We had the same wish for President Kennedy, who was assassinated in November. I was installing chimes on my doorbell when I heard the news.

# CHAPTER V

Our late charge in 1963 saved Johnny Keane's job, thank goodness (after owning the club for more than a decade without a pennant, Mr. Busch was growing impatient), and when he got us together before the 1964 season he had our path to the pennant all laid out for us. The skipper explained that since Koufax had beaten us five times the year before, all we had to do was figure out how to beat Koufax.

As it turned out, we never managed to do that on a regular basis, but it proved to be a small point in 1964 because the Dodgers were no longer the team to beat. It was a strange season—so irregular that the Phillies called it the Year of the Blue Snow. They were the team to beat.

The players on the Cardinals had an uncommon amount of faith in each other, but until very late in the season there was little to justify it. The most optimistic moment was manufactured by Harry Caray, who was so excited during the first week of the season when notoriously weak-hitting Roger Craig—whom we had obtained from the Mets for George Altman—doubled off the center-field wall to drive in a couple of runs that he spontaneously declared, "The Cardinals are going to win the pennant! Holy cow!"

There weren't many other signs to that effect, however, unless mutual admiration and camaraderie counted for something. The Cardinals were the rare team that not only believed in each other but genuinely *liked* each other. We'd go out to eat after a ballgame and a dozen guys would show up, black and white. As a team, we would simply not tolerate any sort of festering rancor between us, personal or racial.

The integration of our hotel in St. Petersburg had established this mood on the Cardinals, and several of us were self-appointed to the role of sustaining it. Even our wives joined in, setting up an integrated day care center in St. Petersburg that openly defied the prevailing Jim Crow practices. If one of the wives caught wind of a racial offense or indiscretion within the ballclub, she would pass it along to the proper authority—which happened to be me or Bill White. We would confront the offender directly and make it clear that there would be none of that on the St. Louis Cardinals. One of my teammates once referred to Mike Epstein of the Orioles as "Superjew," and I chewed him out on the spot. When Charline relayed to me, having heard it through another wife, that some of the players were calling me "Supernigger" behind my back, I checked my anger—the word "nigger" actually makes me perspire—and went straight to the guys concerned to let them know that it would stop immediately. That was our method. We brought our racial feelings out into the open and dealt with them.

As long as I was with the Cardinals, we were like that. I'm confident that I had a lot to do with it, and so did guys like White and Flood. None of the three of us was southern, none of us was uneducated, and none of us gave an inch to racism. The white players respected that. They respected our intelligence and our leadership, and in turn we respected them. McCarver, as I've noted, worked hard at changing his attitude about black people. Shannon didn't give a damn about color, and if I didn't always agree with Boyer—he took a hard line, for instance, against interracial marriage—at least we could discuss our respective positions in a climate of friendly tolerance. Those guys had as much to do with the Cardinals' racial disposition as Flood and White and I. In his book, *The Way It Is,* Flood wrote (and I wholeheartedly agree): "The men of that team were as close to being free of racist poison as a diverse group of 20th-century Americans could possibly be."

Having signed on with the team before it was integrated in Florida, I was able to watch our efforts toward racial harmony mature into a Cardinal tradition. White and Musial and Boyer and Bing Devine started the legacy by breaking down the segregationism of St. Petersburg, and the same attitude was alive and well when I retired nearly a generation later. By then, virtually the entire team conspired to educate any among us who might be derelict on the racial question. The best example of that was in 1973, when we acquired a pitcher from the Red Sox named Ken Tatum. During spring training, Tatum was talking with reliever Al Hrabosky, the Mad Hungarian, when he spotted Dave Ricketts and his wife. Ricketts, who had remained with the team for a long time as bullpen coach, was light-skinned but apparently of mixed racial heritage, and his wife was clearly black. Tatum said to Hrabosky, "I know what Ricketts's wife is, but what's Ricketts?" Hrabosky took the conversation straight to the team, and I confronted Tatum with it. I said, "Look, we don't have any of that crap on this team." The remark had probably seemed innocent enough to him, and he was shaken by our strong reaction. A little while later, Tatum and I happened to be in the training room together and one of our trainers, Gene Gieselmann, pointed out a scar on my knee. "See this scar?" he said to Tatum. "Gibson got that in a knife fight." Tatum was released the next day, and he probably still thinks it was because of what he said about Ricketts.

Of all the teams I was on, though—of all the teams I've ever *seen*—there was never a better band of men than the '64 Cardinals. We were convinced of that. Whether it translated into a pennant was another matter, however, and one about which there was considerable doubt when we found ourselves in seventh place two weeks before the all-star break. First off, the pitching was slumping, led by me: After a 4–0 beginning, I gave up six runs in five consecutive starts. There were many who thought I ought to go to the bullpen to work out my problems, but Keane said he was sticking with me because the Cardinals wouldn't win big unless I did. Bob Bauman, the trainer, noticed that I was tiring in the late innings, so he con-

tacted a nun he knew who liked to take movies and asked her to film me
pitching. The films suggested that my velocity was stable in the late innings but my control wavered. It turned out that my legs weakened after
a hundred pitches or so, and when that occurred, I released the ball too
soon. The manager's prescription for this problem was running the stadium stairs. I didn't like it, but I got stronger. My shoulder was also sore,
and the remedy I found for that was to loosen it up by waxing my car before a game.

I was extremely irritable during my tailspin, of course, and to his
credit—although I didn't see it that way at the time—Gene Mauch, the
Philadelphia manager, effectively took advantage of my temperament one
May night in St. Louis. I was leading the Phillies 7–1 in the fourth inning
when Mauch ordered his pitcher, Dennis Bennett, to knock down Javier.
It seemed that the Phillies had been indiscriminately throwing at several
of our players all night, and after Javier went down I was compelled to toss
a couple of hard ones over Bennett's head. Mauch knew I would do this,
and he also knew that I was at the boiling point. He had been agitating me
all night from the bench, trying his best to get me angrier and angrier.
The next time I came to bat, he called in Jack Baldschun from the bullpen.
According to what I was told by Dick Allen, the Phillies slugger who later
played a year with us in St. Louis, Mauch had called down to his bullpen
coach, Cal McLish, and ordered McLish to warm up both Baldschun and
Ed Roebuck. Then, as Baldschun walked to the mound, Mauch called
McLish back and told him to have Roebuck ready because Baldschun was
about to get thrown out of the game. The way I heard it—and the way it
appeared to me at the time—when he met Baldschun at the mound
Mauch told him he had four chances to get me. The first three came close
and the fourth one nailed me in the left thigh. Without thinking, I flung
my bat in Baldschun's direction and headed for the dugout looking for
Mauch, who was long gone by that time. Naturally, I was ejected, which is
exactly what Mauch was counting on. We won the game anyway, 9–2, but
I hadn't lasted the five innings required to pick up the victory, which
would haunt me later in the season when I was closing in on twenty.

While my troubles were conspicuous and my failures ranked high
among the causes of the Cardinals' slow start, there was no shortage of

other reasons. Broglio didn't seem to be the pitcher he had previously been, and the only guys consistently winning were the lefthanders, Sadecki and Simmons. Right field had not been claimed and the left-field situation was still unresolved after Musial's retirement and the trade of Altman. The shortcomings were obvious, but fortunately they were not overwhelming in every case. It seemed as though the pitching would come around once I did and in right field the Cardinals liked the strong arm and bat of Mike Shannon, leaving left field as the only problem without an apparent answer at hand.

In order to purchase a solution for left field, Bing Devine was willing to pay the price of Broglio, who had won eighteen games in 1963. Bobby Shantz and Doug Clemens were also expendable, and for the three of them Devine fetched two undistinguished pitchers from the Cubs, Paul Toth and Jack Spring, and a young left-handed hitter named Lou Brock who, although he had done very little in Chicago, seemed to have enough raw speed and power to be worth a shot in left field.

Presto. We were transformed.

None of us could believe this Brock fellow when he put on the Cardinal uniform. In batting practice he hit balls as far as White and Boyer, and on the bases he was mind-boggling. When Keane and his coaches were able to convince Brock that his speed would take him and the team much further than his power, he condensed his game and as a result refined it, much as Flood had done a couple of years before. What he did was hit .348 the rest of the way, with thirty-three stolen bases.

An aspect of the Brock trade that has been lost over time was what it did for Ken Boyer, who responded with the year of his life. In spite of the picture painted by Harry Caray, who feuded with Boyer ("Here's the pitch to Boyer . . . and I'll be back with the wrapup after this message." "Ground ball to third—right through Boyer's legs! I don't know how we lose some of these games, but we do"), our third baseman was already an all-star and had driven in 111 runs in 1963. In 1964, he would ring up 119 RBIs and be named the National League's Most Valuable Player.

White drove in 102 to boot, and Flood and Groat benefited significantly from the hitting hole on the right side created by the first baseman holding Brock close to the bag; and from the distraction Brock created for the pitcher. We all benefited from the presence of Brock. We had a new energy. We took more chances.

Still and all, there were two things holding us back. One was the Phillies, who latched onto first place about three weeks after Brock joined us and held it. The other was an internal problem that fundamentally had to do with Groat and Keane but was affecting the whole team. At the start of the season, Keane had given Groat the go-ahead to use the hit-and-run play whenever he chose. But it wasn't working out very well, and after a screwed-up game in Los Angeles when Groat tried the hit-and-run three times and it backfired each time, Keane revoked the privileges. Groat rebelled and the two of them stopped talking. The tension divided the club for a while.

In a way, Groat was never caught up in the spirit that distinguished the Cardinals. Make no mistake, he was an invaluable member of the team—in addition to his obvious skill with the bat and glove, he was a teacher to young players like Shannon and McCarver and Dal Maxvill—and he wasn't a bad guy at all, but his personality didn't seem to blend with everybody else's. On a club that preferred to bring things out in the open, he was more of a hush-hush kind of guy. If he had anything to say to you, whether it was confidential or not, he'd get up real close and almost whisper it, so that you had to lean forward to hear him. (He also carried a pocketful of change with him wherever he went and was constantly making calls from pay phones.)

I'm sure Groat didn't intend to undermine the ballclub in his dispute with Keane, but it was working that way and Keane knew it. Just after the all-star game, Keane called a team meeting in the clubhouse at Shea Stadium and let it all out. Notwithstanding the fact that he had studied for the priesthood, Keane could cuss in the best tradition of major-league managers. He had a gravelly voice and when he was serious he would pace and nervously tug on his pants as he spoke. "You guys might get me fired, goddamnit," he said that night in New York, "but if you do you can bet your asses that I'm taking some of you bastards with me!" He let it be understood in no uncertain terms what he thought about players second-guessing him and grumbling behind his back. The veteran Cardinals were used to frank meetings like that, but newcomers like Brock and Shannon were stunned. There was nothing delicate or half-assed about what went on that night. But when Keane was finished, the air had been cleared. Afterwards, Groat went up to him, apologized, and confessed that he had been one of the chief offenders of what Keane had been talking about. Those two were finally on the same page, and with that, the ballclub caught fire.

There was a long way to go, though. The Phillies showed no sign of faltering through July and August no matter how much heat was put on by us and the Reds and the Giants. It was frustrating, but on the other hand their big lead made us loose and untroubled. We had no reason to be upset about the way we were playing, which was very well (at last), and no reason to be uptight about the pennant race because it looked as though the Phillies had made it academic. So we enjoyed ourselves.

With Bob Uecker on the team, it was hard *not* to enjoy ourselves. He did dead-on imitations of nearly everybody in the organization from Harry Caray to Johnny Keane to Auggie Busch, and for his more elaborate routines he enlisted Roger Craig as a straight man. Uecker wasn't the only comedian on the club, however. Sadecki and McCarver did a damn good rendition of Crazy Guggenheim and Joe the Bartender from the Jackie Gleason Show. Those two were also responsible for getting us started on rubber masks. They stayed up late watching a horror movie in Milwaukee one night, and the next day Sadecki came into the clubhouse with a wolfman mask and McCarver showed up as a hunchback. That sent me out for a Frankenstein mask, and pretty soon we had a whole squad of freaks. We wore the masks on airplanes and on buses to the ballpark, and in heavy traffic we would stick our monster heads out of the windows of our taxicabs. (I never said we were *mature*.)

The only thing that soured our mood—and did it big-time—was when Bing Devine was fired in August and replaced by Bob Howsam. Our internal problems were worked out by then, but Busch was furious when he heard about them belatedly at a brewery convention—and from a Miller rep, no less. He was deeply embarrassed and took out his humiliation on Devine for not keeping him informed. Eddie Stanky, our player development director, and business manager Art Routzong were also sent on their way. Busch was not impressed with Devine's trades, reasoning that a pennant could not be won in that manner, and believed furthermore that our farm system was not developing enough championship-caliber players. His frustration stemmed from the fact that the Cardinals had not won a pennant since he bought the team in the fifties. It apparently didn't count for anything that Devine had been named major-league executive of the year in 1963, and in fact would receive the same honor again in 1964, in absentia. Nor did it have any bearing that Devine was respected by all the players despite having to negotiate contracts with us (this was in the days before player agents). On top of all that, he was conscientious beyond the call of duty, spending night games at Busch Stadium on top of the grandstand roof with a transistor radio in order to catch broadcasts from Chicago, Cincinnati, Kansas City, Houston, and Schenectady, New York, where he could sometimes pick up Mets games. Devine thought that by keeping in touch with other teams he could gain insights about what certain players did in certain situations. He'd had a good feeling about Lou Brock, for instance.

The players were hurt by Devine's firing, but we decided that instead of packing it in for the year, we would dedicate ourselves to redeeming Devine with a strong finish. Brock was certainly doing his part, and our so-called "Million-Dollar Infield" (White claims that the sum of their salaries wouldn't have exceeded two hundred thousand dollars) was playing all-star ball around the horn. I also hit my stride in August, winning six straight complete games in which I gave up a total of six earned runs.

We still weren't gaining much ground on Philadelphia, but by the first of September we were playing so well that we started to believe the weird predictions of Fifi Latour. Some were of the opinion that Fifi Latour was actually Bob Bauman, our trainer, but I'm more inclined to believe what Bauman later confessed about Fifi—that she was actually a male physician from Venice, Florida. The Fifi thing started innocuously with a few notes mailed to the clubhouse, encouraging us to hang in the race and predicting various victories. They were written in red ink and signed *Fifi Latour, an Old Stripper*. Fifi claimed to be a psychic, as well, and her (his, whatever) predictions for our ballgames got to be uncanny after a while. Bauman was not above suspicion—he had been known to disperse placebos that he called "energy pills," which didn't help much—but whoever or whatever Fifi was, she seemed to have an effect on us. When she predicted that we would win the pennant, some of us began to wonder.

Nonetheless, we were still 6½ games behind the Phillies on September 21. That was the best shape we had been in all summer—we were twice as far out at one point, and just a month before had been closer to eighth place than first—but the mathematics were not in our favor. There were less than two weeks left in the season. The Phillies, in fact, were so certain of winning that they used part of their anticipated World Series money to buy expensive hunting rifles during a September trip to Houston. It was around that time that Mauch inexplicably decided to use his ace pitchers, Jim Bunning and Chris Short, on two days' rest. The Phillies were playing the Reds on the first night of the Mauch maneuver, and Cincinnati won when a reserve infielder named Chico Ruiz stole home.

On that note, the Reds went on to sweep the Phillies, and then the Braves swept the Phillies, and then we swept the Phillies. Bunning and Short were finding it extremely hard to win every three days, and Philadelphia's star right fielder, Johnny Callison, was suffering from a virus. In a game against us, Callison hit a pinch single and while standing on first he was shaking so badly that White had to snap his jacket for him. It almost seemed as if the season had been too much for the Phillies and was finally catching up with them. Or maybe the baseball gods were making their presence felt. On an August night in Philadelphia, with Koufax scheduled to start for the Dodgers, the Phillie front office had called off a game on the mere rumor of rain. In the makeup several weeks later, Philadelphia outfielder Frank Thomas broke his thumb—an injury that cost the Phillies severely when Callison took ill, leaving Dick Allen virtually alone in the middle of the lineup.

While the Phillies, incredibly, were losing ten games in a row, we won eight straight, including a five-game sweep of the Pirates in which Craig threw a shutout in the final game. Our starting pitchers were doing the job, but we were getting invaluable relief help from a thirty-eight-year-old knuckleball sensation, Barney Schultz, who had spent most of the season in the minors. Inspired by Brock, Schultz, and our loyalty to Bing Devine, we finally caught and passed the Phillies in the final week—the only complication being that Cincinnati was also on a tear, winning eight in a row, and had moved into first place.

I pitched against Short in the Phillie series and won 5–1, with relief from Schultz in the ninth. At that point, I had broken Sam Jones's team strikeout record and had lost only once (beaten on a three-run homer by Frank Robinson of the Reds) in the last two months of the season. Like everybody else on the club, I was caught up in the momentum that seemed to be escorting our club all the way to the flag . . . but for a small problem called Cincinnati. We had no doubts about our destiny, but the way the Reds were going, we couldn't fulfill it without help from somebody somewhere. It was provided by Pittsburgh, which shut the Reds out twice to set up a frantic final weekend. Heading into the last series of the season, we led Cincinnati by half a game and the Phillies were 2½ out—just one victory ahead of the fourth-place Giants. The situation was still hairy, but it really didn't seem like we could lose. We were supremely confident, we were extremely hot, and we were playing the Mets. The Reds and Phillies, meanwhile, had to go against each other, with a day off on Saturday.

I was called on to pitch the opener of the Met series, facing a skillful little lefthander named Al Jackson. Despite the Mets' pathetic record—they had lost eight in a row and would finish forty games out of first—they had given us a hard time all year. They hadn't beaten me, however, and I was quite certain they wouldn't. But I hadn't taken Alvin Jackson's sinker into consideration. We couldn't hit it. I got out of a bases-loaded, no-out situation in the fourth, but the Mets had put up a run in the third on a single by George Altman—the man whom we had traded for Roger Craig—a stolen base, an infield hit, and an opposite-field single by their nineteen-year-old first baseman, Ed Kranepool. Jackson never allowed us even that much. The only consolation was that the Reds lost to the Phillies 4–3, leaving us still alone in first place.

We were unable to defend that position the next day, however. The Mets pounded Sadecki and beat us 15–5, pulling us back into a tie with Cincinnati, which was idle. The Giants had been eliminated by losing to the Cubs, but suddenly the Phillies were back in the picture. Going into the final day of the season, only one game separated the top three teams.

Curt Simmons started for us against New York's Galen Cisco and was victimized by Bobby Klaus's windblown double in the fifth, which gave the Mets a 3–2 lead and brought in an unlikely relief pitcher—me. I had taken Friday night's defeat very hard, and had been unable to sleep that night. My body was worn out from pitching three times in ten days. My shoulder throbbed. But when Keane called down to the bullpen and our coach there, Bob Milliken, told me to start throwing, there wasn't a damn thing wrong with me. Adrenaline has a way of making an athlete forget about his problems. I got out of the fifth without any more damage, and in the bottom of the inning we scored three times to knock out Cisco. About that time the news went up on the scoreboard that the Phillies had jumped ahead of the Reds 4–0. That seemed to leave the matter of the pennant up to me, which is exactly the way I wanted it.

There's really no way to explain the velocity I had that day without bringing in extracurricular influences. I'd say the Phillies helped, beating up on the Reds by a final of 10–0. I'd say Josh helped, instilling a competitiveness in me that was deap-seated and unrelenting. I'd say Johnny Keane helped, putting his faith in me the way he did. I'd say the pressure helped. I loved pitching with pressure.

White hit a two-run homer in the sixth, we piled up eleven runs, and I hung on until the ninth, working four innings of two-hit relief. The Mets scored a run on me early and another before Barney Schultz took over for the last two outs of the game. The victory was my nineteenth, but at the time I didn't give a damn about the one Gene Mauch cost me in May. I cared only that we would be playing the Yankees in the World Series.

Bing Devine was in the clubhouse after the game, and when I met him at the door I told him how sorry I was that he couldn't share in the pennant he'd had so much to do with. I knew, though, that if we won the World Series, he would at least have one of the championship rings to represent his contribution to the team. During the last week of the season, the players had held a meeting to determine how our bonus shares would be divided after the season. At the time, we didn't know if we would finish first or fourth, but it was necessary to work out the details in any event. Most of the discussion revolved around what to do about Devine. Bill White pointed out that a lot of people were taking and getting credit for our success but we all knew we were Bing's team, that he was the one who put the club together. Roger Craig followed up on White's remarks, but suggested that Devine might find it insulting to receive money from us. He said that if we were to go on and win the Series, what we ought to do is give him a ring.

Uecker said, "Okay, I'll call him."

I think often of the '64 Cardinals, mostly because they're everywhere. There has never been a baseball team whose players have remained so prominent for so long. Turn on network television to watch a game, and there's Tim McCarver, the most popular announcer going. Listen to the Cardinals on radio and it's Mike Shannon doing the color commentary. Dal Maxvill runs the club as general manager. Boyer managed it before he died of cancer. Roger Craig managed the Giants to a couple of division titles and a World Series. One of our bit players, Joe Morgan, managed the Red Sox. Uecker became rich and famous doing the same kind of shtick on television that he practiced in the clubhouse thirty years ago. Flood touched off the current generation of free agency when he challenged the reserve clause—the archaic rule by which players were bound to one team—upon being traded by the Cardinals to Philadelphia. After broadcasting for the Yankees for many years, White became the first black president of the National League. Despite the unparalleled demand for '64 Cardinals, however, Bill is the only black player from our ranks who has found a permanent place in the game. Flood has been persona non grata for obvious—if not good—reasons (more on that later), and our two Hall of Famers, Brock and I, can't seem to catch on anywhere, try as we might.

It's really no wonder that so many of the '64 Cardinals became announcers and managers. (Counting me—I did some commentary for ABC and ESPN a few years back—plus Brock and Flood, who have done a little color work here and there, and Groat, who broadcasts University of Pittsburgh basketball games, eight of us became announcers, to go along with the three managers.) The guys on that team talked baseball to the point of making it an art form. We talked it on the bench, over dinner, on the plane, at the hotel. During a ballgame, most of us did our own managing from the dugout. Keane and later Red Schoendienst—especially Schoendienst—might not have always welcomed our opinions, but we had no shortage of them. We simply were a bunch of guys with things going on inside our heads. Maxvill has referred to "an uncommon intellect" on the '64 Cardinals, and it's true. In addition to the baseball thinkers, we had three electrical engineers among us—Maxvill, Ron Taylor, and Charlie James. And unlike most big-league teams, we had an active, collective social conscience. Although the phrase had not yet been coined, we were, without a doubt, baseball's best and brightest.

This, however, did not make us favorites against the Yankees. They were nearing the end of the era in which they dominated baseball, but they still had Mickey Mantle and Roger Maris and Whitey Ford, and they had won the American League pennant five years in a row and fourteen out of the last sixteen. They seemed to overshadow us in nearly every respect. Their top three pitchers—Ford, Jim Bouton, and rookie Mel Stottlemyre, who won forty-four games among them—rated higher in most estimations than Sadecki, Simmons, and me, despite Sadecki's twenty victories and the fifty-seven games we won together. Brock and Flood were brilliant, but in the eyes of the press and public they were a far cry from Mantle and Maris. Despite the manner in which Johnny Keane had turned our team around, even in St. Louis the fanfare was heaped upon the homecoming of the Yankee manager, Yogi Berra, a more famous product of the city. The only significant advantage we seemed to have was in the battle of the Boyers, Ken and Cletis, the respective third basemen for us and New York.

Actually, there were seven ballplaying Boyers in the family that hailed from a little Missouri town named Alba, where their father, Vernon, was the mayor and their mother, Mabel, was city clerk. Although I never saw him play regularly, word had it that Clete Boyer was the defensive equal of any third baseman in the game—maybe in history. But I was more than happy to have the National League's MVP on our side. In addition to being a good guy and our captain—and despite what Harry Caray thought, not to mention the worst cigarette habit I've ever seen—Kenny Boyer was a consistently dependable player, having hit twenty-four home runs in each of the past four seasons. His defense was not quite up to his brother's

standard, but the hard infield at Busch Stadium had something to do with
that. Before the Series, Kenny saw fit to send Clete a telegram warning
him to watch out for wicked bounces.

My preparations for the Series, which opened in St. Louis, included
resting my arm for a couple of days—which was not enough—and helping
my brother Josh and my friend Rodney Wead with hotel accommodations.
St. Louis was not a segregated city in the blatant tradition of the South, but
that was of little relevance when we attempted to find hotel rooms for two
black men. This was not entirely unexpected. Until Houston and Atlanta
joined the National League, St. Louis and Cincinnati had been the southernmost cities in baseball, a fact that was all too evident to black players.
It wasn't until the 1950s, when Jackie Robinson and Don Newcombe
pressed the point, that the Chase Hotel in St. Louis admitted black
players—and only then on the condition that they stay away from the
swimming pool. Management was careful not to give them rooms that
overlooked the pool, making sure that black men weren't peering out their
windows at white ladies in bathing suits. In October 1964, the only place
I could find for Josh and Rodney was the George Washington Hotel,
where I had previously lived. (I was still unable to buy a satisfactory house
in St. Louis, but for the summer of 1964 I had been invited to stay in the
home of a professor friend on the campus of a suburban private school
called Priory.)

I was not accustomed to the microscope under which the World Series
places a ballplayer, but was not uncomfortable with it, either. Outgoing as
we were (except, of course, for me on game days or after defeats), the Cardinals were a media-friendly team. When a reporter asked about my hitting slump in 1964—I had fallen to an unproductive .156 after leading
National League pitchers in RBIs the previous year and batting average
the year before that—Curt Flood answered for me, pointing out that I was
not in a slump but rather in a nonhitting streak. The writers toasted our
humor, and we feasted on the attention. I'll never forget watching Uecker
parade around Busch Stadium with a tuba he had borrowed from a band
member before the first game.

Sadecki pitched the opener and won it 9–5 as we came from behind
with a four-run sixth inning centered on Mike Shannon's two-run homer.

My maiden World Series assignment came in the second game against Stottlemyre, and although neither I nor my teammates (with the notable exception of Groat, who had played for the champion Pirates in 1960) had any precedents to draw from—it was the Cardinals' first Series in eighteen years—I liked our chances and mine. My experience in the Interamerican championships had given me big-game confidence, and I placed plenty of it in Boyer and Brock and Flood and White and Groat and McCarver and Javier and Shannon, as well.

The game began in a promising manner. I struck out the side in the first—Bobby Richardson, Maris, and Mantle—then got Tom Tresh and Elston Howard in the second. We scored one in the third but the Yankees tied it in the fourth and went ahead with the benefit of a bad call in the sixth: I had walked Mantle with one out, which I didn't mind much, but with Joe Pepitone batting next and a count of one ball, two strikes, American League umpire Bill McKinley said that my slider brushed Pepitone's pants. The pitch definitely deflected off something, but I heard a noise that sounded like a ball hitting a bat, and there were plenty of others who perceived it the same way. Pepitone never made a move for first until McKinley sent him down there. After a long argument, Tresh singled in Mantle. They got two more in the seventh, and I left after the eighth inning, trailing 4–2. The Yankees added four runs in the ninth against our bullpen and the final was 8–3.

The urgency of the situation had enabled me to pitch through my weariness and pain during the last week of the pennant race, but the arm of a tired pitcher aches much more after a defeat. My first Series start had come three days after pitching four hard innings of the last game of the season, which had come two days after pitching nine hard innings against Al Jackson. The Wednesday game against the Yankees gave me twenty-one innings—the equivalent of three starts by today's standards—in six days. I was whipped. But on the bright side, I could take it easy until the fifth game, when I would have three days of rest and the rush of Yankee Stadium behind me.

By then, the Series was tied at two games apiece. The Yankees had taken the lead after the third game, a pitchers' duel between Simmons and Bouton, when Mantle hit a gargantuan home run off Barney Schultz into the third deck of Yankee Stadium on the first pitch of the bottom of the ninth. (As Mantle's ball dropped high into the shirts, I noticed our right fielder, Mike Shannon, poised with one leg on the fence as if he were going to jump up and catch the damn thing. Afterwards, I asked him, "Mike, the ball was in the third deck; what the hell were you doing?" In perhaps the first of many memorable quotations by which I would come to identify Shannon, he replied, "You never know, Big Boy. You never know.") There was some danger of being demoralized by that defeat, because Schultz had been our savior through August and September, but Ken Boyer responded with an even bigger blow in the fourth game. The Yankees had knocked out Sadecki with three cheap runs in the first and still had the 3–0 lead in the sixth when Boyer overcame it with a grand slam. We were on the ropes at the time, and as Boyer's ball slipped over the left-field fence I had the distinct feeling that we were going to win the Series. Confidence in our bullpen was restored that day when Roger Craig and Ron Taylor held the Yankees scoreless over 8⅔ innings of relief to complete a 4–3 victory.

It was sunny and cool for game five, and with the momentum from Boyer's grand slam and three days' rest—only one short of normal—I would have felt pretty good except for the sore throat and cold that kept me up most of the night before. In the bullpen before the game, there was no snap to my pitches. But Yankee Stadium is the kind of place that brings out a player's best—your first encounter with it is sort of like your first taste of something else—and I was sufficiently stimulated to prevail over my aches and fatigue for a few hours.

Stottlemyre was my opponent again, and a worthy one. We reached him for two runs in the fifth when I blooped a single into left field (it should have been a double, but I tripped over first base), Richardson made an error on a double-play ball by Flood, and we scored on a single by Brock and a force-out. We would have pushed across another run or two if Clete Boyer hadn't robbed his brother to end the inning.

It was still 2–0 in the bottom of the ninth, which Mantle led off with a bouncing ball that caught Groat between bounces for an error. After I struck out Howard on a fastball over his head, the next batter was Pepitone, who had been at the plate when things started going wrong in game two. This time, with the count two and two, he stroked a line drive that caught me on the spot my mother used to whip. My follow-through had me spinning toward first base, but the ball bounded off in the other direction. I reversed my course and caught up with it not far from the third-base line, reaching out barehanded with my back to first base. There was no time to brace myself, so instinctively I pivoted in the air, managing to get a good look at Bill White, if only for an instant, and threw as hard as I could. White caught the ball a split second before Pepitone's foot hit the bag. It was a controversial call by the umpire, Al Smith, but replays showed that he was right. I think the Yankees argued mainly because they couldn't believe the play. Bob Broeg, the longtime sports editor of the *St. Louis Post-Dispatch* who had been on hand for Willie Mays's famous catch and throw on Vic Wertz's long drive in 1954, said it was the best play he ever saw in a World Series. Another veteran baseball writer, Fred Lieb, wrote in *The Sporting News* that I had reacted with "reflexes that were almost supernatural." Without repeating the superlatives, I can only verify that he was right in talking about reaction and reflex, because that's what it was. When a player reflects on a play like that, he does it with a certain degree of detachment, almost as if he were a spectator along with everybody else. There was nothing practiced or premeditated about that play—unless you count the days and hours I spent contorting my body while shooting a basketball in the neighborhood gym.

*The ball caromed off to the right, and he couldn't find it initially—for a nanosecond. I saw it unfolding, and by the time he recovered I didn't think it was possible for him to get Pepitone because I thought the ball was too far away from him. The ball was going toward the third-base line, and Pepitone ran well. But I always think of Larry Bird and a description of the way Bird played basketball, and I think it's a perfect description of how Bib Gibson played the game. It's asserted of Bird that when he played, he was a level above everyone else, that all of the other players were in slow motion—because of his intensity, his concentration. That's what happened on that play with Gibson.*

—TIM McCARVER

As it turned out, it was a damn good thing we got Pepitone, because on the next pitch Tresh hit a two-run homer that tied the game and otherwise would have won it. Keane stuck with me into the tenth, when I took the mound revitalized by a three-run lead thanks to a godsent homer by McCarver that came on a three-and-two pitch following a walk to White and a bunt single by Boyer. I told Tim in the dugout that I loved him—a spur-of-the-moment thing that I trust he didn't take too seriously. Anyway, I was feeling frisky in the tenth and struck out pinch hitter Mike Hegan to start it off. It was my thirteenth strikeout, a team record for World Series competition. More important, Boyer reached into the stands to catch a pop fly by Maris and close out one of the best games I, or anybody else, was ever involved in. McCarver, who had a very personal stake in it, has said that the fifth game of the 1964 World Series summarizes, for him, what makes baseball the sport that it is. Drama, heroism, theatre—it had it all, including, from our viewpoint, an extremely happy ending.

Rummaging through some old clippings of the game not long ago, I was interested to read a story about it—more or less—that appeared in the *Post-Dispatch* under the byline of Neal Russo. It took a little different twist from the others: "Gibson, limping from the clubhouse with an assortment of bruises, was able to relax at least as he listened to a Bob Gibson vocal recording with Hoot accompanying himself with a ukelele . . . 'It's called, *Send Me Someone to Love,*' said the Gibson boy." I had forgotten about making the recording earlier that year—hell, I'd practically forgotten about playing the ukelele—and was also surprised to read how recently I'd actually become a *man*. Apparently, I was not there yet at the age of twenty-eight, even with an extra-inning World Series victory under my belt.

Thankfully, Johnny Keane considered me enough of a man to start me in the seventh game in St. Louis, which became necessary after Maris and Mantle hit back-to-back home runs in the sixth inning of the sixth game and Pepitone added an eighth-inning grand slam for an 8–3 victory behind Bouton. My opponent in the final game would again be Stottlemyre, who was being counted on to take up the slack for Whitey Ford after Ford developed a bad shoulder in game one. I wasn't sure that I didn't belong on the shelf with Ford, having pitched four grueling games in ten days, but

I couldn't beg off with my manager and teammates depending on me and Josh scrutinizing me from the George Washington Hotel. Don't get me wrong—the world championship had its appeal and I wanted to win it as much as anybody, but nothing motivated like the wrath of Josh.

As might be expected, I didn't have my best fastball or slider for the seventh game, but I had some of my best adrenaline. So did Stottlemyre, and as a result the game was scoreless through the first three innings. I ran into a predicament in the second, when an error by Groat loaded the bases, but Stottlemyre was up and I fanned him. That enabled us to take the lead in the fourth when Ken Boyer singled, Phil Linz threw away a double-play grounder by McCarver, Shannon singled, and then McCarver and Shannon—both of whom ran well but neither of whom would be confused with Lou Brock—pulled off an unlikely double steal to bring in a run with Maxvill at the plate. Almost as unlikely was the single by Maxvill that scored Shannon. Shannon, whose main asset in right field was a world-class throwing arm, had helped keep the Yankees scoreless in the third by catching a low line drive by Linz and gunning the ball to second to double the runner.

The double-play ball that the Yankees botched in the fourth had been hit to first base and required that Stottlemyre cover the bag for the return throw, but he landed on his shoulder while diving for it and couldn't answer the bell for the fifth inning. Al Downing took over, and Brock met him with a long home run onto the pavilion roof. White singled, Boyer doubled and moved to third on a ground out, McCarver brought him in on a short fly to right center—Mantle was not healthy enough to throw him out—and when I returned to the mound the score was 6–0.

At that point, I was being told by Keane and McCarver to simply throw strikes and let New York's big boys hit the ball out of the park if they must. It was sound advice in light of the fact that I wasn't capable of anything more at the moment. Obviously, I wasn't going to shut out the Yankees under those conditions, but a six-run lead is like another device in a pitcher's repertoire and I intended to use it to full advantage.

*When we got ahead 6–0 I told Gibby to just pour the ball over the plate—and boy, he showed me something. Talk about raw meat!*

*He just threw it in there, like, "There it is, buddy, if you want it.*
*If you don't, it's a strike."*
        —TIM MCCARVER

The idea behind that method of pitching, however, is to keep runners off the bases to minimize the damage from long balls. This didn't happen when Bobby Richardson opened the sixth with an infield single—his record thirteenth hit of the series—and Maris followed with a single to bring up Mantle. The book on Mantle was that he liked to extend his arms and hit outside fastballs, but it seemed to me that his bad knees were buckling a little bit when he tried to reach out with the bat, and as a result I was having good luck with him away. I had tried one change-up on him just to see what happened, and he pulled it way foul. I figured my best bet was to stay on the corner, but what I didn't take into consideration was the fact that Mantle had become the great player he was by playing over pain. Somehow, he braced those wobbly knees long enough to lift my outside fastball into the opposite-field bleachers in left center for his third home run of the Series. In the third game, Mantle had broken Babe Ruth's World Series record with his sixteenth homer, and added another in the sixth game. This home run, his eighteenth, would be his last in a World Series. The Yankees wouldn't win another American League pennant until 1976, eight years after The Mick's retirement. We were playing out the end of a historic era in baseball that day; but that, of course, was the furthest thing from our minds. We had another three innings to get through.

After Mantle's home run, Keane came to the mound to ask me how I felt. Naturally, I lied. He reminded me that Mantle's ball was the first one hit hard all day and told me to go ahead and try my luck with Elston Howard. When I struck Howard out, it convinced Keane to stay with me. I don't know if there was another manager in baseball who would have shown that degree of faith in me or any pitcher. The ultimate compliment I can pay to Johnny Keane is that, in an entirely different way, he motivated me damn near as much as Josh.

Boyer gave us another run in the seventh with a home run against Steve Hamilton, and I took a 7–3 lead into the ninth. By this time, I was simply throwing as hard as I could on every pitch, grunting up my best frazzled-arm fastballs. Keane had sent me out there with the advice to throw nothing but fastballs, remarking that he didn't think the Yankees could hit four home runs in one inning. With one out—a strikeout of Tresh—Clete Boyer jumped on the fastball he knew was coming and sent it over the fence. With two outs, Linz did the same. It was 7–5, and I looked over to the dugout at Keane, wondering if perhaps he had overestimated my speed and underestimated the Yankees' power. But Keane didn't waver. He left me in to pitch to Richardson, who sent a pop fly that hung over Maxvill at second base. Groat yelled, "Don't let it hit you on the coconut, Maxie," and he didn't.

The celebration that followed was out of the ordinary for several reasons. On the surface, there was the fact—of little significance to the players, actually—that the Cardinals hadn't won a World Series in eighteen years. Below the surface, there was the deep satisfaction of winning for Bing Devine and Johnny Keane. Besides that, we knew that our triumph was not a product of hitting and fielding and pitching skills alone, but, in an almost tangible sense, of the mental, social, and spiritual qualities that made the Cardinals unique—of intelligence, courage, brotherhood, and faith. I know that sounds corny as hell, and believe me, the last thing I aspire to be is corny. But I can't honestly explain the '64 Cardinals any other way. That's what and who we were.

Uecker—who hit all of .198 that season with a homer—was of course at center stage in the clubhouse, wearing an usher's cap, dancing a polka, mimicking Auggie Busch, and grabbing Harry Caray's microphone to interview himself. Flood, always one to take a cosmic view of things, declared, "We are the champions of *el mundo*, the galaxy, the solar system!" Johnny Keane celebrated more quietly, excusing himself from the reporters in order to share the moment with his players one by one. When Bill White was on his way out the door, Keane pulled him aside and said, "Bill, I wanted to give you this." It was a hug.

He was even warmer to me, telling reporters, "You can't say enough about Gibson. He didn't pitch only with his arm; he pitched with his heart. And he's got lots of heart. He gave it all he had and more. I went all the way with him because I was committed to this fellow's heart." I've often thought that Keane's long, arduous struggle to become a big-league man-

ager, his vast experience with adversity and setbacks, enabled him to understand and deal intuitively with me and other black ballplayers. He always seemed to know the right words for the situation. Privately, he said
to me after the seventh game, "Hoot, you're on your way."

A reporter for the New York *Daily News,* Phil Pepe, wrote something
the morning after the Series that I appreciated and that hit home: "The
story of the Cardinals' world championship is the story of Johnny Keane
and yesterday it was the story of Bob Gibson. It is the story of faith . . . of
John Keane's faith in Bob Gibson and of Bob Gibson's faith in himself.
There had been some remarks by another National League manager
questioning Gibson's courage. Gibson had heard them and he had chosen
to remain silent. But yesterday he spoke. He spoke by pitching nine cou-
rageous innings under the greatest pressure and with only two days' rest."
Pepe was referring to a comment by my friend Gene Mauch, who had re-
portedly said late in the pennant race that the Cardinals would never win
a league championship with me as their main pitcher. I don't know if
Mauch said that or not—it sounds like something he would say—but I had
refused to be drawn into it. Mauch's opinion had nothing to do with my
ability to do my job, which was to win ballgames. In the end, I saw a great
deal of justice in the fact that Johnny Keane had a World Series ring and
Gene Mauch didn't.

What's more, we had been a manager's kind of team, the kind that performed under pressure, executed by the book, and did exactly what it had
to do. As Bob Broeg described us in the *Post-Dispatch:* "The incredible
1964 Cardinals will go down in baseball history as the ballclub that never
won a game it could afford to lose and never lost a game it had to win."
That was damn true. Broeg also said that the front page the day after the
1964 World Series, carrying headlines about the Cardinals' victory and
Khrushchev being replaced by Brezhnev and Kosygin in the Soviet Union, was the greatest in the history of the *Post-Dispatch.*

For me, the news got better before it got worse. My thirty-one strikeouts had set a World Series record—eclipsing the mark of twenty-eight set
by some guy named Bill Dinneen of the Red Sox in the 1903 World Series,
which was the first ever—and for that and my two victories, I was named

Most Valuable Player of the Series by *Sport* magazine. The prize was a Corvette.

Before I touched the wheel of my new sports car, however, I was whisked off in a chartered plane to Omaha, where it had been arranged to honor me with a motorcade and a ceremony that was unprecedented for a black man in Nebraska. It would have been a grand and glorious occasion but for one jolting development: As I stepped off the plane that morning, word came that Johnny Keane had resigned. A day or two later, he replaced Yogi Berra as manager of the Yankees.

# CHAPTER VI

For a guy who had come out of the ghetto to win a Corvette as MVP of the World Series, I had a horseshit winter. It started with the Johnny Keane bombshell and continued four days later in New York, when a reporter innocently informed me that I was only the second black pitcher—Joe Black of the Dodgers being the first in 1952—to ever win a World Series game. Bill White was with me that day, and he jumped in to say, "It doesn't matter that he's colored. He's a ballplayer and he's my teammate—that's all that matters. Is he colored? I didn't notice. He could be Japanese or Hawaiian, I don't care. What I care about is: Does he want to win? I thought we had gotten away from that. I thought we didn't use labels anymore."

The thing was, I didn't *want* to make an issue of race but couldn't avoid it. I would have much preferred to just pitch and talk about pitching in the manner that white pitchers did. Sandy Koufax wasn't beset with questions about being white, or about being Jewish, when he was World Series MVP the year before.

In fact, a lot of things were different for Koufax the year before, not the least of which was endorsements. While Koufax was able to cash in nicely, the only thing I got out of my minor celebrity was a trip to the Rose Bowl. (Charline and I and McCarver and his new bride, Ann—they were married on Christmas Day—spent a week in California and rode on the Budweiser float during the parade.) My financial status was so unaffected by commercial benefits from the World Series and regular season that I sold the Corvette because I needed the money more than the transportation. Besides, I couldn't drive my wife and daughters around in a two-seat sports car.

My initial experience with the Corvette was a bad one, anyway. Just after I got it, I was driving from St. Louis to Omaha when a policeman pulled me over in a small town in Missouri. He said there was a report of a stolen Corvette that matched the description of the one I was driving. I said, "Bullshit." I knew he was just messing with me because he didn't believe that a black man could come by a Corvette honestly. When he asked to see the title papers I said that I didn't have any yet because I'd just won the car for being Most Valuable Player in the World Series. He then apologized, which policemen and others tend to do when, and only when, they find out they're hassling a public figure.

Through baseball, I was able to travel and circulate much more freely than the average black man, but even for me it was not uncommon for bigotry to come barging through. I was with friends and teammates at a suburban St. Louis nightspot around 1964, for instance, when a customer walked over and said to me, "We don't allow niggers in this place." There's no use talking with somebody like that, so I stood up and knocked him over the table.

Now and then, I was given a hard time even back home in Omaha. In the winter following the '64 season I played basketball with an otherwise all-white local team that traveled to small towns in Iowa for games and tournaments. We usually met at a bar on North Thirtieth Street, and while I was waiting there one evening—not long after the city had observed Bob Gibson Day—I asked the bartender for a Coke. He said, "This is to go, isn't it? You know you can't drink in here." Instead of responding physically again, I fetched the boss, which I figured was the best way to strike back at the bartender. After some words from his employer, the bartender grudgingly brought me the Coke, which I left on the table when I walked out with my friends.

When it came to expressing my grievances with the Cardinals—concerning the resignation of Johnny Keane, in particular—the options unfortunately didn't include walking away or punching somebody out. I confess, though, that it gave me a little perverse pleasure to make the club reshoot the 1964 world championship team photograph. The retake was ordered after the first picture had been printed and packaged for distribution to the media, at which point somebody in the front office finally looked closely enough to notice that Uecker and I were holding hands in the front row.

My anger toward the ballclub—and it was tangible—stemmed largely from the needless nature of Keane's departure. It bothered me, also, that I hadn't seen it coming. Or maybe I saw it coming but figured that the world championship changed everything. At any rate, it was apparent, in retrospect, that Keane's decision had been quite a while in the making.

The Groat situation had taken its toll on him, but more unsettling to Keane, like the rest of us, was the manner in which Bing Devine had been undermined and terminated. Even before he was fired, Devine's authority as general manager had been compromised by the heavy involvement of Branch Rickey in personnel matters. Devine and Keane had worked closely to build a championship team and Keane was well aware that his security did not exceed Devine's. It was no secret, either, that, on the urging of Rickey, August Busch had tried to bring Leo Durocher (whom Rickey had hired to manage the Brooklyn Dodgers) to St. Louis to take over for Keane earlier in the 1964 season. Harry Caray escorted Durocher one morning to Grant's Farm, a family theme park owned by Busch, to interview for the manager's job. This, of course, occurred before our big push to the pennant and world championship, which prompted Busch to offer Keane a new one-year contract during the final weekend of the regular season. At the time, Keane told Busch that he wanted to wait and discuss his future after the season. But Keane had already made up his mind. His resignation was dated September 28, the Monday before the season ended. He handed it in the day after the World Series. A press conference was held for the announcement, which most reporters—and perhaps even Busch himself, who sat next to Keane—mistakenly believed would make public the particulars of the skipper's new Cardinal contract. I, for one, was deeply upset that it didn't, and I stayed mad through the winter.

My reaction, however, had little to do with the new manager, Red Schoendienst. The only problem I had with Schoendienst was that he wasn't Johnny Keane. But he was a good man and a good man for us. Being a gang of independent thinkers, we would have resisted a manager on the order of Gene Mauch, who knew everything and wasn't reluctant to tell you so. Schoendienst, like Keane, respected our intelligence and our professionalism. His only rules were "Run everything out" and "Be in by twelve." Somehow, we got the words tangled up and lived instead by the motto, "Run everything in and be out by twelve."

In a way, the transition from Keane to Schoendienst may have been less difficult for the players than the one from Bing Devine to Bob Howsam in the general manager's office. While Schoendienst was passive by nature, willing to treat us as the capable, self-motivated group of grown men we had proven ourselves to be in 1964, Howsam felt compelled to assert complete control over the ballclub. He imposed rules about such petty things as how high we were supposed to pull up our baseball pants. If he looked down from the press level and saw one of our guys slouching in the dugout, he would fire down a memo ordering him to sit up straight. I suspect, although I can't say for sure, that it was Howsam's idea to institute periodic bed checks. The unfortunate foil for this duty was Dick Sisler, a coach who was very pleasant and spoke with a stutter. It was Sisler's bad luck to come around one night when I was trying to rest up and prepare myself for pitching the next day. As my roommate Flood has often attested, I was not a sweetheart on those occasions.

> *Around 2 A.M., there was a rap at the door. I got up to answer it and Sisler poked his head in. "J-just checking," he said. With that, Gibson flew out of his bed, stuck his nose right in Sisler's face, and said, "If you ever come to our room again, you'd better be prepared for a good time, because we're going to drag you in, we're going to force liquor down your throat, and then we're going to get you raped. Is that perfectly clear?"*
> —CURT FLOOD

Anyway, the spying was not necessary because most of us were responsible enough to get the sleep we needed and in the dugout we were tuned in to the game regardless of our posture. Especially in Schoendienst's long tenure as manager, we stayed attentive in the dugout. Red was uncertain of himself in the beginning, a fact of which the ballplayers were well aware. McCarver and I would make it a point to sit on either side of him, and when a certain situation developed on the field, Tim would say something like, "What do you think, Hoot? This looks to me like a good opportunity for Flood to lay down a sacrifice." I'd say, "Yeah, although with Brock on first I could go for a hit-and-run." McCarver would say, "I think you're right. Hit-and-run is probably the ticket here." About that time, Red would stand up and flash the hit-and-run sign. We never actually *told* him to make a move; we were just there as birdies in the ear, now and then providing the information he needed to make his decision. Once, Schoendienst inadvertently let a pitcher go to the plate to hit in a key spot, and McCarver shouted, "Hey!" Red jumped. He knew something was wrong, but he didn't know what. So he started looking around, noticed the pitcher getting into the batter's box, and quickly sent up a pinch hitter.

Schoendienst obviously knew how to play the game, though—he was a Hall of Fame second baseman for the Cardinals, primarily, and the Braves—and it wasn't his fault that our lineup came up lame in 1965. McCarver and Javier broke fingers early in the season, Flood stayed on the field with a pulled muscle, White and Boyer struggled with various afflictions, and Brock played with a left shoulder that Koufax cracked in May—just when he had figured out that he could drive Koufax crazy by bunting.

Until then, we hadn't come up with any solution to Koufax. For years, Johnny Keane had been on a personal mission to find a way to get to him, without any luck. At one point Keane had been convinced that our problem was trying in vain to pull Koufax's fastball, and he announced before a game that anybody who tried to pull Koufax that night would be fined five hundred dollars. He ordered everybody to try to hit the ball to the opposite field. We got one hit that night—a double that Groat pulled over the bag at third.

Brock's bunting was the only thing that threatened Koufax, and when he put a stop to that, he and the Dodgers were home free. Koufax and Drysdale would win a phenomenal forty-nine games between them in 1965. They were easily the toughest left-right combination the National League has seen as long as I've been following the game, and the Dodgers played this strength to full advantage. I noticed that whenever we faced Koufax at Dodger Stadium, the left-field bleachers would be closed so that our right-handed batters would be trying to pick out Koufax's fastball in the horizon of shirts packed into right field. When Drysdale pitched—and it was hard to follow the ball from his sidearm delivery, anyway—the right-field bleachers were shut off.

When I say that I consider Juan Marichal to have been the best pitcher of my time, I mean no disrespect to either Sandy Koufax or myself. In fact, I *respected* both of us—and Drysdale—more than Marichal; I just thought he could do things with the baseball that nobody else could. I have to say, though, that Marichal didn't have my will to win, he didn't have Drysdale's mean streak, and he never dominated the league like Koufax did for five years.

As far as I'm concerned, no other pitcher in the history of baseball ever put together five years like Koufax did from 1962 to 1966. But in light of the fact that Koufax put together nothing more to speak of than those five years, I'm unwilling to take a backseat to him as a pitcher. I don't question his courage or his competitiveness, nor do I mean to imply that he didn't realize all the potential in his arm, but there is simply no way to judge a ballplayer except by what he accomplished. I believe, for what it's worth, that I accomplished a little more in my career than Koufax did. For that reason, it bothers me somewhat, as I'm sure it also bothers Marichal, to hear and read so often that Koufax was the leading pitcher of our generation. A generation lasts more than five years.

But I'll concede to him at least the Dodger pennant years—1963, 1965, and 1966. For different reasons, all of those were difficult seasons for the Cardinals, and none more so than 1965. After the inspired manner in which we had taken it all in 1964, we had every reason—except, perhaps, for the absence of Johnny Keane—to expect the best in 1965. It just didn't work out that way. For the first time in four years, neither Boyer nor White drove in a hundred runs, and neither even came close. Also for the

first time, I was unequivocally the ace of the staff—which was a good sign
for me but a very bad sign for the rest of the team. Sadecki lost it, plum-
meting from twenty wins to six. Simmons's victory total was severed in
half, from eighteen to nine. The only starters other than me with winning
records were a couple of veterans we acquired by trade, Tracy Stallard
and Bob Purkey, who won eleven and ten games respectively.

For completely different reasons, I enjoyed having both of those guys
on the club. One of my primary recreations as a ballplayer was agitating,
and Stallard was a guy who enabled me to exercise the considerable talent
I had in this area. He was best known as the guy who gave up Roger
Maris's record-breaking sixty-first home run when he was pitching for the
Red Sox in 1961, and as long as he stayed in the American League he
didn't seem able to get over that stigma, but he was a competent pitcher
for us in 1965 except for one prominent shortcoming—his fielding.
Stallard was very slow afoot, and our fearless announcer, Harry Caray,
took it upon himself to make this fact known to the world. Harry would
wonder on the air why more teams didn't bunt on Stallard to take advantage of his weakness with the glove. After silently suffering the insults for
a while, Stallard finally blasted Caray in an interview that appeared in the
*St. Louis Globe-Democrat.* Not long after that, Stallard was sitting with a
young lady at a table in a local tavern when she noticed Harry at the bar
and asked Tracy to introduce her. That was probably the last thing
Stallard wanted to do, but he swallowed his pride, walked up to Harry, and
asked if he would come sit with him and his date for a minute. Harry said,
"Drop dead." That was the last straw for Stallard. He wanted nothing more
to do with Harry Caray, which was fine except that a week or two later
Stallard pitched a shutout in Chicago. This created an interesting little situation with respect to Harry's star-of-the-game show. After the game,
Harry was down on the field going, "Where's Stallard? Where the hell is
Stallard?" Naturally, I was eager to help. I sprinted to the clubhouse, found
Tracy there, and cheerfully passed along the information that Harry
wanted to interview him. He said, "Fuck Harry." Dutiful messenger that I
was, I then raced back to the field with Stallard's reply. "Hey, Harry," I
said. "Tracy says, 'Fuck you.'" By this time, the veins were standing out

in Harry's neck and he wanted to fight Stallard on the spot. Of course, Tracy would have killed him, but that didn't matter to Harry. He had a show to do, but he was itching to go into the clubhouse to fight Stallard. Meanwhile, Stallard came out of the clubhouse to deliver his own message, and while they were screaming at each other I was laughing my head off. (Some time later, Harry told me that he didn't understand why ballplayers worried so much about what he said on the radio. I explained that some guys didn't appreciate public criticism. He said, "I've never hurt you, have I?" I said, "Harry, the only way you could hurt me would be if you had a bat in your hands and knew how to use it.")

Stallard stayed with us for a while in 1966, but he didn't do much. Purkey, who was nearing the end of a productive career spent mostly with Cincinnati, lasted only one season with the Cardinals, a strange one in which he had a 10–9 record despite a horrible 5.79 earned run average. The record was not all luck and coincidence, however, because Purkey knew how to pitch and win. In fact, I learned more about pitching from Purkey in one season as his teammate than I did from any pitching coach I ever had.

Purkey actually taught me a way to take advantage of my bad curveball. I seldom threw my curve because I was afraid of hanging it, but Purkey convinced me that a hanging curve can oddly enough be an effective pitch to left-handed hitters, who dive into them expecting the ball to break their way. And so I'd leave the curveball hanging inside now and then to left-handed hitters.

Another pitch that Purkey added to my repertoire was the backup slider—a slider that doesn't break away from a right-handed hitter but holds its course and maybe even bends back a little like a screwball. Purkey explained that, especially in day games, hitters will recognize the spin on a pitch, and when they identify a slider they will instinctively lean out in anticipation of the ball breaking *away* from them. A quick backup slider, consequently, ought to result in broken bats and balls hit weakly off the fists. It sounded good when he described it, and in fact I had often thrown sliders that backed up accidentally, but I had no idea how to do it on purpose. Purkey asked me if I knew when my slider backed up. I thought for a minute and said it was usually when I tried to throw it too hard. So I started deliberately overthrowing the slider on occasion, and just like that I had a nasty new pitch.

The hanging curve and two sliders completed my pitch assortment by complementing the two fastballs I had been depending on. I held one type of fastball across the seams to make it sail away from the right-handed batter, and the other I held with the seams to create a sinking, screwball action. Most important, though, was the fact that my control was improving measurably each season. While my strikeout pace remained basically the same from year to year, my walks dropped steadily from five for every nine innings in 1961 to less than three a game in 1964. My reputation as a competitor was also in full flower by then. With all of those things going for me, I fully expected to do in 1965 what Gene Mauch tricked me out of doing in 1964—win twenty games.

Johnny Keane had been absolutely right when he told me after the seventh game of the World Series that I was on my way. He knew that it was a matter of maturity and confidence, and I'm sure he knew, also, when he stepped down, that I was ready to leave the security of his wing and fly on my own. I won my first eight games in 1965. My pattern in past years, though, had been to slump around midseason. Since Keane wasn't around to see me through the hard times anymore, my mother took it upon herself to give me some advice. She suggested that if I didn't try to throw the ball so hard, maybe I wouldn't get tired halfway through the season. Hell, no. That way, I'd be back in Omaha by the Fourth of July, unemployed.

Except for certain batters and rare occasions—like the seventh game of the '64 World Series, when I was pitching on fumes—I actually didn't try to throw the ball as hard as I could on every pitch. But I worked to maintain my speed throughout a game, and my opponents would sometimes comment that, although I seldom threw quite as hard as the hardest pitches from Koufax or Jim Maloney or Bob Veale, my velocity might have been the highest when measured over the course of nine innings. And I was never consistently faster than I was in the early part of the 1965 season, when I threw three shutouts in the first two months. My only loss in my first nine decisions was 2–0 to Drysdale, who pitched a one-hitter against us. I'd had one of those earlier against the Phillies, prompting

As a switch-hitting jack-of-all-trades, I finished second in the city in batting average while in high school, then, as an outfielder for Creighton, led the Nebraska College Conference. Fortunately for the righthanders of the National League, I gave up switch-hitting in the minor leagues at the behest of the Cardinals, who were afraid I might get hit on the right arm while batting left-handed.
*(Collection of the author)*

Most of the amateur teams I played for in Omaha were coached by my brother Josh and operated out of the YMCA. Occasionally another team, like the one sponsored by a local tavern called the Chicago Bar, would borrow me for a big game or tournament. My catcher here was Andy Sommer. (Omaha World-Herald *photograph*)

The basketball team that Josh coached, the Y-Travelers, was every bit as strong as his baseball team. Josh was a legend on the north side of Omaha.
*(Collection of the author)*

I broke the color line on Creighton's basketball team and held the school career scoring record until Paul Silas broke it six years later. When I became the first athlete inducted into Creighton's sports hall of fame, it was mostly for basketball.
*(Collection of the author)*

Although I'd been with the Cardinals off and on since 1959, my major league career effectively started midway through the 1961 season, when Johnny Keane took over as the St. Louis manager. (Omaha World-Herald *photograph*)

LEFT: One of the pleasures of playing for the Cardinals was that guys like Keane and Tim McCarver would stick their necks out on my behalf—or for just about anybody on the club, for that matter. *(Collection of the author)*

RIGHT: My daughters, Annette and Renee, weren't just holding those pennants— they were serious Cardinal fans. Renee *(right)* wanted desperately to be a big-league ballplayer. *(Alfred Fleishman photograph)*

Mickey Mantle's three-run homer against me in the seventh game of the 1964 World Series was his last and eighteenth in series competition, still a record. I gave up two more home runs in the ninth inning but hung on for a 7–5 victory that carried both me and the Cardinals to the next level. *(Collection of the author)*

Ken Boyer, our captain, and I had been through some lean years with the Cardinals before the 1964 world championship made local heroes out of us and the other St. Louis players. *(United Press International photograph)*

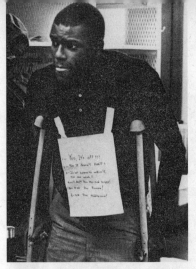 

LEFT: I got a little tired of answering questions about my broken leg in 1967. I was grumpy when I pitched, and when I didn't pitch, I was grumpier. *(Collection of the author)* RIGHT: Orlando Cepeda, bending my ear during the seventh game of the 1967 World Series (nobody could tell me *anything* when I was on the mound), was the spirit behind our drive to the world championship. For the second time, though, I got the Corvette as World Series MVP. (Sports Illustrated *photograph by Herb Sharfman*)

Although the Detroit Tigers brought the firepower into the 1968 World Series, *Sports Illustrated* pointed out that we brought the bucks. That money today would buy one utility infielder. (Omaha World-Herald *photograph*)

With this long ball against Boston's Jim Lonborg in the 1967 World Series and another one against the Tigers in game four of the 1968 Series, I became the first pitcher—including Babe Ruth—to hit two home runs in postseason play. Moments such as this were very useful when I discussed relative batting prowess with my position-playing teammates. *(Collection of the author)*

My ninth-inning strikeout of Norm Cash in the first game of the 1968 World Series set a single-game Series record. I fanned Willie Horton for the final out and went on to also set the record for most strikeouts in a full Series, but we surrendered the world championship when Mickey Lolich outpitched me in the seventh game. *(Collection of the author)*

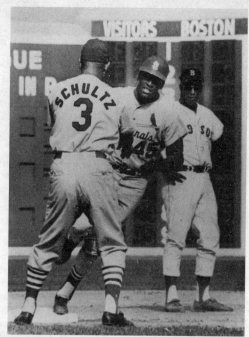

LEFT: My right leg was vital to my pitching delivery. I pushed off of it so hard that the momentum spun me a couple of steps toward first base. *(Collection of the author)* RIGHT: People tend to remember Lou Brock only for his base-stealing, but he was a full-fledged Hall of Famer—a deadly competitor and one of the most cunning players in the game. *(Collection of the author)*

August Busch, the owner of Anheuser-Busch and the Cardinals, gave me, my mother, my daughter Annette, and Mrs. Busch a ride around the ballpark in the motor home he presented me on Bob Gibson Day in 1975. (St. Louis Globe-Democrat *photograph by Jack Fahland)*

Willie Mays wandered into the New York dugout one day in 1981 when I was coaching for the Mets. By that time, we were observing a game entirely different from the one we'd played. *(Collection of the author)*

Since I've been out of baseball, I've been able to devote full-time attention to my family—Wendy and Christopher—and my home in Bellevue, Nebraska, a suburb of Omaha. (Omaha World-Herald *photograph*)

Dick Allen to comment that I had by far the liveliest arm in the league. It was a heady stretch of pitching for me. In May, on the way to my seventh straight victory, I fanned Jim Pagliaroni of the Pirates for the thousandth strikeout of my career. That came the night after Flood had picked up his thousandth hit, at which point he was a few months younger than Musial had been when Stan the Man, the National League's all-time hits leader at the time, got his thousandth.

Maybe I should have listened to my mother after all, because once again I hit the skids before the all-star break. Actually, I was able to thank her for the advice and chuckle at it privately, but my brother's recommendations were a more serious matter. I recognized all that Josh had done to make me a pitcher, and he recognized it too, but we couldn't seem to leave it at that. In the same way that a parent never stops being a parent, Josh could never stop being my coach. I was deeply grateful for his support and acknowledged that he had been and still was my inspiration as an athlete, but the fact is, Josh didn't know a hell of a lot about pitching in the big leagues. In all fairness, how could he? It was hard for me to tell him that, though, and harder for him to understand it. So we argued. He would tell me what was wrong with my mechanics and what pitches I ought to be throwing in certain situations and to certain batters, and the chances were not good that he would be right. Josh could coach desire and competitiveness and basic baseball skills, but he was out of his element when it came to the fine points and technical aspects of the game, especially the fine points and technical aspects of pitching in the big leagues. The down side of my professional progress was that the more skill and knowledge and success I acquired as a pitcher, the further apart I grew from Josh.

It was a no-win situation with Josh, because when I was going good I didn't want advice from him or anybody, and when I was going bad I wasn't in the mood to be gracious. Josh's advice was never of the take-it-or-leave-it variety. He didn't operate that way. I suppose we were too much alike to get along—headstrong and stubborn and brutally honest to the complete exclusion of any subtle quality like tact. I was giving up a lot of home runs during my midseason slump in 1965, losing six in a row, and the last thing I wanted was more bashing from my big brother.

What I really needed was sharper control and a strong game to get my confidence back. The cure was an 8–0 shutout over the Cubs in which I hit a two-run homer. Then I struck out thirteen Mets in my next start and after that worked thirteen innings against the Giants, losing 4–2 on a two-out single by Tom Haller in the thirteenth and a home run by Mays.

It was unusual for Mays to hurt me that way. I had pretty good success with Willie by brushing him back and then throwing fastballs away, but I had to work at it extremely hard. The funny thing is, he told Mike Shannon a few years ago that he more or less conceded when he batted against me.

> *When Gibson came in tight on Willie, he would just bail out of there. But if Gibby or any other pitcher got it out over the plate a little bit, he'd smoke it. When I was talking to him about Gibson one time, Mays said that he used to just go up there stepping in the bucket and taking wild cuts at anything Gibson threw in the strike zone. He said if he happened to hit it, great, and if he didn't, that was okay too because he knew he'd get two or three hits the next couple of days against our other starters. He'd light those sumbitches up.* —MIKE SHANNON

When I heard what Willie said, I thought, damn—I wish I'd known that when we were playing! Because when he stepped up there, I was giving it everything I had. I mean, my hemorrhoids were hanging out, and I was grunting so hard my throat would be sore. And to think that Willie was practically surrendering. I don't really believe it, though. Mays has a way of exaggerating the truth. When I was working for ESPN, I ran into Jesse Barfield and he told me a story he'd heard through the grapevine about Willie and me. Supposedly, Willie was in the batter's box digging a good foothold and I screamed at him, "What are you doing?" Well, that's a lie to begin with because I never talked to batters. Anyway, the story goes that when I yelled to him, Willie quickly began refilling the holes he had made and saying, "Excuse me, Mr. Gibson, excuse me." Believe me, there wasn't a pitcher in the world that Willie Mays had to call "Mister." But Willie's been telling that tale and it gets bigger and better as the years roll along.

Another reason I don't believe Mays conceded anything against me or any pitcher is that he never gave in; he never stopped looking for an edge. For example, Willie was one of the great "peekers" of all time. By this, I mean he would steal a glance behind him before the pitch was thrown to see where the catcher was positioned and what he was signaling for. Aaron was a peeker, too, but true to his character he was a little more subtle about it. Once, at the time when catchers were just beginning to use their shinguard flaps to give signs and location instead of doing everything by fingers, Mays was peeking at McCarver and saw something he didn't understand. So he stopped his warm-up swings, stepped out of the box, and said to McCarver, "Now, what was that pitch? What in the hell are you doing back there?" I couldn't believe the guy.

I caught up with Willie again at the 1965 all-star game, which was the one in Minnesota that Torre loves to tell about, where I refused to talk to him on the mound or in the shower. I hardly even talked to Mays at all-star games, and I had traveled all over the South with him. Among all the players on other teams, the only guy I had anything to do with was Roberto Clemente, who was a special case. One reason I talked to Clemente was to explain to him why I always threw at him. He swung way too hard against me, flinging himself at the ball and spinning around in the batter's box like he was on the playground or something. I had to demonstrate to him that I was no playground pitcher, and to that end I made a point of throwing at least one fastball in his direction nearly every time he came to the plate. In most cases, I wouldn't have felt compelled to provide a reason for knocking a batter down, but somehow Clemente brought out my soft side. It was virtually impossible to ignore him because he was always talking. Usually, it was to complain about how much his back or his shoulder or some other damn thing was hurting. "Oh, my back," he would say, "ees keeling me." He would go on and on until you had no choice but to say, "Clemente, shut the fuck up!" Then he would step in the batter's box and swing so hard that the flagsticks on top of the stadium would bend. He was so full of shit that you had to laugh, and you couldn't help liking the guy.

I was the only Cardinal at the Minnesota all-star game, which tells you all you need to know about our season. For some reason—it's a good bet that Harry Caray was the reason—the fans took it out on Boyer. As soon as he was announced, they would start booing. The Cardinals' field announcer, Charlie Jones, would call Boyer's name, and in the dugout I'd count "one, two, three . . ." On three, the boos would start heaping down from the upper deck. And this was for the man who had been the MVP of the league only a year before.

We were out of the race by August, after which the only remaining questions were whether I would win twenty games and who would take the fall at the end of the year. My nineteenth victory came against the Giants in a game in which I hit my first grand slam, one of five home runs I managed during the season. I was pleased that my stroke had returned after an off year in 1964, and was actually used for a pinch hitter now and then. I also won my first Gold Glove award. Dizzy Dean, who was the color commentator for the *NBC Game of the Week* every Saturday, declared one afternoon that I was the best fielding pitcher he ever saw after I saved a game against the Giants by chasing down a chopper over my head and flipping backhanded to White at first base while my momentum carried me toward second.

I had to beat Houston on the last day of the season to win twenty games for the first time in my career, and in the clubhouse beforehand Schoendienst showed me the lineup and asked what I thought about it. None of the regulars were in it. So I scratched out the names Red had put on the card and penciled in Boyer, White, Flood, Brock . . . to no avail. Red exercised his managerial prerogative over my objections and I had to go out there with the reserves. We won anyway, 5–2, but that still left us a game short of .500 for the season and in seventh place—the deepest plunge a World Series champion had ever taken.

The conclusion of a season like that is its best part, and we were feeling pretty chipper after the final Houston game—especially me, for whom twenty wins was something new and terrific. I was enjoying the moment, joking around with our equipment manager, Butch Yatkeman, when I was ambushed by the Cardinals' publicity director, Jim Toomey, who walked into the clubhouse and started raising hell. He came right over to me, glared, and said, "Why are you playing around in here, Gibson? That's why we had such a horseshit season." I truly felt like knocking his fucking head off and started to do it, but White stopped me and said, "He's not worth it."

With the issue of my twenty victories having been resolved, attention turned to the other question that had hovered over the late stages of the Cardinal season. It was answered within a month, when Howsam traded Boyer to the Mets for my old pitching nemesis, Alvin Jackson, and a third baseman named Charley Smith. With that move, roughly half of our power was gone. Howsam got rid of the other half a week later when he traded Bill White to the Phillies. Groat and Uecker were also in the deal, which brought us Pat Corrales, a catcher; Art Mahaffey, a pitcher; and Alex Johnson, a young outfielder.

In seven days and two trades, Howsam had disposed of three-quarters of the infield that had started the all-star game two years before. And although Uecker was a weak hitter, he was more than adequate as a defensive catcher and one of a kind in the clubhouse. Among his many imitations, Uecker did a hilarious rendition of Howsam, who was very bland and nasal, and in turn Howsam's dislike for Uecker was so intense that he wouldn't make the deal with the Phillies unless they agreed to take Uecker.

Groat's productivity, like Boyer's, had begun to fall off, and defensively Dal Maxvill represented an improvement at shortstop. We would miss the professionalism and leadership of the two men who had been the left side of our infield, but we would miss everything about White, who, in addition to being such a solid guy and all-around player, would drive in more than a hundred runs for Philadelphia in 1966. The steep cost of the Phillie trade made me awfully curious about Alex Johnson, who was alleged to be the key to the deal.

Of all the men I played with in my Cardinal career, few could equal the talent of Alex Johnson. Physically, he had it all—strength, speed, and skill. He could hit a ball hard enough to be frightening at the plate. He was also the most contrary man I've ever known in my life—which is a hell of a statement coming from Fred Gibson's brother. There was something deep down in Alex Johnson's personality that made it impossible for him to go along with anybody anytime for any reason. When he got hit in the arm with a pitch once, the trainers told him to soak the arm in ice to keep the swelling down. So Alex dropped it in the whirlpool and watched it puff up to twice its size. If he were shipwrecked and being carried to safety by the tide, Alex Johnson would swim the other way just to show the ocean who was boss.

Mostly because he was his own worst enemy, refusing to make the adjustments necessary to succeed in the big leagues, A.J. fared poorly in his two seasons with the Cardinals. Ultimately, after he was traded to the Reds and his talent took over, he had a few .300 seasons in spite of himself and even won an American League batting title in his first year with California, but with us he was a complete and exasperating disaster. On the rare occasions—three, to be exact—when he hit a home run, he ignored the attempts of his teammates to shake his hand, explaining, "You don't shake my hand when I make an out; don't shake my hand when I hit a home run." A.J. accepted the hand or the advice of no man. When he was playing the outfield, the coaches, as they did with all outfielders, would wave a towel from the dugout to show him where to position a particular batter, and similarly, when I was pitching, I sometimes motioned to the outfielders to move them one way or another. But it didn't matter to Alex who the instructions came from: If he saw the towel, or if he saw me waving, he would acknowledge the order by turning around in a circle without budging an inch from the spot where he was standing. His favorite saying was, "Trying to tell me how to play the outfield is like trying to tell Einstein about science." I don't know how A.J. was at physics, but I suspect Einstein was a better judge of fly balls.

I'm really not sure what kind of sense of humor Johnson had, because it was hard to tell if he was serious or not. Once, when we were boarding the bus after an exhibition game in the spring, Alex was sitting with his legs crossed and I accidentally bumped his foot as I walked past. I said, "Oh, excuse me, A.J." He never even looked up. Instead, he stared right at his foot, pointed to it, and said, "You don't have to apologize to me, 'cause that's who's gonna kick yo' ass."

Needless to say, I missed Bill White a lot.

I didn't *miss* White, however, the first time we played the Phillies in 1966. I've already described what happened when he leaned over the plate and pulled my first outside fastball, but for his benefit I should add a footnote to that story. When we had been teammates and I first advised White of what I would do if he ever took liberties with the outside corner when I was pitching, he responded with a warning that he would take great pleasure in running on me when he reached first—particularly if I put him there with a purpose pitch. I have to say that he made good on his threat, several times hauling those stiff old bones to second base at my expense.

The man designated to replace White at first base for the Cardinals was a twenty-six-year-old Oklahoman named George Kernek. In the event that Kernek should fall short, the insurance was veteran Tito Francona, a decent player on the down side of a journeyman career. It was soon apparent, though, that Howsam had created a problem and the answer was not at hand. Our lineup was completely devoid of a home-run threat, and we were scoring runs at the most lethargic pace in the league. Perhaps Howsam had stripped the team of power in the anticipation that our circular new stadium, roomy and symmetrical and ultimately unencumbered by a single blade of grass (although the artificial turf would not be installed for another four years), would emphasize speed. We had Brock and Flood and Javier to satisfy that requirement, but nobody was left to drive them in.

We were scheduled to move into Busch Memorial Stadium on May 12, 1966. Fortunately, Howsam finally awoke to the grim prospect that our offensive deficiencies would be highlighted against the wide-open spaces of the new ballpark unless we found a first baseman with a little thunder in his hands. Old Busch Stadium had been one of the best hitting parks in the league, but its concrete replacement was sure to be less generous. The way we were going, we might never make a scratch on Busch Memorial's home plate. Hence, Orlando Cepeda.

The Baby Bull, as they called him—Cepeda's father, the Babe Ruth of Puerto Rico, was the original Bull—had been the National League's Rookie of the Year in 1958 with the San Francisco Giants and peaked in 1961 with forty-six home runs and a whopping 142 RBIs. He was a ferocious hitter and an extremely likable guy whose only enemies seemed to be the San Francisco manager, Herman Franks, who apparently didn't appreciate Cepeda's Latin nature; the San Francisco public and press, to whom he was not Willie Mays or Willie McCovey; and his knees, which were as fragile as Mickey Mantle's. Cepeda's knees had disabled him for most of the 1965 season, and Franks had no patience left for him. He also had no place to play him. McCovey, a quiet and indisputable superstar, had taken over at first base during Cepeda's absence in 1965 and was better there than in the outfield. Cepeda was too hobbled for the outfield, of dubious durability, and therefore expendable. Howsam took him off the Giants' hands in exchange for Ray Sadecki.

Cepeda was not yet in full swing after his latest surgery, and his production for 1966 was comparatively modest. But he at least gave us a power presence for the middle of the lineup, leading the team with seventeen home runs. As a pitcher, I appreciated that. I had been 2–3 without Cepeda despite an earned run average around 2.00. With Cha-Cha on first—he left the "Baby Bull" label back in San Francisco and took on a new persona with the Cardinals—I won eight of my next nine decisions before slipping into my customary midseason slump. An arthritic elbow contributed to the tailspin this time, causing me to sit out the all-star game, which I wouldn't have minded except that the game was played in front of the home folks, showcasing our new accommodations next to the Mississippi River.

Although Busch Memorial has always been a pitcher's park and I'm glad to have played in it, even when it was brand spanking new it was not a place to stir the emotions—except possibly for the view beyond left field, where the top of the arch loomed at a greater height than the Eiffel Tower. It was little different from other new parks of the period—Atlanta, Philadelphia, Pittsburgh, Cincinnati—and even the Houston Astrodome was much the same but for the roof, which was a novelty for the players as well as the fans. Our contribution to Astrodome lore was supplying the first player to hit the roof with a fly ball from a fungo bat. The honor went to Joe Hoerner, who became an outstanding relief pitcher for us in 1966 after falling short previously (both as a reliever and a fungo hitter) with the Colt .45s.

In a less visible manner, Hoerner would become nearly as important to the rebuilt Cardinals as Cepeda. He gave us the relief ace we had lacked since the departure of Lindy McDaniel, and he was very much a Cardinal at heart. This required a certain degree of immaturity, which Hoerner didn't lack. His favorite stunt was pouncing on a teammate who was trying to tie his shoe. That was the cue for about eight others to pile on top, creating a common scene that must have been puzzling to visitors in the Cardinal clubhouse. Hoerner was also a willing companion to anybody who wanted to go anywhere, whether it was hunting or fishing or bar-hopping. He didn't like to sit around. After a ballgame in Atlanta one hot day, we were all sitting on a bus waiting for the driver to show up, and after about half an hour Hoerner couldn't take it any longer and crawled behind the wheel. With Cepeda urging him on, he managed to maneuver safely to our hotel, only to forget about the height of the bus and smash into the overhanging exit sign in the hotel driveway.

Hoerner's favorite occasions were Saturday nights, which he enjoyed so much that he extended them into Sunday mornings. Schoendienst was aware of his reliever's Saturday habit and made it a practice not to pitch Hoerner on Sunday, if possible. The times he had to deviate from this policy were memorable. One Sunday against the Pirates, Red was compelled to bring Hoerner into a one-run game to pitch to Maury Wills, who was a bothersome hitter but not strong enough to present any immediate danger. Wills hit the first pitch about five hundred feet. With that, Red jumped up, shouting, "See, I'll never pitch that son of a bitch again on Sunday! Never!"

Schoendienst kept his promise, but when Hoerner was traded to the Phillies a few years later it was a different story. He was brought in to pitch against us one Sunday, and even in a Philadelphia uniform he still haunted Red's sabbaths. Hoerner had an unusual condition in which his circulation would be cut off if he raised his arm too high—which I suppose is why he pitched sidearm—and this particular day he somehow got his arm too high and passed out right on the mound. Everybody was hovering over him, going crazy, and Red was in the dugout screaming, "I told you! It's Sunday! That man should *never* be pitching on a Sunday!" Somebody whacked Hoerner on the chest and he was fine, which was more than could be said for Red.

In addition to being a very tough lefthander, Hoerner was also a skillful agitator, and when he was with the Cardinals he had warned Lou Brock that if he ever pitched against him he would saw the bat off in Lou's hands. Brock told him he was full of shit, but damn if the first pitch he threw to Lou didn't snap his Louisville Slugger right in half. After I stopped laughing, I carried an armful of bats out to Brock at home plate.

As much as I appreciated Hoerner, I didn't take too much advantage of him in 1966 because I completed twenty out of the thirty-five games I started. The time off around the all-star break helped, and when I returned to the rotation I won nine out of my next ten. It was my best season of pitching overall, and although my numbers still fell short of Koufax's and Marichal's, they were the best any Cardinal pitcher had put up in nearly twenty years—since Harry Brecheen won twenty games and the ERA title in 1948. My earned run average was 2.44, and after giving up more home runs than any other pitcher in 1965, I cut the number by more than a third, thanks in large part to the deep fences of the new Busch Stadium. As a result of better control, I was also reducing the number of pitches I threw, which in turn enabled me to remain stronger in the late innings and finish more games. I was strong enough to pitch on three days of rest toward the end of the season—although we were out of the race by then, finishing sixth as the Dodgers again beat out the Giants for the pennant—and the extra starts allowed me to win my twentieth game in mid-September, 3–1 over the Cubs and former teammate Curt Simmons, who had been sold to Chicago in June. My twenty-first victory was also against the Cubs.

Along with Drysdale, I continued to be, I suppose, the best hitting pitcher in the league—or at least the proudest. I had two hits against Koufax in a game in which we reached him for thirteen in all, the most he ever surrendered. (He beat me, anyway, 4–2, capitalizing on four runs the Dodgers scored in the first inning on a series of hits that rolled and dropped into just the right—wrong—spots.) I did more pinch-hitting that year than ever before, which stands to reason considering our lackluster offense. Charley Smith came up way short of Boyer at third base, and although I felt good about Maxvill's glove behind me, his bat was sorely lacking. One of the worst days of my career, in fact—I don't remember the year, because I've tried to block it out of my mind—was when Schoendienst sent Maxie up to pinch-hit for me. I told him, "Red, if you ever want to get me out of a ballgame, come out to the mound and do it, please. Whatever you do, don't send Maxie up to the plate for me." I had five home runs playing every fourth or fifth day in two different seasons, 1965 and 1972, and Maxvill had only six in his entire fourteen-year career! I was completely humiliated to have him at the plate swinging the bat for me. Of course, he popped up.

That was only professional humiliation, however, and, like most baseball-related tribulation, left no permanent scars on my psyche or my wife's or children's. It hardly compared with the personal humiliation the whole family suffered after the season in Omaha, when we bought a house in a white neighborhood called Rockbrook.

Charline had been shopping around for houses during the summer and liked this one, so I told her to go ahead and buy it and we'd move in when I got home. The house had to be painted in the meantime, and halfway through the project a neighbor across the street, in a last-ditch effort to discourage us from integrating the block, ordered the painter to gather up his crew and leave. The house stood there partially painted until we could find a workman with enough backbone to finish the job. The neighbor later apologized, but there was never a time in that house when our race ceased to be conspicuous. When a new family moved in down the street, they were told that there was a Negro living on the block, but it was only Bob Gibson, the ballplayer.

The appearance of a successful, middle-class, or even well-dressed black person invariably required an explanation in the white portions of Omaha. I walked into a store once wearing a suit and tie, and the sales clerk asked if I was a minister. I said, "Why do you ask? Because I'm not dirty?" Charline and I were prepared to handle that sort of thing because we had made the choice to move where we did, but Annette and Renee were a different matter. It wasn't uncommon for Renee to come home crying or in trouble because a teacher had considered her impudent and grabbed her behind the neck or because she had been fighting with a boy who called her names.

Although we were the only black family in our corner of town, the Gibsons were not alone in the attempt to integrate Omaha. Charline and the girls marched in front of city hall that year with ten thousand other blacks to show support for a local fair-housing ordinance. I stayed in the car and watched, afraid that if somebody spit or threw something at me or a mem-

ber of my family, I would become violent. I greatly admired Dr. Martin
Luther King, Jr., but I couldn't do as he said. The Gibson clan, as nearly as
I can figure, has consisted over the years of two basic types—those who
practice passive resistance and those who don't. ———

My mother, who was not the kind of lady to take any crap and could be
downright militant when it came to whipping her children, belonged to
the latter. Her nature, nonetheless, was fundamentally tranquil. For instance, she kept all of us far away from the branch of the family that was
well known to curse, drink, play cards, and carouse—the rowdy cousins,
as they were referred to in our house. We stuck to the strain of Gibsons
and Browns in which there was a preacher or deacon in every
generation—a tradition that has been carried on by my sister Barbara
Jean's son, who is a minister. My father, who was a deacon and met my
mother in church, was also the kind who rebelled peaceably. Back in Louisiana, his father had remarried a mean woman, but instead of having it
out with her, as I later did with my surly stepfather, Pack Gibson merely
gathered his things and moved to Nebraska. (After he found work in Lincoln, my father returned to Louisiana to spring his brother Josh, for whom
the firstborn of our family was nicknamed; contrary to what many people
assume, my brother was not called Josh in deference to the Josh Gibson
who was a famous Negro League catcher. Uncle Josh and another uncle,
Ira, were Christian people who were highly regarded in our family and
maintained a warm relationship with us. My mother wanted nothing to do
with the rest of my father's relatives, however.)

The part of the family that I took after—as did Josh and Fred and
maybe even Barbara Jean—was on the Brown side of my mother's line,
which was part Creole and part West Indian. Unfortunately, the story that
best illustrates this point is sketchy because there are no written records
of it, only the oral version that my mother told Barbara Jean when they
worked together in the garden during the spring. It's about my mother's
mother, who not long after the Civil War was working as a sharecropper
on a large plantation outside Lecompte, Louisiana. Apparently, there was
a dispute between my grandmother and another woman that turned violent, and the other woman was badly hurt. That meant trouble for my
grandmother, whose only recourse was to take a horse in the night and

steal away to the relative safety of a friendlier plantation where she had grown up and her mother still lived. Along the way, she was overtaken by the straw boss or overseer or whoever the hell enforced the policies of the plantation she was escaping. (Since slavery had been abolished, I've always presumed that this all took place independent of federal law but in strict compliance with local custom.) The overseer informed my grandmother that it was his duty to punish her with a whip, but she answered by showing the pistol that she gripped in her apron pocket and advising the gentleman not to get off his horse. He obliged, and with the gun as her escort, she made it to her mother's plantation. Although freedom had officially been conferred by the outcome of the Civil War, hers was effectively won astride a stolen horse, with a gun in the apron. In later years, we knew our grandmother as an Indian-looking woman who made corn liquor and drove a wagon and a mule, singing in broken English, "I don't drink no whiskey. I don't drink no wine, I don't drink no strong drink, just a little toddy sometimes." She was my kind of relative.

In retrospect, it's interesting how guns in aprons have made such a dramatic difference in my life. My mother might have saved my skin when she hid my stepfather's pistol in her pocket, and my grandmother set the course for family history by packing iron in her domestic apparel. At the risk of stretching the point, I suppose it could be said that, for my part, I sort of pitched with a gun in my apron.

# CHAPTER VII

The good news after the 1966 season was that Bob Howsam left the Cardinals to become general manager of the Cincinnati Reds. Stan Musial, three years out of uniform, took his place, which indicated right off the bat that we would again be a player-oriented organization, as we had been with Bing Devine and Johnny Keane running the show. The bad news was that Keane, who had been unable to rouse the declining team he inherited in New York and (with the Yankees on their way to last place) was fired early in the 1966 season, died in January.

The news that Sandy Koufax had retired was both good and bad. It was obviously helpful for the Cardinals and the other National League teams with pennant aspirations, but unfortunate for baseball in general. Koufax was still very much in his prime, having blown away the league for twenty-seven wins and a 1.73 earned run average in 1966—his fifth straight ERA title—at the age of thirty-one. It was regrettable that his last game was a World Series loss to Jim Palmer and the Baltimore Orioles in which the Dodgers' incredibly fast center fielder, Willie Davis, had made three consecutive errors. The Orioles swept the Series, and Koufax never got another chance. The way his arthritic elbow felt, though, I don't suppose he was eager to get out there again. The pain was so intense, and he had endured it for so long, that he was able to walk away at the top of the game without second-guessing himself.

From the Cardinals' standpoint, while Koufax's retirement was encouraging it would require much more than that for us to overtake the Dodgers and various other teams that had finished ahead of us in 1965 and 1966. Realizing this, Musial made a bold move, trading Charley Smith, our only third baseman, to the Yankees for Roger Maris, who was going on thirty-four years old and seemed to be fading fast.

Like most of the Yankees we had faced in the 1964 World Series, Maris hadn't had a good year since. But he had always been a far better player than was suggested by his reputation, which had been warped when he practically came out of nowhere to break Babe Ruth's single-season home-run record in 1961. Maris was actually much more than a home-run hitter, playing solid defense and doing with the bat what was required to win. His baseball intelligence was well suited to the Cardinals, and in St. Louis we didn't give a damn about the fact that he had become unpopular and unappreciated in New York, much as Cepeda had in San Francisco. The similarity was not lost on Cepeda, who in the spring pulled Maris aside one day and said something like, "It's you and me, Roger. You know what I mean?" I knew what he meant. I felt so good about having those two veterans on the field that when I met Ed Bressoud, a shortstop we acquired before the season from the Mets for Jerry Buchek, I said, "How do you feel about picking up an extra $10,000 [World Series money]? Just stick around all year and it'll happen."

The acquisition of Maris bumped Mike Shannon from right field and the absence of Smith created a neon vacancy at third base for the 1967 season. Shannon, although available, was not an obvious answer at third because his strength was his outfield defense—mainly his arm—and a positional setback might negate the improvement he had begun to make offensively. But Schoendienst liked Shannon's guts and competitiveness, as did I, and put his stamp on the team by committing third base to his former right fielder.

A good athlete, Shannon was a former University of Missouri football player, a strapping, handsome guy with an unrefined manner of speaking and an extremely original mind. We called him Moon Man. I understand that he got the nickname in the minor leagues, when he left his feet once to elude an inside fastball and looked briefly as if he were floating in space, but he could just as well have earned it on the merits of his personality. It often seemed as though Shannon existed in another dimension, talking about things that nobody else was in touch with. We had a diathermy machine with lights that flashed on and off and periodically would go crazy, prompting Flood to remark, "There goes the machine talking to the Moon Man again." The common reaction to Shannon's cosmic conversation was, "Okay Mike, whatever you say," but sometimes, always to our astonishment, he made sense to the point of being uncanny. I remember him telling me as far back as around 1962—for no particular reason, of course—that there would be a man on the moon before the decade was out. Okay, Mike, whatever you say. Then there was the day in Chicago when the game was droning along with no score into the middle innings. They had a left-handed pitcher going—I think it was Rich Nye—and about the fifth or so Shannon turned to me and said, "Ya know, we're not gonna get any runs off this guy until the ninth inning, and then I'm gonna hit a home run offa him because he's gonna hang a fuckin' curveball." Okay, Mike, whatever you say. Well, the game went on without either team scoring a run, and in the ninth inning the lefthander hung a curve and Shannon hit it out. I guess he was motivated. In situations like that, he was always saying, "We've got to get this game over with so I can go out and have a toddy."

To Shannon's credit, he worked hard to learn third base. It was in my best interest to make it as easy for him as possible.

> *During spring training, I went up to Hoot and asked him if there was any particular place he wanted me to play for certain batters or certain situations, whatever. He said, "I don't give a shit. The only time you're going to get the ball is in a double-play situation. If there's a runner on first base with less than two outs and a right-handed batter up, look for the ball." So I started paying attention, and I'll be damned if it didn't happen six or seven times in a row. Runner on first, less than two outs, bang, a one-hopper right at me*

*and I throw to second to start the double play. I went to Gibson and said, "How did you know that?" He said, "I'm smart, that's how."*    —MIKE SHANNON

By 1967, I was clearly the veteran of the Cardinal pitching staff, the only starter with any appreciable experience except for Ray Washburn, who was still trying to work his way back after blowing out his arm in 1963. He would never regain his speed entirely but eventually learned to work with what he had, which provided a useful lesson for our young starters—a twenty-nine-year-old rookie named Dick Hughes; a jocular, guitar-strumming righthander named Nelson Briles (who actually started the season in the bullpen after a 4–15 performance in 1966); a bonus-baby lefty named Larry Jaster, who made a living by shutting out the Dodgers time after time; and a tall, promising, extremely confident southpaw named Steve Carlton whose style of pitching was similar to mine. I thought Carlton might benefit from my experience and relative wisdom, but when I approached him in that vein it seemed that he had little respect for either (although he later acknowledged that he learned a lot about pitching from quietly observing me).

Despite the apparent indifference of Carlton, I warmed up to the role of elder statesman (I was thirty-one) and demonstrated my paternalism toward the young staff by bestowing nicknames on most of them. I called Washburn "Deadbody" because he moved as if every last particle of life had been sucked out of him; Hughes earned the nickname "Sniper" when he bought a hunting rifle in Atlanta and checked out the scope by zeroing in on pedestrians from the window of his hotel room; Jaster's moniker was "Creeper" for the way he seemed to sneak around; Hoerner was "Bulldog" because he looked like one; and his partner in the bullpen, Ron Willis, had a weak chin that prompted me to call him "Gomer" or "Andy Gump." Andy Gump had a strong arm, though, and gave the team a much-needed righthander to complement Hoerner in late-inning situations.

Although he was an effective reliever, Willis was not the kind of pitcher who would enter a game and blow people away, nor was he the type to try to outwit the opposing batter. I recall a team meeting in Pittsburgh that year when Schoendienst was going over the scouting report on the Pirate hitters and Willis was sitting in the back of the room reading a newspaper. Red said, "Hey, Willis, we're having a meeting here. You might want to listen." Willis said, "Naw, I don't need to. I'm just gonna throw my good slider anyway." Red must have had faith in Willis's good slider, because he brought him into a key spot that night to face Maury Wills, who had been traded from the Dodgers, and Wills smoked one of those good sliders over the right-field fence to win the ballgame.

We didn't lose very often, though—especially early in the season. We won our first six games out of the chute, including two in which I beat Marichal. With Koufax out of the picture, the question of the best pitcher in the league was effectively narrowed down to me and Marichal, and I think I relished our confrontations more than he did. One of the victories was a 6–0 shutout in which I struck out the first five Giants—Ken Henderson, Jesus Alou, Mays, McCovey, and Hart—and thirteen in all. I figured it was my time to step to the front.

After eight seasons in the big leagues, I felt by 1967 that I had finally mastered all of my pitches. I could challenge the best hitters with my sailing fastball, induce the double play with my sinking fastball (how about that, Moon Man?), finish off strikeouts with my slider, and do some funky things with the junkball tricks Purkey taught me. My control was sharp, and there wasn't a batter in the league who thought he could take the outside corner from me without paying a stiff price.

But I wasn't the only one throwing the ball well for the Cardinals that year. Dick Hughes, who started the season in the bullpen, suddenly put it all together after a long, undistinguished career in the minors, and Carlton began to rack up strikeouts with his surprising fastball and even better slider. None of the starters pitched poorly, and the offense was getting it together, as well. Maris, though his numbers were modest, proved to be the piece we needed in the third spot of the batting order to take us from Brock and Flood to Cepeda.

It all made for a hell of a fun season. I was caught up in the spirit of 1967, but nobody appreciated it more, or was more responsible for it, than Cepeda, who was bubbling over with cheerfulness about our club, his role on it, and his liberation from Herman Franks and San Francisco. He was also driving in the runs that White and Boyer used to take care of, and as a direct result we were in the pennant race from the beginning, jockeying with the Giants, who had finished second to the Dodgers two years in a row, and the surprising Cubs, who despite finishing last in 1966 had put together a strong lineup (Ernie Banks, Billy Williams, Ron Santo, etc.) and were making noise under Leo Durocher.

As we neared the all-star break, our team was taking on a special chemistry, with Cepeda as the chief chemist. Other big-league teams might not have considered it cool to show enthusiasm in the clubhouse, but Cepeda couldn't suppress his. After a ballgame, win or lose, he would stand on the money trunk, where we all stored our valuables during a game, and lead the whole team in a round of cheers. Losing, in fact, seemed to pump him up with purpose and, in turn, bind the team closer together.

"All right, we lost tonight, El Birdos," he would say, using the mangled Spanish nickname (authored by coach Joe Schultz) that we took on because of him. "Anybody gonna quit?"

We'd all answer, "No!"

"We coming back tomorrow to kick some ass?"

"Yes!"

Of course, the cheering was more creative, and more fun, when we won.

"All right, El Birdos! Who made the greatest play out there tonight? Was it Heinie Manush?"

"No!"

"Was it Toulouse-Lautrec?"

"No!"

"Was it Curt Flood?"

"Yes!"

"El Birdos!"

"Yes!"

The *most* fun was when we beat the Giants, who were considered the favorites to supplant the Dodgers at the top of the league. Cepeda had a big finish for the nights when we showed up the team that dumped him. For what he meant to us, we were happy to indulge his personal feelings.

"Who's the best team in the league?"

"El Birdos!"

"Is it the Giants?"

"No!"

"Fuck Herman Franks!"

"Fuck Herman Franks!"

Even Maris, who by nature was not a sunny kind of guy, joined in the clubhouse high jinks, singing out nicknames of various El Birdos. We all shared in the camaraderie of that uncommon group of ballplayers, the effect being that we came to consider ourselves a special team, much as we had in 1964. Implicit in that was the fact that we considered ourselves foremost a *team*. There were stars on the 1967 Cardinals, but no star mentalities. If a player was caught looking at the stat sheet, for instance, we fined him on the spot.

The team concept manifested itself conspicuously on the field. McCarver has said that the '67 Cardinals were the most remarkable team he has ever been associated with because we never made a mental mistake. We never threw to the wrong base and we always took advantage of every inch the opponent would give us. When it came to intangibles— execution, resourcefulness, sacrifice, etc.—we were the equal of any team in modern baseball.

Although a pitcher works in relative isolation from the other eight men on the field, there were specific ways in which I was able to contribute to the teamwork that characterized the Cardinals. Lou Brock provided me with that opportunity in abundance. A significant part of my job when I took the mound was to protect Brock.

By 1967, Brock had surpassed Maury Wills as the premier base-stealer in the game, and it was an identity that he worked diligently to maintain. Until that time, baseball etiquette had dictated that it was not appropriate to steal bases when one's team was ahead by more than about three runs, but Brock was paid to steal bases and figured, furthermore, that if a four-run lead is good, a five-run lead is better. There were many, even on the Cardinals, who disagreed with this philosophy and thought that Brock often stole for the sake of the statistic. In this regard, it didn't help Brock that, of the regulars on the team, he was the most independent. While I regarded Flood as a brother, I thought of Brock merely as my teammate. We seldom talked, less often at length. At the same time, though, I admired Brock's skills, appreciated what he did for the team, and couldn't argue with his attitude toward stealing bases. Brock was a winner because he was a competitor, and a competitor doesn't stop competing just because his team has pulled reasonably ahead. If I hadn't respected Brock as I did, I would have been less likely to stick my neck out in his behalf.

Much of my reputation as a badass pitcher resulted from the fact that Lou Brock was on my side. There was no other player who irritated the other team as Brock did, and consequently no other who was knocked down quite as often. When somebody on the other team threw at Brock, I considered it my duty to throw at somebody on the other team. That's simply how the game was played—at least in my book.

The worst baseball fight I ever saw started that way. We were playing Cincinnati in St. Louis early in July of 1967 and I was coming off possibly the worst start of my life four days earlier, giving up eleven runs to the Giants (Fuck Herman Franks!) without finishing the first inning. This, of course, put me in the mood to take it out on somebody, and the opportunity quickly presented itself against the Reds. We jumped all over Milt Pappas in the first inning, two of our runs scoring on a throwing error by a young second baseman named Pete Rose, and when Brock batted for the second time in the inning the score was already 7–0. He reached first base and not surprisingly tried to steal second. It's certainly reasonable to operate on the premise that even a seven-run lead is not secure in the first inning, but the Reds didn't care to see it that way. Even though Brock had been thrown out in the steal attempt, the gauntlet had been dropped.

Don Nottebart was the relief pitcher who took over for Pappas, and he responded to Brock by knocking down Javier. When Brock batted again in the fourth inning, Nottebart hit him. This could not go unanswered, and the unlucky Red leading off the fifth inning was Tony Perez, Cincinnati's personable power hitter by the way of Cuba. My first pitch buzzed past Perez's ear, which should have been an indication that I wasn't trying to hit him. If a pitcher is trying to hit a batter, the last place he wants to throw the ball is at the head, because it's the easiest thing to move. When I wanted to hit somebody, I threw slightly behind him because a batter will instinctively jump backwards when he sees the ball coming toward him. The brushback of Perez was merely a message to lay off Brock. A pitch or two later, Perez flied to left, and as far as I was concerned the moment had passed. But on his way back to the dugout, Perez trotted past the mound and said something uncharacteristically nasty in his barely discernible English. I returned the compliment and informed Perez that if he had anything more to say he knew where I could be found. We stared at each other in that menacing baseball way, and then Cepeda moved in from first base to get between us. That was the signal for the benches to empty, but even then there was no heavy action until Bob Lee, a Cincinnati relief pitcher known as Man Mountain, came charging in from the bullpen shouting, "Where's Cepeda? Where's Cepeda? I'm gonna punch his fucking lights out!" There was a tangle of people on the field, and as Lee was looking around and ranting, Cepeda tapped him on the shoulder and coldcocked him with a single punch. From his position on the ground, Lee missed a hell of a fight. It was so wild that nineteen cops came onto the field to try to stop it, which they couldn't. The brawl spread all over the field and even into the dugouts. I ended up in the Cincinnati dugout with Rose and Tommy Helms under me and Perez somehow involved.

> *I'll never forget the sight. There was Gibson in the Reds' dugout, visibly manhandling about three Reds and tossing them bodily out of the dugout and onto the field. That was just a sample of something you saw from Gibson every time he went out there. He was the toughest athlete mentally I ever saw, and the greatest competitor.* —Cardinal announcer JACK BUCK

We were all wrestling around in the dugout, doing very well, thank you—I actually got in some good licks on Rose and Helms—when all of a sudden we looked up and there was Bobby Tolan, one of our young outfielders, on the top step, poised to dive on the pile with a flying leap. He must have been watching too many cowboy movies or something. I yelled, "Look out, that fool's gonna jump on us!" We moved just as Tolan left his feet, and he landed headfirst on the dugout bench. He came out of it with hand and head bruises. One of the cops got a dislocated jaw in the melee; Dave Bristol, the Reds' manager, picked up a spike wound; Nottebart's face was messed up; I jammed my thumb; and most of the other players were black and blue. Everybody recovered quickly enough, although

Bauman refused to treat Tolan. He said, "How the hell did you get hurt? You didn't even play!"

Lee was the only one ejected from the game, and I wasn't about to let a sore thumb deprive me of a seven-run lead. I lasted eight innings and we won 7–3. The victory was my tenth and it kept us in a tie for first place with the Cubs. It also lit a flame in our bellies. As the midpoint of the season approached, we felt that we had it in us to torch the rest of the league in the second half. There was concern when Flood crashed into the center-field wall in the last game of the Cincinnati series and had to go on the disabled list, but Tolan, none the worse from his dugout debacle, was a talented replacement. We put together a little streak and led the pack by three and a half games at the all-star break.

The all-star game was in Anaheim, and this time I felt good enough to pitch in it. In fact, all of the pitchers on both sides felt pretty good that day. Richie Allen homered for us in the second inning, Brooks Robinson matched him in the sixth against the Cubs' Ferguson Jenkins—who tied a record by striking out six batters in his three innings—and that was it through nine. I worked the seventh and eighth innings, joining Marichal, Chris Short of the Phillies, Mike Cuellar of the Astros (who had been with the Cardinals in 1964), Drysdale, and a kid from the Mets named Tom Seaver as pitchers against whom the American League couldn't score in fifteen innings. My feelings for Tony Perez softened somewhat when he homered for us in the top of the fifteenth, and the longest game in all-star history was finally over when Seaver checked the American League in the bottom of the inning.

My arm felt strong enough at the all-star break that I decided to take my turns thereafter on three days' rest instead of four, as I had been doing since my elbow problems the season before. As a result, my next start came four days later, July 15, against the Pirates in St. Louis. Our lead was four games at the time, and although half the season remained to be played, there was nothing on the horizon that seemed likely to get between us and the pennant. The stars appeared to be lined up in our favor.

I came out throwing hard against Pittsburgh, and we were ahead 1–0 when my old pal Clemente led off the fourth with the Pirates' first hit, a line drive off my right shin. I couldn't get up right away, and Bob Bauman rushed out to check my leg and spray ethyl chloride on it. I said, "I hate to tell you, Doc, but you're spraying in the wrong place." He advised me to take a look, and I saw what he saw—a dent in the skin the shape of a baseball. It was odd that I couldn't feel where I had been struck, but since I couldn't feel it I wasn't particularly worried. I told Doc to put a little tape on it and let me get back to work. Willie Stargell was the next batter, and I walked him. Then Bill Mazeroski popped out, and the count was three and two on Donn Clendenon when I tried to put a little extra on the payoff pitch and collapsed. The fibula bone had snapped above the ankle. I was taken to Jewish Hospital, my leg was put in a cast, and I was out of the pennant race for nearly eight weeks.

Those who witnessed the Clemente game—which we eventually lost—perceived it much differently than I did. While it was true that I didn't surrender easily to pain or injury (Josh had seen to that), at the time I didn't fully realize what I was doing. I assumed that I had picked up a hell of a contusion, which was of little consequence in a 1–0 game in a pennant race. Long before, Josh had taught me that if there was any way I could continue to play, it was my duty as a ballplayer to continue. Initially, the bone had been fractured but not separated. It was only when I came down on it so hard—my motion concentrated a lot of weight and spinning momentum on my right leg—that it broke cleanly in two. If that hadn't happened, I believe I might have continued the season uninterrupted.

I felt a little awkward with all the gushy rhetoric that accompanied the incident, but if it provided a constructive example for the ballclub, so be it. The reaction on the Cardinals was summarized, I suppose, by Dal Maxvill, when he spoke years later to baseball writer Roger Angell for an article in *The New Yorker*. Maxie said, "That was the most extraordinary thing I ever saw in baseball—Gibby pitching to those batters with a broken leg. Everyone who was there that day remembered it afterward, for always, and every young pitcher who came onto our club while Gibson was still with us was told about it. We didn't have too many pitchers turning up with upset stomachs or hangnails on our team after that."

While the highfalutin praise was nice and everything, it didn't take the pain away. The ache was not in my leg, but in my whole being. It's good form, I know, and standard practice for a ballplayer to say that he can't stand being out of commission, but believe me, I *couldn't stand* it. There was a pennant to be won, and I was hobbling around with crutches and a goddamn cast.

The day after my injury, we were swept by the Mets in a doubleheader. A week later, we had fallen back into a tie with the Cubs. Everybody on the club knew that it was time to see what we were made of, but everybody *else* had the chance to go out on the field and prove it—including the pitcher who took my spot in the rotation. That turned out to be Nelson Briles, who had a good arm but was only twenty-three years old and hadn't yet shown himself to be capable of winning in the major leagues. In his first start for me, Aaron beat him with a home run. That wasn't a disgraceful thing—Aaron had beaten *me* with a home run before, and nearly every other pitcher in the league—but it was enough to bring out the doomsayers. It looked to most people as though the Cardinal magic had spilled out of the bottle.

The next day we lost again to the Braves, this time in thirteen innings. We obviously needed something, anything, to get us believing in ourselves again, even if it was something absurd like Fifi Latour. Bob Bauman, of course, dutifully embraced the challenge of a psychological gimmick. He never seemed to run out of schemes and potions, going so far as to label vitamin bottles to suit every situation—one marked "RBI," for instance, and another "hit-and-run." This time, he responded with a large pot of tomato rice soup. We ate the soup in the clubhouse and the next day swept the Braves in a doubleheader. I can't begin to offer a reason why Bauman thought that tomato rice soup would get us going again, but we were willing to latch onto anything at that point. It wasn't practical for Doc to mix up a pot of tomato rice soup every day, so in its stead we borrowed the red-and-white theme by painting a baseball red on one side and using it for infield practice. The tomato-rice ball became sacred and was attended, like most sacred things, by a ritual. When Cepeda tossed the ball into the dugout after throwing grounders to the infielders before every inning, the only one allowed to catch it was Dick Sisler. When we lost a game, the tomato-rice ball was thrown away and a new one was made. We put a lot of faith in that ball. Once, Cepeda accidently chucked it into the stands and we had to give a fan two balls to get it back.

While the trainer was doing his part to hold us together, about the only thing I could offer was help for our young pitchers. Briles, in particular, was in the market for a little encouragement or counsel or something, and since I had put him in the spot he was in I took a special interest in him.

> *I was struggling as a young pitcher, and Gibson sat me down and asked, "Do you think you're a strikeout pitcher?" I said, "I can strike people out." He said, "No. Do you think you're a strikeout pitcher?" And I kind of said yes. Then he asked, "Do you think I'm a strikeout pitcher?" "Yes." "All right, who do I strike out? Let me tell you who I strike out. If I get nine strikeouts in a game, I'll probably strike out the sixth and seventh batters once or twice. I might strike out the eighth batter twice and I'll strike out the pitcher every time. That's about seven or eight right there. The good hitters are going to hit the ball most of the time no matter what I do. If you try to strike out the good hitters, that's when you make mistakes."* —NELSON BRILES

Briles was the kind of competitor whose best was brought out by a challenge, and not surprisingly he was equal to the task of his next start, which happened to be against the Cubs. Ray Washburn also beat Chicago, and it restored the confidence of the club to seize first place again. We— maybe I should say "they"—never let go of it after that. In two weeks, we won five of six from the Cubs while sweeping three games each from the Braves and Reds for an eleven-of-twelve run. A month later, we swept the Cubs in St. Louis, by which time our lead had opened up to 10½ games. Flood was back in the lineup, playing the best ball of his life, Briles got on a roll, Cepeda had returned to the powerful form of his earlier days in San Francisco, the tomato-rice ball was working like a charm, and El Birdos were flying high.

It was a heady time for the Cardinals and one of the most difficult periods of my professional life. I grew antsier with every game and had the disposition to prove it. It wasn't that I was lacking for activities. I've always kept several hobbies going at once, and while on crutches I was able, at least, to fiddle around with my ukelele and build a couple of model cars that I still have, including a 1918 Ford Runabout and a 1941 Lincoln. I also wrote a sports column for the *St. Louis Post-Dispatch* and did a considerable amount of yelling at Charline and our basset hound, Snoopy. I hope I spared the girls. I was not as sympathetic toward the sportswriters, however (despite my unsophisticated attempts at joining their ranks), and didn't think twice about snapping at their tiresome questions regarding my leg. Finally I composed a sign to hang around my neck and save us both a little aggravation. It said:

1. Yes, it's off!
2. No, it doesn't hurt!
3. I'm not supposed to walk on it for one week!
4. I don't know how much longer!
5. Ask Doc Bauman!
6. Ask Doc Middleton!

The sign was intended (half-intended, anyway) as a joke, but the press was not amused. I didn't really care, though, and it wasn't in my nature to put on a happy face when I hadn't won a ballgame in over a month.

The pennant was virtually in hand when I finally returned to the mound on September 7 against the Mets. Briles, Hughes, and Carlton had taken up the slack like champions while I was out, going 19–6 between them, and our lead had been holding at around ten games since late August. There was no reason to rush back except for the fact that I couldn't tolerate another day of not pitching. I went five innings, knocked off some rust, and won the game 9–2 as Maris and Javier homered and Maxvill, believe it or not, went four for four. Afterwards, Joe Hoerner said, "Big deal. You rest for two months and pitch five innings." Flood was also compassionate, adding, "So what? Anybody can pitch when the other team doesn't score many runs." Like I said, the Cardinals were sensitive guys.

My next start was better, nearly seven shutout innings against Philadelphia for my twelfth win. Six days later, I faced the Phillies again with a chance to clinch the pennant. I was well aware that I had done nothing for eight weeks while the rest of the guys pulled away from the field, and this was my chance to make a contribution to the second half of the season and the push toward the World Series. On a personal level, the game was also important to me as a test of my endurance. My leg had felt weak and sore in the two previous starts and I needed to prove to myself that I could pitch on it into the late innings. Fortunately, the guys got me five runs and I went the distance for a 5–1 victory that climaxed a memorable regular season.

We finished with 101 victories—eight more than we had in 1964—and blew away the Giants (second for the third straight year) by 10½ games. To our great satisfaction and the embarrassment of Herman Franks, Cepeda was the National League's Most Valuable Player with a .325 batting average, 111 RBIs, and the immeasurable credential of rebuilding a ballclub's morale. I'd like to think that we might also have come away with the Cy Young award if my leg had stayed in one piece. In the three previous seasons, I had increased my victory total by one each year to the point that I was due to win twenty-two games in 1967. I was in good position to do that when Clemente gained his revenge, and if I had, the Cy Young vote would have been a close call between me and the eventual winner, San Francisco's Mike McCormick, who finished the season 22–10.

It would be a while before we found out our World Series opponent. Detroit, Minnesota, and Boston battled down to the last day of the season, when the Red Sox, who had finished in ninth place the year before, overtook the Twins by completing a sweep of their two-game weekend series while Detroit split a Sunday doubleheader with the Angels. Carl Yastrzemski, a New Englander whose Triple Crown season had been the talk of the American League, was heroic to the end for Boston, going seven for eight with six RBIs in the final two games, winning the first with a three-run homer and tying the last with a bases-loaded single.

In the excitement of their much-celebrated victory, Yaz predicted that the Red Sox would polish off the Cardinals in six games.

It seemed that every time we made it to the World Series, we were overshadowed by the superheroes on the other side who were the real story. In 1964, it was Mantle, especially, and Maris and Ford. In 1967, it was Yastrzemski and Boston's Cy Young award winner, Jim Lonborg. My reaction was always the same:

Fine. Now watch this.

For that and other reasons, I loved the World Series. I loved being the underdog, as it seemed we always were. I loved the competition, the challenge of playing the best the other league had to offer for the honor of being the best of the best. I didn't love all the media nonsense that went along with the territory, but I loved the spotlight when I was on the mound. I loved the fact that the world championship would be decided when and only when I let go of the ball in my hand.

A lot of the Cardinals were like that. Brock, too, fed on the pressure of the World Series because it was his nature to take advantage of the moment and do whatever was necessary to reach the top. Flood was not as comfortable with tension—he admitted once that he sometimes broke out in a cold sweat while waiting for an important fly ball to come down—but I never thought of him as anything less than a money player. McCarver and Maris and Cepeda and Shannon and Javier and most of the others were the kind of guys you'd want in your foxhole.

We respected the Red Sox, who, in addition to Yastrzemski—and despite the absence of Tony Conigliaro, who was suffering dizzy spells after being struck in the face by a pitch in August—had an enviable lineup of sluggers that included George Scott, Reggie Smith, Ken Harrelson, and Rico Petrocelli. But they played in the slower American League fashion, and the feeling in our clubhouse was that they would soon find out what a real ballclub was all about. Of course, being a little more circumspect than our opponents, none of us dared say so publicly. We were content to leave that sort of thing to Yastrzemski and his cohorts, who succeeded over and over in prodding our competitive nerves. If it wasn't Yaz, it was Lonborg, and if it wasn't Lonborg, it was Scott.

The entire city of Boston was like that, it seemed. It was a fascinating place, and one that I wish had been on the National League circuit, but the people there, friendly as they basically were, could be downright nasty when it came to baseball. The night before the first game, for example, several of the Cardinals went to a party at the home of Bill Russell, the great basketball player for the Celtics. A few other Celtics were there, along with some luminaries from the jazz world, Les McCann and Nat and Cannonball Adderley. Everybody there loved jazz, including Nelson

Briles, who was the only white guy in the place. (The party, by the way, was the first time Briles ever ate soul food.) It was a great evening, with music and good conversation, and after we had been wined, dined, and entertained, we were told in no uncertain terms, "All right, now we're going to kick your asses."

The particular ass that the Red Sox intended to kick in the first game was mine. I looked forward to the occasion (Fine. Now watch this) and in fact felt so good about it that I wasn't even grumpy on the way to Fenway Park. Instead, I sat at the front of the bus, and as mounted police escorted us through traffic, I opened the window and hollered out, "The Redcaps are coming! Spread the word!" A little Massachusetts humor.

Lonborg had pitched the final game of the regular season against Minnesota, which meant that my opponent would be Jose Santiago, who, although not Lonborg's equal on the mound, was a better hitter. He homered against me in the third inning for the only Red Sox run. They hadn't had a baserunner to that point, and when he hit the ball in the air toward left, I started to walk off the field for our turn at bat. Then I noticed Santiago running around the bases and I thought, "Where the hell is he going?" I couldn't believe the ball had dropped into that damn screen on top of the Green Monster.

We scored in the third and the seventh as Brock went four for four with two stolen bases and came across with both of our runs, which were efficiently driven in on a pair of ground balls by Maris, who was playing with a fever and a shoulder so sore he took shots of cortisone and Novocain after the game. I struck out ten and gave up six hits, staying out of trouble for the most part.

> *Here we are in a tight game in the World Series, and I'm playing a new position. They've got runners on first and second with one out, I think, the situation in which Gibby told me to always look for the ball. It was a high bouncer this time, and I tried to come in and get the big hop. Instead, I wound up getting the short hop and was caught in between. I kicked it, and now we're in a jam. So I picked up the ball and tried to go in to say something to Bob and he says, "Just give me the fuckin' ball. Just give me the fuckin'*

*ball." I say, "Here, you got it." He struck out the next two batters*
*with six or seven pitches. We weren't much for hugging on the*
*field, but at that moment I was very tempted.*
　　　　　　　—MIKE SHANNON

The final was 2–1, but the Red Sox were not the least bit humbled. Yaz, who was oh for four and didn't hit the ball hard, commented afterwards that his hands had been slow after two days off, that his six-year-old son could have gotten him out, and that he couldn't wait to face me again. Fine, I thought. Lonborg was also on the offensive, opening game two by brushing back Brock with the first pitch (and later boasting about it).

It was soon evident that the cockiness of Yastrzemski and Lonborg was not idle. Boston's superstars proved in the second game that they were the real thing, Yaz hitting a home run off our starter, Dick Hughes, who was not up to the sensational form of his 16–6 regular season, and another against Hoerner; and Lonborg retiring the first nineteen batters on his way to a 5–0 one-hitter that evened the Series.

We were back in St. Louis two days later and countered with Briles, who, using a no-windup style that he and Hughes developed that summer with the encouragement of pitching coach Billy Muffett, had won his last eight decisions of the regular season. He continued his roll against the Red Sox, holding them to seven hits as Shannon homered in a 5–2 victory that reasserted our presence in the Series—an important item in light of Boston's chest-pounding in game two. Briles not only put us ahead two games to one, but demonstrated that the Boston pitchers would not get away with throwing at Brock. The first time Yastrzemski batted, Briles hit him in the leg. On his way to first, Yaz shouted, very sarcastically, "Thank you." He was starting to bother me.

The timing for this was just right, because I was next in line and eager to get out there again—partly because of Yastrzemski but mostly because it was the World Series. I had become convinced, by this time, that a World Series situation was to my advantage for several reasons, many of them psychological and competitive but one technical. Because of the reputation of my fastball and the fact that I threw everything hard—and possibly because of poor scouting—American League batters seemed to walk up to the plate anticipating fastballs and only fastballs from me. They apparently didn't realize that I got many of my strikeouts on sliders. Even in the batter's box, it seemed that they often mistook my slider for a fastball because I threw it nearly as hard. By the same token, the action on my sinking fastball sometimes misled the batters into thinking it was a slider and consequently swinging late. I sometimes wondered what it would be like to pitch in the other league for a whole season.

These helpful dynamics were never more evident than in game four. My fastball was not at its best that afternoon, but the slider was working fine and my intensity was at its highest level. We scored four in the first against Santiago, two more in the third, and the rest of the day was mine.

> When I faced Gibson in game four of the 1967 World Series, it was the closest I ever came to being intimidated. I hit a long foul that would have been a home run to make the count two and two, and after that foul I'll never forget the look he gave me. It scared me to death. He sent a stare right through me, like, Who do you think you are? I thought for sure there was a knockdown coming, but he fooled me with a slider that I tapped out in front of the plate. McCarver picked it up and tagged me.
> —REGGIE SMITH

Yastrzemski had a couple of hits among Boston's five, but failed to avert a shutout despite some interesting extra effort. The score was 6–0 in the ninth inning and he was on second base after a double—the first Boston player to reach second all day—when Scott hit a fly ball to Maris in right. There was no percentage in going for third base when down by six runs in the ninth, but Yastrzemski did, and Maris damn near threw him out. Yaz said after the game that he did it to make me work a little harder for the shutout.

That should have been a tip-off that the Red Sox would not go down easily, but we fully expected, nonetheless, to close out the Series in game five and save ourselves a trip back East. All of our charms seemed to be working. One fan was sending Brock lemon pies for good luck, and Flood was receiving fried chicken from another. Everything was going our way and the mood in the clubhouse reflected it. Even Maris, who had a two-run double in the first inning of game four, was practically chatty with a two-game lead, telling a reporter that we didn't want to be compared with the Gas House Gang (the Cardinals' famous World Series champions of 1934) but sought to carve out our own historical niche as El Birdos. Meanwhile Cepeda, El Birdo numero uno, was in good voice, standing on the trunk and yelling, "One more to go!"

"One more!" we answered.

"Do you want to go back to Boston?"

"No! No! No!"

We were unable, however, to bring Lonborg around to this point of view. He and Carlton squared off in game five and neither team scored until the Red Sox pushed across an unearned run in the third inning. Schoendienst, figuring that we were yet to cross the plate against Lonborg in the series, sent up a pinch hitter for Carlton in the bottom of the sixth, to no avail. Washburn held the score at 1–0 with a couple innings of scoreless relief, but the Red Sox got two runs in the ninth against Willis and Jack Lamabe. Maris homered in the bottom of the ninth to break Lonborg's spell, but the momentum—and the home-field advantage—had swung back to Boston.

Our objective there, of course, was to avoid a sudden-death situation at Fenway Park by winning game six, and the chances seemed favorable with Hughes pitching against a Boston rookie named Gary Waslewski. That changed when Yastrzemski, Smith, and Petrocelli homered in the fourth inning to knock out Hughes. Petrocelli had also homered earlier for the first run of the game, after which Brock had singled in one run and scored another to give us the lead. Brock then tied the game with a two-run homer in the top of the seventh, but they scored four more in the bottom of the seventh and we ultimately went through eight pitchers in an 8–4 defeat.

The only pitchers who *didn't* pitch for us in game six were Carlton, who had started the day before, Al Jackson, and me. Red hadn't hesitated to use Briles, Washburn, and Jaster in relief because he knew all along that

I would be pitching the seventh game, if there was one. The only question was who would pitch against me. It was Santiago's turn, and Dick Williams, the Boston manager, also had the option of Lee Stange. But with the world championship on the line, he wanted the ball in the hands of Lonborg, however tired he might be on two days' rest.

To get my mind off the game for a few hours—I'd been thinking about the Red Sox for ten days and there wasn't much left to think about—I went the night before the seventh game to hear my friend Les McCann wear out the piano at the Jazz Workshop. It was a perfect, relaxing diversion, and I was back at our hotel, the Sheraton Motor Inn of Quincy, in plenty of time to get my sleep. That was not an easy proposition, however, because for some reason the air-conditioning hadn't been turned on there since we arrived, in addition to which I had a bothersome toothache. I got as much rest as I could expect under the conditions, and the next morning left myself about an hour to have some breakfast downstairs and catch the bus for the ballpark.

I sat down at the breakfast table with Charline, the McCarvers, and the Maxvills, and ordered scrambled eggs. They didn't come. Charline's breakfast came and the McCarvers' came and the Maxvills' came, but the waitress said that my order had somehow been lost. After forty-five minutes and several complaints, she brought me some burnt toast. I called her back and said, "This toast is burnt. Please take it away." She replied, "We'll take *you* away." The bus had been delayed for me on the premise that it might be useful for the starting pitcher to have something in his stomach, but after the toast episode I got the hell out of there and left hungry for Fenway Park. When we paused at a stoplight, Bob Broeg of the *Post-Dispatch* hopped off the bus, hailed a cab, and took it to a local diner for two ham-and-egg sandwiches, which he delivered to me in the clubhouse. I ate one of them and saved the other. Broeg has always been very proud of the role he played in the 1967 World Series and was crushed to find out years later that I often pitched on an empty stomach. In some ways, it helped to stay hungry.

It was evident by that time, and to my good fortune, that Boston didn't understand me. Anger was part of my preparation. The people at the hotel, despite their best efforts to the contrary, were getting me extremely ready for the ballgame, and so were the Red Sox and the Boston newspapers. After their triumph in the sixth game, Dick Williams announced (as reported by a headline in the *Boston Record-American*), "It'll be Lonborg and then champagne!" George Scott, in a poor imitation of Cassius Clay (as Muhammad Ali was known at the time) predicted that "Gibson won't survive five," which the *Boston Herald Traveler* passed along in bold type. Flood responded to that one with his own private variation: "Gibson will be drunk by five."

> *I thought the 1967 Series was extraordinary in the way it brought out the competitive aspect of Gibson. After he missed nearly half of the season with his broken leg, I have always thought he took the World Series personally that year—as if he had to stamp his imprint on the team and win the Series single-handedly if he had to. I remember him before the seventh game, reading the Boston paper with the headline about Lonborg and champagne. Bob looked at that headline and paused for several long seconds after seeing it. I think he responded, again, by taking it personally.*
> —JOE HOERNER

My state of mind before the seventh game pretty much reflected the way the team felt. As long as I was with the Cardinals, I don't think we ever wanted to win a game as badly. It would have taken something monumental to stop us that day. The throbbing tooth in my mouth was certainly not up to the task.

In fact, my toothache and the Quincy Sheraton notwithstanding, I felt pretty good in the knowledge that I was better rested than my opponent for a change. My condition improved when we scored two runs in the third and I was feeling no pain at all after I hit a 380-foot home run in the fifth, gaining my revenge (for Santiago's mini-homer in the first game) on the Green Monster and giving us a 4–0 lead. I can still see Lonborg's hanging slider.

Scott, who had declared I would be gone by the fifth, got Boston's first hit that inning, a triple on which he scored when the relay throw was mishandled. But Javier hit a three-run homer in the sixth to send Lonborg back to the clubhouse, where quite a bit of champagne was presumably going to waste.

The Red Sox added a single run in the eighth to make the score 7–2, and by the ninth there was so little left of my fastball that I was mostly throwing sliders. Yaz, who still wouldn't quit, caught one of them for a single, and then Harrelson pulled a hard grounder to Maxvill, who threw to Javier, who threw to Cepeda for possibly the fastest double play I'd ever seen them pull off. I had the pleasure of striking out Scott to end the series with a three-hitter.

Cepeda, undaunted by a personal slump that tried in vain to spoil his World Series, had the pleasure of leading the cheers in the celebration that followed, which I joined after scarfing my other ham-and-egg sandwich and washing it down with bubbly:

"Lonborg and champagne!"

"Yeah!"

"We'll win in six!"

"Yeah!"

"Gibson goes in five!"

"Yeah!"

There was no such thing as an ordinary, run-of-the-mill, booze-and-backslap victory party in the Cardinal clubhouse. My jazz friend, Les McCann, joined us there after the seventh game and attracted some stares when he stood on a stool, held up a clenched fist, and shouted, "Black Power!" This was a full year before Tommie Smith and John Carlos made the same sort of gesture on the medal stand of the Olympics, and although I was generally uncomfortable with public displays of a racial nature, I didn't feel it was an inappropriate tribute to our club. I think, too, that the white players understood. They were our pals and partners. I've never lost my pride in the special, colorless character manifested so uniquely by the Cardinals. Long before Jesse Jackson moved to Washington, we were the rainbow coalition of baseball.

This is not to imply that black and Latin players were not prominent on other teams. (In fact, as a group we dominated the National League, if not in number—Latins and blacks were still in a severe minority because most of the marginal roster spots were unofficially but undeniably reserved for white players—certainly in numbers. The records of the sixties show that the minority combination of black and Latin players competed collectively on a statistical level well above that of the league's white players. A white player did not lead the National League or even finish second in home runs during any season of the 1960s, and only three white players—Groat, Koufax, and Boyer—were MVPs. The exception was in pitching, where blacks remained rare.)

What made the 1967 Cardinals different—in addition to our balance and fundamental excellence, that is—was that we had leadership and executive material of all shades: a black man as the go-to pitcher; a Puerto Rican (Cepeda) as our leader on the field and in the clubhouse; a popular southerner (McCarver) calling signals behind the plate; and two brilliant black outfielders at the top of the lineup. Flood, whose defense was second to nobody's, batted .335 for the season, and Brock led the league in stolen bases for the second year in a row.

Brock also drove the Red Sox crazy in the World Series, batting .414 and setting a record with seven stolen bases, three in the final game. It was a performance worthy of the series MVP award, which I frankly thought he should have won. The voters, however, bestowed the honor upon me for the second time, citing the facts that I tied a World Series record held by old-time Yankee Red Ruffing with five straight complete-game victories (including 1964) and another one held by Christy Mathewson since 1905 for the fewest hits (fourteen) surrendered in three Series starts. The Red Sox never managed more than one hit in any inning against me, and I struck out twenty-six of them.

In a genuinely fine gesture, KMOX radio in St. Louis gave Brock a car, anyway, matching the one I received from *Sport* magazine. I'm sure that *Sport* ultimately wished that it, too, had honored Brock instead of me, because when I showed up at the dealership in St. Louis to receive my Corvette, I refused to pose for the publicity pictures, fearing that my participation might tie me in commercially with the dealership and constitute an association that would restrict me in pursuing other business arrangements. After failing to cash in on the series MVP award in 1964, I was determined this time to make a little hay for my family. I started by selling the car to another Chevy dealer. (In retrospect, I wish to hell I had kept both of my Corvettes as investments. They would be worth a lot of money today.)

The episode at the dealership was one of many examples of a special talent I had in those years for alienating people in the Establishment. I managed to do this several times in St. Louis, nearly always on what I considered to be matters of principle. The South Side Kiwanis Club, for instance, held an annual banquet honoring a Cardinal player, and for some reason—I suspect that somebody in the Cardinal front office had something to do with the Kiwanis Club—everybody on the team was expected to attend. This was awkward for the black players because the club was in an Italian part of town (the Hill, where Yogi Berra and Joe Garagiola grew up); a black person would be taking his life in his hands to be caught walking there and at the least might be put in jail. One year I was chosen to receive the award, but I declined by telling the club officials that I simply didn't think I would enjoy receiving it and explaining why. They didn't take kindly to my response, and neither did the Cardinals.

I did accept an award given by the Downtown Athletic Club in the first year it allowed blacks inside the door, but even then managed to make some enemies by commenting during my speech that if I had received the award a year before, they would have had to throw it to me out the window. I was expecting a laugh, but the room fell absolutely silent when I made my little joke.

The winter after the 1967 season was not unpleasant on the whole, however. It began with another Bob Gibson Day in Omaha, and I was made an honorary governor for the day by Governer Norbert Tiemann, who, seizing the moment like any good politician, claimed that he once had a hit against me in the Elkhorn Valley League, one of many in which I made brief appearances during my itinerant boyhood summers. More meaningful to me were the handmade gifts I received from students at Lake Elementary School in the heart of the north side ghetto.

After the day in Omaha I headed straight back to St. Louis for a three-day party that started at Musial's restaurant. When we were finished eating but not drinking, Musial whipped out his harmonica, which he was seldom without, Briles played the accordion and sang, and Dick Hughes yodeled in a way that sounded like he actually knew what he was doing. Then it was off to New York with Brock for *The Ed Sullivan Show.*

Thanks in large part to the efforts of my friend Sandy Bain and his boss Marty Glickman, president of Sportsplan in New York, I was finally able that winter to realize some of the spoils that were supposed to come with the territory the Cardinals and I had conquered. I was on Joey Bishop's TV show, Pat Boone's, and *To Tell The Truth,* and even did some acting (they tell me I wasn't bad) in an episode of *Gentle Ben.* My celebrity was not such that I was in high demand for commercials, but I did enough of them to pay some bills. I also had weekly radio and television shows in Omaha, and stirred some memories by doing color commentary on Creighton basketball games.

I dropped everything, though, when President Johnson invited me in mid-November to the White House for a state dinner with Premier Sato Eisaku of Japan. I observed that Johnson looked tired and drawn, chatted with Kirk Douglas, and apparently impressed Premier Sato, who held up my hand and measured his own against it. Vice President Hubert Humphrey, noticing that I was wearing a blue shirt under my tuxedo, as he was, commented that we were the only ones in the joint with any class.

The evening at the White House was unquestionably the highlight of the winter, and although my off-seasons, as a rule, were visited regularly by lowlights, a letter from a man in Tampa that year stands out in my memory. It said: "I guess this will make you and your swollen head several times larger. Why don't you and the other blackbirds on the Cardinals move to Africa where you belong? If you and the other darkies can't read this because of your low mentality, get one of the white players to do it."

Hate mail was not uncommon for me or any of the top black players—on the Cardinals, Brock and Cepeda received their share—but we never made a fuss over it because we didn't want to let the assholes think they bothered us. However, there was a small batch of it waiting for me when I arrived at spring training in 1968, and I happened to be reading one of the letters in front of my locker when a sportswriter noticed me and asked to see it. He then asked if I had more letters like that one and if he could print some of them. I didn't mind showing the world how ignorant some people could be. After a sampling of the hate mail ran in the paper, I received about three thousand letters from around the country apologizing for the hateful minority.

I appreciated the outpouring, but actually I didn't consider the hate mail to be all bad. I regarded it as my motivational correspondence. After winning the World Series and being treated like a big-shot all winter, it sort of came in handy as we headed into 1968.

# CHAPTER VIII

It was said that I threw, basically, five pitches—fastball, slider, curve, change-up, and knockdown. I don't believe that assessment did me justice, though. I actually used about nine pitches—two different fastballs, two sliders, a curve, change-up, knockdown, brushback, and hit-batsman.

Although the first half-dozen are standard fare, an explanation is probably in order regarding the last three, which are distinct and very different pitches in terms of both strategic purpose and technical execution. The brushback is the most common and least severe in this family of inside pitches, and a good place to start the discussion.

If hitters respected the pitcher's right to claim part of the plate as his own, the brushback would not be necessary. In seeking a portion of the plate, however small, the pitcher asks for nothing more than the batter already has, and in fact would be satisfied with less. By his stance and type of swing, every batter demonstrates a partiality toward a certain region of the strike zone, thereby declaring that area as his own. I consider this to be fair and workable. As a pitcher, it's my job to identify the part of the plate in which a hitter prefers to operate, respect him for it, and then try to get him out by taking for myself whatever is left. Fundamentally, this is a matter of every man staking out his territory, which was a lesson first and most effectively brought home to me by Andy Johnson of the Globetrotters when he flattened me during the college all-star game as a way of pointing out the property lines on the basketball court. Baseball works the same way.

The problem arises when the hitter is unwilling to reciprocate with the kind of respect that I have afforded him going in. He does this by neglecting the inside corner of the plate or by moving around in the batter's box or by somehow deviating from his usual methods in order to beat me at my own game; by changing the guidelines that he has already established; in short, by cheating. My task then is to make an honest man of him. I do this by throwing my fastball in the area where he, by taking liberties that are not granted him through the prevailing rules of the profession (as I perceive them, anyway), would like to be moving into. Nobody gets hurt in this exchange. The pitch buzzes inside, the batter flinches, everybody understands each other a little better, and the game goes on.

The brushback is probably the most misunderstood pitch in baseball. It is not meant, first of all—at least, the way I used it—to punish a batter for the pitcher's own mistake, as is often speculated. If I threw a bad pitch, I deserved to get creamed. But if I threw a good pitch and the batter still hit it hard, then I had to find another way to establish myself. In a case like that, pitching inside might be a starting point—to let the batter know, at least, that I'm out there and have to be reckoned with.

Nor is the brushback intended to harm or even frighten anybody. You don't scare a major-league hitter. But by pitching inside, you can alert him to the possibility of being hit, widen the area for which he has to be concerned, and then get him out by pitching on the other corner. If a batter is preoccupied with the inside pitch, he might inadvertently bail out as he swings or, at the least, turn away and open up his front shoulder, a cardinal sin of hitting (because it loosens a batter's power base). Ballplayers refer to that as hitting with your ass in the dugout, at which point the pitcher has effectively won.

If, on the other extreme, the batter is not mindful of the pitch inside and consequently unprepared for it—which is where the problem often begins—he will freeze or be unable to react in time and catch one in the side or the leg. I consider this to be a case of the batter hitting himself. Many batters in my day—I've previously noted cases involving Duke Snider and Mike Shannon, for example—accepted the responsibility for being hit in such instances. Not all of them did, however, and the press invariably held the pitcher accountable. It perturbed me that sometimes the umpires did, also; they should have known better.

In San Diego one time, I was pitching a game in which a brushback battle developed. The home-plate umpire that night was Lee Weyer, who for a big man had a surprisingly high voice, and as I was walking out to the mound to start an inning during this little fracas, Weyer called out to me in that choirboy alto of his, "Gibson, if you throw at anybody, it'll cost you fifty dollars!" I hiked my voice up an octave or two and yelled back, "I got a lot of fifty dollarses!" Then I threw the first pitch at somebody's belt buckle and shouted to Weyer, "There's fifty!" My second pitch bored in on the ribs: "There's a hundred!" It was worth it.

Another umpire warned me once before the game even started about brushing batters back. I was deeply offended by that and considered it tantamount to asking me to throw the game. The brushback is a legitimate piece of hardware in the pitcher's tool belt—one of the few at his disposal—and I resented having it taken away. I resented also the fact that a pitcher can miss the outside corner by six inches and nobody says a word, but if he misses the inside corner by the same amount he's a menace to society and everybody wants to fight. This is the case now much more than it was in my day. Pity the poor pitcher today.

If I had wanted to hit batters on a regular basis, as my reputation suggested, I would have hit a hell of a lot more than I did. My control wasn't pinpoint perfect, and like every other pitcher I grazed a few people on pitches that simply got away, but it was good enough that I could nail a guy if and whenever I really wanted to. That was seldom the case. More often than I appreciated, my brushback and knockdown pitches were misunderstood as attempts to hit somebody.

The knockdown is basically a brushback pitch with an attitude, the difference being that on a knockdown the batter is not supposed to be on his feet when the ball reaches the catcher's mitt. It also serves a different purpose. Whereas the brushback is a strategic device, the knockdown is a statement of retaliation. I consider retaliation to be the only necessary and indisputably valid reason for knocking a batter down, although I confess to having expanded its application to include intimidation.

I make a distinction between intimidating and frightening a batter, because the former is tactical and the latter is practically impossible. Semantics aside, with certain batters—especially new ones to the league—it is in the pitcher's best interest to introduce himself at close range. There were players whom you wouldn't have to worry about for the rest of the night if you knocked them down the first time up. It was important to test every batter in that regard at least once—to familiarize him with all of the possibilities at home plate.

> *I faced Gibson for the first time in the spring when I was a rookie for the Reds, which was late in his career. In the clubhouse before the game, a number of the veterans came over to me and asked if I knew anything about Bob Gibson. The message was that if he knew I was a rookie, he'd try to intimidate me. I couldn't imagine why a Hall of Fame pitcher would bother with a rookie infielder who hit like me, and I said, kind of laughing, "He'd intimidate me? He doesn't even know who I am." They said, "Don't worry. He'll introduce himself." Then they told me just to hang loose. Nothing really happened that day, but the warning alone was enough to make a lasting impression.*
>
> —DOUG FLYNN,
> *former Red*

My attempts to intimidate on the mound were not unlike Brock's on the basepaths. There were many times when I would have preferred to be free of the burden that befell a pitcher on Brock's team—when I would have preferred not to have to throw at somebody for throwing at Brock— but I was more than happy to have the runs he provided, and I could hardly fault him philosophically. When Brock would keep stealing after we had built a three- or four-run lead, guys on the bench would say. "Goddamn it, Brock, you can't do that!" He'd say, "Fuck you. I'm gonna do it." His attitude was to beat the other team as badly as possible, and that was my kind of baseball. It would have been hypocritical for me to balk at my obligation toward Brock. The chore of retaliation was a small price to pay for having him in the lineup. I might have wished that he didn't bicker with the umpires so much because that only served to aggravate the other team even more—Johnny Bench said Brock was the worst guy in the league for hassling the ump—but he was only looking for an edge, to which I should be the last to object.

The bottom line in all of this was that my knockdown pitch took on exaggerated proportions in light of Lou Brock, coming into play on such occasions as the 1967 incident involving the Reds and Tony Perez. I had to deal with the fact that opponents were vicious toward Brock, to the point that he was hit in the head once by Al McBean of the Pirates. In a situation like that, I had no reluctance to draw a bead on McBean's head at the next opportunity. The ball didn't hit him, of course, as I knew it wouldn't. If I'd wanted to hit him, I'd have thrown behind him, between his shoulder and belt. But we never had any more trouble with Al McBean.

I was obliged to protect not only Brock but any teammate who was hit or knocked down by an opposing pitcher. The only time I really objected was when somebody in the dugout would *ask* me to retaliate. That teed me off. Nobody had to ask me to stand up for my teammates, goddamn it. I took care of business on my own.

Now and then—and I want to emphasize that the times were rare—I saw fit to discharge my business by plunking a guy. Please note that I've avoided the term "beaning" because that implies hitting a guy in the head. I hit a few guys in the head, but not on purpose. If I hit somebody on purpose, my target was the body, where nobody really gets hurt.

I once hit Dave Rader of the Giants in the head, meaning either that I missed my destination or he ducked into the pitch, which was intended to catch him below the shoulder. It was precipitated by the fact that Rader was one of those catchers who was always mouthing off to the batters. Some of my teammates said he was a decent guy, but I hated it when players on the other team tried to chat with me. One game, late in my career, I came up to bat and he said, "How's the family, Bob?" His timing couldn't have been worse, because I had just been through a nasty divorce with Charline and was feeling pretty shitty about the whole thing. I said, "I ain't got no fuckin' family. I just got divorced." Then I popped straight up. I don't know whether Rader was getting back at me for my answer to his question or just talking to hear himself talk, but when the ball left the bat he said, "Up the fuckin' chute!" I would have let the family thing pass, but when he said, "Up the fuckin' chute," it was more than I could handle politely. I said, "What are you, some type of smart-ass?" When he came to bat, I hit him. Thankfully, he ran down to first base unhurt.

I don't deny that I played with a chip on my shoulder, operating under the assumption that there was a pointed edge to anything anybody on the other team had to say to me. Everything I did on the field was calculated to gain the upper hand, and I always figured that the other guy had the same agenda. Nobody got the benefit of the doubt from me in the heat of a ballgame.

> *Ron Fairly hit Gibby about as well as anybody did. He didn't hit him* hard, *but seemed to be able to drop in a lot of base hits against him. One night Fairly came up and banged out base hits against Bob in his first two times at bat. Then Gibby got a single, and as he's standing on first base Fairly saunters over and says, "Goddamn, Hoot, you've got such good stuff I don't see how anybody can hit you." Gibson didn't even look at him. He just said, "You asshole." I'm catching, and the next time Fairly comes up he glances back at me and says, "I'm not going to like this at bat, am I?" He took one in the ass that time.*
>
> *Denis Menke was another one who hit Bob a little better than he should have. When he was playing with the Astros he got clipped by Gibson one time, and as he was lying on the ground I said, "Okay?" He said, "Okay," then got up and went to first base. Everybody knew what was going on.*
>
> —JOE TORRE

Ernie Banks was a good example of a guy whom I probably would have enjoyed quite a bit if he had been on my side—I don't doubt that he was as nice a guy as everybody said—but as it was, he talked too damn much. He was always jabbering at me a day or two before I pitched against the

Cubs, trying to get me off my game. One day at old Busch Stadium he came by during batting practice and said, "Hoot, you pitchin' tomorrow? We gonna beat you. We gonna beat your ass tomorrow. Hey, man, we gonna beat you." I said, "Ernie, you'd better leave me alone." It wasn't in his nature to do that, though, and the next day I answered him. The first pitch got him in the ribs. I ended up with a three-hitter that day, and afterwards I watched the Cubs' box score every morning for about two weeks until I saw Ernie's name in it again. He didn't have much to say to me after that.

Clemente was similar to Banks to the degree that he would never shut up, but I threw at him for a more substantial reason. As he and Bill White and others found out, I simply couldn't allow batters to lean across the plate or take wild hacks at my pitches, both of which suggested a complete disregard for the weapons in my possession. John Milner of the Mets was another one in that category. He used to practically fall across the plate, popping buttons when he swung, and I took the opportunity during spring training one year to make sure he understood my feelings about that sort of thing. I hit him in the body, harmlessly enough. Much later, well into the season at a time in which the Milner episode was far from my mind, Tom Seaver threw at me three straight times during a game at Shea Stadium. After picking myself up for the third time, I yelled at him, "You've got better control than that!" He yelled back, "So do you!" That was when I realized he was getting back at me for Milner. Retaliation can take weeks or months, but it always comes. In the 1960s, anyway, it always came. Nowadays, the first team throws at somebody and the second team is not permitted to retaliate, so they fight instead.

All three of the inside pitches—the brushback, the knockdown, and the hit-batsman—played big parts in the intimidation environment that I worked hard to create when I pitched. In my estimation, it wasn't so much the prospect of the ball in the batter's box that did the job in this respect, but the fact that the batter never knew what the hell was going on in my mind. The basis of intimidation, as I practiced it, was mystery. I wanted the hitter to know *nothing* about me—about my wife, my children, my religion, my politics, my hobbies, my tastes, my feelings, nothing. I figured the more they knew about me, the more they knew what I might do in a certain situation. That was why, in large part, I never talked to players on other teams. That was why I never apologized for hitting anybody. That was why I seemed like such an asshole to so many people.

I was so intent on remaining mysterious that I carried it to the extreme. I refused to let the coaches or anybody clock the speed of my pitches, for instance, because I didn't want the information going around. I refused to talk to our team psychologist because all he could do was find out more about me and I didn't want anybody knowing more about me. I asked Schoendienst to pitch me only against American League teams during spring training whenever possible because I didn't want to show myself to National Leaguers. I dressed and left quickly at all-star games so that I wouldn't accidentally make a friend. And I know that late in my career, especially, I was cruel to young players who had heard a lot about and maybe even admired me. When Gene Clines of the Pirates asked me once to sign a ball for him before a game, I took the ball and tossed it over my shoulder into left field. Although I don't remember it, Dave Winfield has said that I blew him off when he approached me as a rookie to introduce himself and tell me that I had been his idol. I do remember a game in San Diego, though, when I pitched and won with a hangover (under the influence of Tim McCarver) in spite of a home run by Winfield. As he rounded second base, he gave me a look as if to say, "What do you think of that, old man?" The next time he batted, I separated him from his yellow and brown cap.

There's no way of telling how much difference all of that stuff made, but I'm convinced it was considerable. For one thing, I saw enough examples to make me believe that pitchers who talked too much to hitters were asking for trouble. Marichal and Cepeda had been good friends on the Giants, and when we got together they were always yakking and yucking it up about something or other. And Cepeda just lit up Marichal—hit him better than any other pitcher in the league. I saw Cha-Cha cream one over the stadium club in St. Louis one time against Marichal, which was something you didn't often see. I just couldn't understand how those two could laugh together the way they did and then Cepeda would go out and kill Marichal and then they'd go have dinner and laugh some more. I just didn't understand it—although, as I found out later, it wasn't easy to turn a cold shoulder on Orlando Cepeda. After the Cardinals traded him to the Braves following the 1968 season, it was difficult even for me not to fraternize with him on the field. I kept up with him off the field, as I did with Bill White after he was traded, but when he was in the other uniform I did my damnedest to steer clear of him.

> *When I played against Gibson in San Francisco, I hated him. Then when I came over to St. Louis, he made me feel wanted. He would fight for you, cry for you, laugh for you, whatever you needed. When I was traded to the Braves and the Cardinals came to Atlanta for the first time, I contacted Gibson and invited him to my house for dinner after a day game that he was going to pitch against us. He accepted. That day, Gibson got a base hit, and as he was standing on first base I said something friendly. He said, "Don't talk to me now. You're my enemy until we get off this field."*
> —ORLANDO CEPEDA

To me, baseball is about winning, and I didn't see how being friendly had anything to do with winning. The fact is, I didn't like the other team. The guys in the other shirts were the enemy. Aside from former teammates, the only opposing player I ever really made friends with was Willie Stargell. I don't have a good excuse for this, except that Stargell's personality left me no choice. I was just fortunate he didn't spread around the league that I was a nice guy or something; I couldn't have that. The very idea was distasteful to my competitive sensibilities—besides which, image was very important to me.

It was to preserve my image that I was never particularly friendly with the press. I got along well enough with the writers—especially those in St. Louis—but if I revealed too much of myself to them, it would tear down that wall of mystery I had carefully built up. My relationship with the press might have hurt me in the long run, because to this day I carry the reputation of being angry and hard to deal with, but it helped my pitching, and that was all I cared about at the time. I believe I succeeded in intimidating a lot of hitters. I know for a fact that they didn't go up there against me confident.

*Gibson was the single most intimidating pitcher I ever faced. I re-member hitting a home run off Mr. Gibson in 1968, when he was at his very peak, and I just sort of watched it for a moment in dis-belief. When I got back to the bench, guys came over and sort of looked at me. They couldn't believe it either.*
>                                        —ED CHARLES,
>                                            *former Met*

*When I was a young player, our manager, Lum Harris, didn't want me to face Gibson. He thought my confidence might not be able to handle it. I pleaded with him to give me a chance, because as a young player I felt like I didn't have to back down from any-body. Finally he said, "All right. I'm worried about it, but you're in there." The first two times up, I stood in there all confident and he blew me away with fastballs up and in and then a slider on the corner. I still told myself I could hit him, but the third time he knocked me down and then struck me out again. It was a miser-able day. Luman was right.*

*Young players look for challenges, though, and the next time in Atlanta I was in there against him again. I struck out the first two times and then, somehow, he got a fastball too far inside and I crushed it. I was standing there watching the ball go out when I suddenly remembered it was Bob Gibson and did something I'd never done before and never did again. I thought about facing Gibson the next time, and with that in mind, instead of breaking into my normal home-run trot I sprinted around the bases—got around as fast as I could, found a seat in the dugout, and sat down.*
>                                        —EARL WILLIAMS,
>                                            *former Brave*

While I went the extra mile to gain every psychological advantage I could muster, I realized at the same time that my ability to intimidate—to use intimidation as an effective pitching device—was in direct proportion to the speed and movement of my fastball. There was no way I could have built up the reputation that I did by throwing junk. In fact, it worked both ways. I could not have intimidated anybody with bad stuff, and at the same time, intimidation made my stuff a little better—my fastball a little faster and my slider a little sharper.

*Gibson utilized every edge he had as a pitcher. His competitiveness showed through in his face, the way he used it to intimidate a batter. He didn't have to throw intentionally at batters to intimidate them, but he made sure they never felt secure up there. What would happen if an inside pitch got away? Then, with all of that going for him, Gibson had a fastball that just exploded in the strike zone. It's what made his fastball impossible to hit. Others, including Koufax and Drysdale and Nolan Ryan, threw a little harder, but Gibson had expert control of the fastball and it moved so much that I rarely caught it squarely in the pocket of the mitt. When Gibson threw the fastball, I could actually feel the heat of the pitch through the glove and the skin and into my bone. In 1969, my thumb was broken and the bone exposed from catching Gibson. It's still distorted. And I still feel nerve damage on rainy days. Every time it flares up, I think of Bob Gibson.*
—TIM MCCARVER

*Tony Taylor, our leadoff man with the Phillies, used to come back to the dugout and tell us what to expect from the pitcher. Once he worked Gibson to a three-two count to start the game and fouled off several pitches to stay alive. Then Gibson threw a wicked yakker and the umpire goes, "Steeeerike three!" Tony takes a seat on the bench, pulls up his sleeves, and says, "Well, boys . . ." I think Gibson got fifteen of us that night.*
—DICK ALLEN

*The first time I played in St. Louis, I went up there against Gibson, and although I was well aware of him, he couldn't have known anything about me, so he just threw me fastballs. I was a good fastball hitter—especially when I was young and very quick.*

*But I went up there against Gibson and struck out three times. Af-*
*ter the third time, I'm heading back to the dugout thinking about*
*my dad. Back in Oklahoma, my dad used to watch big-league*
*baseball on TV and he'd say, "I can hit that guy." No matter who*
*it was, it was always, "I can hit that guy." Walking back to the*
*dugout, I was thinking, "Where's Dad now?" I don't think he*
*could have hit Bob Gibson.*

—Hall of Fame catcher
JOHNNY BENCH

To an extent, I think my reputation as an intimidator obscured a lot of
other things I had going for me as a pitcher. It was almost as if the real me,
or the real pitcher that was me, had been devoured by the monster that I
created. I'm proud of the fact that I used all of my resources as a competitor and perhaps helped define the art of intimidation on the mound, but
I don't appreciate being introduced, as I often am these days, as the
world's meanest ballplayer. I don't think that's necessarily a compliment.
It's as if my tombstone is going to read, "Here lies the meanest son of a
bitch who ever toed the rubber." I really don't want to be remembered as
a bad son of a bitch who pitched a little. That diminishes my game and
trivializes the fact that I set World Series records, won two Cy Youngs and
nine straight Gold Glove awards, was the last pitcher to win twenty games
and bat .300 in the same season, and in 1968 put together maybe the best
season a pitcher ever had. First and foremost, I was a pitcher who did
whatever he could to win.

It seems that about the only time my name comes up these days is
when somebody gets knocked down. The fact is, knockdowns were commonplace in my day, part of the baseball landscape, and guys like Drysdale and Stan Williams employed them more liberally than I did. Drysdale
and I did a talk show a few years ago on KMOX radio in St. Louis, and we
argued back and forth about which of us threw at more guys. I have no
doubt that it was him. Drysdale was mean. He would hit you on a three-
and-two count. The Dodgers as a whole had the most ferocious staff in
baseball history, and while their meanness has been generally acknowl-

edged, it disturbs me that I am so often held up as the all-time champion of ruthless, malevolent pitchers. That misses the point almost entirely. The impression is that all I ever did was knock guys down when in fact my thought process had nothing to do with that. I was focused on winning. I'd much prefer that my name were invoked in discussions about winning.

There's no way to gloss over the fact that racial perceptions contributed a great deal to my reputation. I pitched in a period of civil unrest, of black power and clenched fists and burning buildings and assassinations and riots in the street. There was a country full of angry black people in those days, and by extension—and by my demeanor on the mound—I was perceived as one of them. There was some truth to that, but it had little, if anything, to do with the way I worked a batter. I didn't see a hitter's color. I saw his stance, his strike zone, his bat speed, his power, and his weaknesses.

> *We played in a time when black people were supposed to stick to-gether, so I asked Gibson one time why he always threw at the brothers. He said, "Because they're the ones who are gonna beat me if I don't."*     —DICK ALLEN

My color influenced me, no doubt, to the degree that it influenced Josh and Josh influenced me, but on the mound it was not a part of my mental makeup or my game plan. It might, however, have enabled me to understand and utilize intimidation a little better. As a black man, I was a member of a race that had been intimidated by the white man for more than two hundred years, in which time we learned something about the process. When one is intimidated, he resigns himself to the backseat. He defers to his so-called superior, having no other legitimate choice, and allows himself to be dominated. As a major-league pitcher, I had the opportunity, at last, to push off the mound in the other man's shoes.

This was apparently disconcerting to many white batters, in particular. They seemed to be much more aware of my color than I was of theirs. As a result, I was more threatening to them—more intimidating and unsettling and menacing—than white pitchers whose stuff and pitching patterns might strongly resemble mine.

*Gibson and I share the same loyalties to the state of Nebraska,
and we had nothing against each other, but when the game
started I always had the feeling I was standing there as the Grand
Dragon of the Ku Klux Klan. He was the toughest pitcher for me.
Like Koufax and Marichal, Gibson dominated, but he did it
longer and did it with a vengeance that savaged the batters. His
pitches were devastating. His fastball was equal to Koufax's and
Maloney's and Ryan's, and his slider had no equal. And more's
the pity, Gibson was mean on the mound. He had a menacing,
glowering intensity that more than occasionally deepened into a
sneer. His intimidating demeanor, his lack of concern for the wel-
fare of the hitter, combined with his almost-unhittable pitches, put
Gibson in a class by himself.*
                              —*former Philadelphia Phillie*
                                RICHIE ASHBURN

I'd like to think that the term "intensity" comes much closer to summa-
rizing my pitching style than do qualities like meanness and anger, which
were merely devices. Intensity, to me, was a matter of focus and desire
and energy and power, all packed into nine hellacious innings. When
those innings were over, my intensity shifted toward winning the next
one. Intensity was never letting up—between pitches, between innings,
between starts, or between seasons. It was something that started on the
Omaha sandlots and filled my belly and ran down my arm and came off
my fingers at about ninety-five miles an hour. Intensity, as I knew it, was
the will to win.

*I never saw anyone as compelled to win as Bob Gibson was. Gib-
son hated to lose, and because of that, he hated the competition.
Hated them. I was driven to win, but not like Bob Gibson, not
with his intensity. His desire to win and succeed influenced me
and all of our teammates. We revered him as a teammate. The
guys on the club understood his competitive drive—to the extent
that we could, anyway—and this created a tension for all of us. At
the same time, he loosened us up, too, because when he wasn't*

*pitching he was one of the funniest men on the team. But it was*
*his competitiveness that set him apart. Clearly, that was what*
*made him reside on the next level of athletes.*
— TIM MCCARVER

My pitching career, I believe, offers a lot of evidence to the theory that baseball is a mental discipline as much as a physical one. Physically, I was probably at my peak around 1961 or 1962, before I ever made an all-star team. My desire to win was no less fierce at that time than it was later, but as a young pitcher I wasn't mentally or psychologically ready yet for big things—not to mention the uncertain matter of my control. It was only when my confidence and control and command of the major-league scene fell into line that I was able to fully utilize my physical skills.

I would estimate that, given sufficient physical ability to compete on the major-league level, the part of pitching that separates the stars from everybody else is about 90 percent mental. That's why I considered it so important to mess with a batter's head without letting him inside mine. Psychology represents a major portion of that 90 percent, and the rest is knowledge, strategy, and common sense. If a major-league pitcher uses only his arm and not his head (God, I sound like Solly Hemus!) he is going to get battered around no matter how mean he is and how hard he throws. It's necessary not only to throw intelligent pitches, but to think three or four pitches ahead. At the same time, however, a pitcher should be flexible enough to change his plans relative to the signals given out by the batter. If a batter misses a fastball by a foot, that ought to significantly increase his chances of seeing another one. But if he fouls it straight back, indicating that he has it accurately timed, a breaking ball might be in order next. It's not advanced calculus, but the wheels have to turn upstairs.

There are instances also, as Tommy Davis taught me twice over when I tried to fool him with inside fastballs, when a pitcher can think too much. That was a hard lesson for me, and one on which Dick Allen also took me to school. Allen was a great fastball hitter, but I had been having good luck on him with fastballs one night in St. Louis. Ordinarily, I didn't throw curves to right-handed hitters—just the dinky one to lefthanders that Bob Purkey showed me—but when I got two strikes on Allen this time I thought it was a good opportunity to cross him up. As I expected, the curveball caught him completely by surprise, and after that, he was looking for it every time up there. All season long, he kept waiting for the curve and I wouldn't give it to him. One night in Philadelphia, late in the year, I struck him out two or three times in a row on nothing but fastballs and he never took the bat off his shoulder. We were in a tight, low-scoring game, and about the ninth inning I figured he was probably getting ready to nail my fastball and maybe I ought to sneak in that little curve one more time. So I gave it another shot and this time he hit it over the center-field fence—way the hell over. When he reached second base he kind of looked back at me with a little smirk, and I thought, "Yeah, you tricked me, you cocksucker." I told him it was the last curveball he would ever see from me, and it was.

For the most part—the exceptions being when guys like Davis and Allen went deep to beat me (losing has a way of sucking the pleasure out of things)—I enjoyed the mental challenge and the gamesmanship involved in outthinking the hitter. I was certainly on the right team for that sort of thing because everybody on the Cardinals had their own ideas about strategy and situations and the like. Because he was my catcher, I exchanged ideas most often with McCarver. He usually wanted to go by the book, and I usually agreed—in principle. But we weren't playing in principle, we were playing in St. Louis, and on a team that worked with a very tight budget offensively. There would be runners on first and third with no outs early in the game, for instance, and McCarver would come out and say, "If the ball comes back to you, go for the double play." The Cardinals frequently didn't score more than a run or two a game, though, and I wasn't about to give one up on purpose. I'd say, "No, I'm gonna see if that guy's trying to score, and if he goes, I'm gonna try to get him." He'd say, "Goddamn it, Hoot, that's the wrong way to do it," and I'd say, "You just stay awake."

I generally enjoyed McCarver's company, but not in my office, as Steve Carlton referred to the mound. (Carlton and I happened to share one pet peeve relating to the office. We hated when hitters crossed behind it on their way back to the dugout. We took down names.) Sometimes

McCarver would come out to talk to me and I'd hardly notice him because I was staring off in the other direction concentrating on what I had to do next. He'd say, "Bob! Oh, Bob! Remember me? I'm Tim, your catcher. I believe we've met." Other times I'd have to insult him to get him off my mound so I could carry on with the job at hand. He'd remind me that there was a runner on first and I'd say, "I know goddamn well there's a man on first because I put him there. What difference does it make? If he tried to steal, you couldn't throw him out anyway." If he started to tell me how to work a certain hitter, I'd say something like, "Get back behind the plate. The only thing you know about pitching is that it's hard to hit." It's a good thing I thought so highly of my friend. Poor Tim was caught in the middle—especially when Johnny Keane was managing the club, because Keane was a strong advocate of communication. Keane even had a signal that meant McCarver was supposed to go out to the mound and settle me down. McCarver hated that signal because when he received it he would look out and see me glaring back at him, almost daring him to come out. To appease both parties, he'd go about halfway and pretend like he was telling me something.

My ability to concentrate on the mound was one of my best assets as a pitcher. I believe all successful athletes have a common ability to put distractions out of their mind when they're called on to perform. I recall once when Charline came to St. Louis for Father's Day and we spent the whole morning arguing about a mink coat she wanted to buy. We stopped arguing only to go to the ballpark. I pitched a shutout in the afternoon, and as soon as we got home we resumed the argument. (I won that, too, by the way.)

Because I was so zeroed in when I pitched, I liked to work fast, which was another reason I despised catchers and infielders huddling with me on the mound. Pace was part of my game—getting into a rhythm and going at the hitters hard and aggressively, taking command of the action by pouring the ball in before they had a chance to get comfortable. The most nerve-racking part of the game for me was the national anthem, when I was standing there in the dark with all my muscles itching and twitching to pitch. Ron Fairly told me that when I took the mound against the Dodgers, they used to remind each other to start swinging as soon as they heard "home of the brave." My games were commonly the fastest in the National League.

> *When Gibson pitched, you might as well come out hacking because you knew that either you would beat him or he would beat you in an hour and a half. He didn't let the bars close on him. Most of the time, he was there before eleven o'clock with a victory under his belt.*  —HANK AARON

I believe, also, that working quickly kept the fielders on their toes— often the difference between a play being made and not made—and helped my control because it kept my mind focused. Control is largely a function of concentration, and as a result mine got better as my concentration improved with maturity. As wild as I was early in my career, by the time I reached my prime I was very much a control pitcher. My best years, for the most part, were those in which I walked the fewest batters. The control of my slider was particularly instrumental in my improvement. When I was able to throw it consistently for strikes, everything else fell into place. Most important was the fact that I was ahead in the court more often than not, which enabled me to keep the batter on the defensive.

Getting ahead in the count was a priority for me. When I watch young pitchers today, I'm constantly baffled by their inability to get ahead in the count. It's not so much that they're unable to do it—nearly all of them can throw a strike when they have to—but they don't even *try.* It appears to me that their whole purpose is to get the hitter to miss the ball. In most cases, that's wrong. Pitchers should try to make the batter hit the ball as soon as possible, but without authority. When they try to make the hitter miss, invariably their first pitch will be some half-assed breaking ball that bounces six inches off the plate. Then they're struggling for strikes and the guy in the box is sitting back waiting for a pitch to unload on. I was so intent on getting ahead in the count that I frequently started the batter off with a fastball right down the middle of the plate. Most hitters take the first pitch anyway, and even if they don't, you learn quite a bit from their reaction. If a right-handed hitter fouls the ball off into the right-field stands, you know he hasn't caught up with your fastball. There were times, certainly, when a batter hurt me by clobbering the first pitch, but the percentages were greatly in my favor. When I was on top of my game, I was *always* ahead in the count.

(While the hitter's responses provide useful data, it would be a mistake to assume right off the bat that if he has trouble with a certain pitch one time, he'll have trouble with it every time. This is especially so in the case of breaking balls, where the element of surprise is very instrumental. With the bases loaded one time, Gaylord Perry threw me a nasty slider that started out at my chin and darted sharply over the plate. I wheeled around toward the umpire and said, "God, what was that?" Then I stole a glance at Dickie Dietz, the Giants' catcher, to see if he was paying attention. He was. Sure enough, he called for the same pitch and just as it started to break I leaned into it for a grand slam.)

Another advantage of throwing the first pitch down the middle is that you don't have to rely upon getting a marginal call from the umpire. Casual fans probably don't realize that a home-plate umpire can be the most influential factor in the development and outcome of a ballgame. The umpire can change a pitcher's entire thought process. The pitcher might throw what he thinks is a perfect pitch—the very pitch he had been depending on and hoping to produce in that situation—only to have the ump call it a ball. When he does that, the umpire takes away your best pitch.

I loved when Ed Sudol umpired my games because he always called strikes on the black part of the plate. His opposite number, and the umpire who gave me the most difficulty, was Al Barlick. Damn him! He would *never* give the pitcher a strike on the black. Technically, the black is out of the strike zone, and I can't say that Barlick was wrong, but shit, if the ball is that close and the batter takes it with two strikes on him, he deserves to be called out. The hitter can't tell if it's on the black. If he lets that pitch go by, he's beaten. Call him out! I'll give Barlick credit for being consistent, but God, he made you throw that ball.

Another umpire who aggravated the shit out of me was Doug Harvey. He was a good umpire, but there was no way he could possibly be as good as he thought he was. He was absolutely convinced that every call he ever made was right. I loved to raise hell with a guy like that.

I argued with the umpires quite a bit because I wanted them, like I wanted the hitters, to know I was out there. If I got the benefit of the doubt just once or twice a game because of my protests—and who knows whether I did or not—it was worth it. Most of the umps tolerated my temperament because they understood I was rude to everybody when I pitched. They also liked the fact that I could get them showered and dressed in about two hours. I don't suspect they were eager to see me leave the game. Unfortunately, that didn't mean I got all the breaks from the umpires. I remember one night Tom Gorman was giving me a rough time on balls and strikes, and when I came up to bat I thought I'd give him a little razzmatazz back. The first pitch was high—at least it was what he had been *calling* high when I threw it there—and Gorman said, "Strike one." I said, "Goddamn it, Tom, the pitch was high." He just stood there looking at me and tapping his ball-strike indicator. The next one was in the same spot and Gorman said, "Strike two." This time I turned around and faced him, which umpires hate (it tells the whole stadium that they're being questioned), and said, "Tom, goddamn it, the pitch was high." He said, "Bob, why don't you take just one more?" I decided not to accept his advice and popped up on the next high fastball.

The best I ever saw at messing with an umpire was Bob Uecker. He was catching for the Braves against us one night in Atlanta, and with Shannon at the plate the umpire, Billy Williams, called a strike that was three or four inches outside. Uecker ripped off his mask and started arguing like mad. Williams argued right back, and then, after a little while, he figured out that Uecker was arguing on behalf of Shannon. He said, "What the hell are you talking about? I called the pitch in your favor." Uecker said, "That's beside the point!"

The best and really only way to cope with any umpire is to learn his strike zone, respect it, and then put him out of your mind—which is relatively easy as long as the umpire is consistent in his calls. If he is, then you can give your full attention to the batter and the target. Actually, there were times, for me, when the batter *was* the target, but most of the time I concentrated on the catcher. Not the catcher's *glove*, as you might expect, but the catcher. I always thought that the glove was too small a target and I would end up missing it half the time, then overcompensating by aiming the ball—not a good idea—to put it where I wanted.

Control is not as precise an art as it's often purported to be. For my target, I picked out a big square between the catcher's knees and shoulders and tried to deliver the ball into the middle of it. That way, I found I usually hit the glove without really trying. Because I threw at the catcher, it was important for McCarver or whoever to move his whole body inside or outside instead of just his glove. The glove is impractical as a target anyway because it would be awkward for the catcher to move it to the high and low borders of the strike zone. For the vertical extremities of my square, I used the batter's knees or belt, mentally transferring the area to the corresponding region of the catcher. (For that reason and also on basic sartorial principles, I hated the beltless polyester pants that so many teams adopted in the seventies.) It's a little trickier to line up a breaking ball, of course, but once a pitcher knows how much his ball is going to break, he can start it at the middle of the plate to hit the outside corner (on a right-handed batter for a right-handed pitcher) or at the batter to clip the inside corner. The most troublesome location challenge for me was throwing the backdoor slider to a left-handed hitter. There was nothing to aim at on the outside part of the plate except the catcher, and I didn't want to start the slider directly at him because then it would cut comfortably over the middle, right into the hitter's power. So I would throw it at some vague space to the catcher's left and try to pull it back into his mitt.

No matter how much it moves or breaks, a pitch doesn't do a pitcher any good unless he can throw it where he wants to throw it. That was why I never screwed around much with pitches that had unpredictable flight patterns, like the spitball and knuckleball. I was tempted by both, but not severely, realizing that I wouldn't be able to execute a pitching plan using pitches that I couldn't locate with reasonable accuracy.

My experience with the spitball was restricted to one game against the Mets in 1965. Dave Ricketts was the catcher that night, and I told him that if I got two strikes on a batter and he fouled a pitch off, the next one would be a spitball. When a ball is hit foul, everybody instinctively turns to watch it, which would give me a second or two to spit on my hand without being seen. I remember throwing a spitter to Jesse Gonder, a catcher for the Mets, and he whirled around to the umpire and said, "Did you see that? He's throwing a spitball!" I forget who the umpire was, but he must have been a veteran because he assured Gonder, "Gibson doesn't throw a spitball."

I did, however, take advantage of natural conditions very often to legally create a spitball-type effect. Particularly on hot days, I made it a point to wear long sleeves so that sweat would roll down my arms onto my hands and the ball, adding a little extra dive to my sinking fastball and slider. I was fortunate, though, that by flicking down hard on my forefinger and middle finger, I was able to create downward movement on my fastball whenever I needed a ground ball, cold days or hot. My cut fastball, as I called it, was sort of a cross between a hard slider and the split-fingered fastball later popularized by my old 1964 teammate, Roger Craig. Although few if any pitchers threw the split-finger in my day, I probably couldn't have mastered it anyway because my hands are not big enough. (They are unusual, though. I don't know if it made a difference in my pitching but, unlike most people's, my fingers are symmetrical; that is, my index finger and little finger are the same height, and my two longer fingers in the middle are the same height.)

While I used various means to approximate a spitball, there was nothing in my working repertoire that even faintly resembled a knuckleball. I *had* a knuckler, and was fairly proud of it, but I didn't dare throw it in a game—with one exception. Pitching against Hank Aaron once, I figured I had nothing to lose. Aaron was the best fastball hitter the world ever saw anyway, and I was always looking for something different and funky to try on him. So I said "what the hell" and tossed him my bullpen special. He hit a bullet that Javier caught at second. On his way back to the dugout, Aaron caught my attention and said, "What was *that* pitch?" I told him, "Man, that was my best knuckleball!"

Aaron probably gave me more problems than any other right-handed hitter because he could match my speed. It was all but impossible to get a fastball past that man. My teammate, Curt Simmons, used to say that trying to throw a fastball past Hank Aaron was like trying to sneak the sun past a rooster. For me, it was like trying to slip an excuse past my brother

Josh. Aaron could pound the slider, too, and although there were plenty of occasions when I had to get him out and did, the only basic strategy I was comfortable with against him was to pitch around him. When we played the Braves, I tried to make damn sure that neither Aaron nor Eddie Mathews beat me. It was my policy and nature never to fear any hitter, but guys like Aaron and Mathews demanded a pitcher's utmost respect.

Aaron and I never said much to each other, but I believe—in large part for that reason—that we maintained a mutual admiration. We approached the game much the same way, keeping our mouths shut on the field and operating with a powerful dislike for whoever (pitcher in his case, hitter in mine) would try to reach into our pocket. Other than the knuckleball incident, the only personal communication that I recall between us on the field was when he was on second base and Rico Carty hit a sharply bouncing ball that I backhanded. Aaron was trapped between second and third, and we both knew that I had him cold. I ran directly at him and he stared at me for a second with one of those uh-oh looks on his face. Then he began feinting and dodging and the old Globetrotter shadowed every move he made. He wasn't getting out of it and all at once, realizing the impossible nature of his situation, he stopped. I stopped, too, and when our eyes met we both broke out laughing. Then I walked over and tagged him.

On the Cardinals' staff, Simmons was the only pitcher who seemed to have Aaron's number. He'd float his lollipop change-up toward the plate, and the whole dugout would crack up watching Aaron trying to hit that thing. I mean, we laughed *hard*. The same thing happened nearly every single time: Aaron would take a mighty rip at that slowball just hanging there in front of him and bloop it about ten or twelve feet in the air, right to the catcher. Once, he couldn't wait any longer and ran up toward the mound to knock one of those lollipops onto the pavilion roof at old Busch Stadium, only to be called out for leaving the batter's box. Simmons taught Sadecki the same pitch but Sadecki was afraid to throw it. One day he finally got up the nerve to use it and sure enough, Aaron blooped it ten or twelve feet in the air, right to the catcher. I had a half-baked change-up slider that I got Aaron out with a few times, but if I didn't put it in the right spot he'd knock the shit out of it.

As determined as I was not to allow the best hitters to beat me, I also wanted to let them know who they were up against. In the early innings, before the game was on the line, I tried to raise the level of competition and go straight at them—even Aaron. It's not possible to maintain that level of effort and intensity for every batter over nine innings, so I saved a little extra for the superstars. There's a certain egotism required to be a great pitcher, and against the great hitters I took the challenge personally—to say nothing of the fact that they'd jump all over anything that wasn't my best stuff. In a game situation, however, there was no place for personal considerations of any kind and I gave the big men a wide berth.

In my book, the great hitters were all power hitters and they were all fastball hitters. They were also every bit as egotistical as I was. The funny thing about power hitters is that they don't mind looking silly, swinging off their front feet and falling on their faces hacking at curveballs, but they don't want anybody throwing the fastball by them. That's an insult to their manhood. As a result, they're always ready for the fastball, just in case.

Most of my energy was spent working on and worrying about the guys with the biggest sticks. Although the ping hitters may have put more nicks in me from game to game, I didn't fear them whatsoever. Singles hitters were made to order for me because I could groove the first pitch, as I was fond of doing, without worrying about it leaving the park. I was known as a strikeout pitcher, but I much preferred to get a guy out quickly—on pitch number one, if possible. (When I did have a batter set up for a strikeout, I usually went for it right away rather than waste a pitch and fool around with him. This was contrary to most theories on pitching, and Red Schoendienst didn't approve. He once called a meeting to tell the Cardinal pitchers that they would be fined a hundred dollars if anybody got a hit against us with a count of no balls and two strikes. I piped up and said, "Red, I might as well quit right now because most of my strikeouts come with two strikes." He said, "Oh, all right. Forget it.") If I *wanted* the batter to hit the ball, as I wanted singles hitters to do in most cases, I didn't see the merit of throwing pitches that weren't strikes. With hitters on the order of Larry Bowa, Matty Alou, and Cookie Rojas—even Richie Ashburn, although he was very bothersome to me because he would foul off pitches for half the night and outlast me for walks—I had no reservations about laying in a high fastball and letting them hit it to the warning track.

(It didn't concern me too much, either, if one of those little fast guys reached first base. After I'd been in the league a few years, I stopped wasting my time and energy by throwing to first to hold runners on. I'd done a lot of that as a rookie, and it seemed like the runner always ended up at third after the ball bounced around the right-field corner for a while. I eventually learned that I didn't have to throw the ball to keep the runner close. I just held it a little longer. That drove Maury Wills crazy. I'd stay in the stretch position and after two or three seconds Wills couldn't wait anymore. He'd take off for second and I'd turn and toss the ball to Groat or Javier for the tag.)

With power hitters, my pattern was to pitch outside, then come in on their hands to ensure that the outside corner remained outside. If a homerun hitter wanted to reach out and guide the outside pitch to the opposite field, that was fine with me because it meant he wasn't turning his body into the ball. My objective was to prevent him from extending his arms and putting his hips into the outside pitch, which I accomplished with strong doses of the inside pitch.

Aaron aside, right-handed hitters didn't trouble me terribly. Against the Cubs, for instance, I would much rather pitch to Ernie Banks or Ron Santo than Billy Williams. Williams might have been the toughest all-around hitter for me. He could handle both the fastball and slider, controlled the bat well, and had more than enough power to cause concern. But the scariest hitter I faced had to be Willie McCovey, the third member (Williams and Aaron being the others) of the awesome pyramid of sluggers from Mobile, Alabama.

As dangerous as he was, I loved pitching to McCovey. He was so long and tall that he liked the ball away from his body so that he could unwrap himself and get his big arms in motion. Once in St. Louis, I gave him a pitch away that he could handle and *Boom!*—he crushed it off the left-center field wall so damn hard you could hear the ricochet all over the park. Imagine what that ball would have done to me if he'd hit it back through the box! He once got hold of one against Al Jackson that had to be the longest ball I ever saw hit. It landed somewhere over the scoreboard at new Busch Stadium, one of those shots where everybody in the dugout just kind of leans out, turns their heads, and watches in silence. Whenever I go to the ballpark in St. Louis nowadays, the first thing I think about is that ball McCovey hit over the scoreboard.

Most of the time, I tried to pitch McCovey inside. I'd go outside once in a while just to keep him guessing, then come back in again. I always threw the first pitch to him as hard as I could and down in the strike zone just to get ahead in the count. He was a low-ball hitter, but there wasn't a way to pitch to McCovey without substantial risk. Often he'd foul my opening strike. My second pitch was always a little higher, and on we went up the ladder. He knew exactly what I was doing, but he couldn't quite catch up with the ball. By the time I got two strikes on him, he'd be almost on his toes. He couldn't hit a ball that far up, but it's against the nature of a thoroughbred slugger like McCovey to resist a high fastball, and he couldn't afford to take it, anyway, with two strikes.

Willie Stargell was comparable to McCovey, and like McCovey, if I got behind him in the count, it was time to pitch and duck. In the opening game of 1969, after the Cardinals had traded for Joe Torre, Torre was at first base when I got behind Stargell and gave him a pitch down and in. He scorched the ball down to first on two hops, and Torre took it off the shoulder. I wasn't sure if he was trying to prove himself on a new team or if he was just dense, so I called Joe over and said, "Look, don't ever get in front of a ball like that when Willie Stargell hits it. *Don't ever!*"

Torre was a pretty dangerous hitter himself, and I worked him in a fashion similar to McCovey except that instead of going higher and higher I would pitch Torre increasingly inside. Each time he'd come to bat, I'd bring the ball a little farther inside, and each time, I could see him inching a little farther back in the batter's box. When I got him back far enough, I'd slip a slider on the outside corner—which is exactly where he would have wanted it if he had stayed put.

I had good luck with Orlando Cepeda the very same way, and when he came over to the Cardinals I told him how I'd taken advantage of the way he crept back in the box against me. He said, "You *saw* that?" He couldn't believe it; and I couldn't believe he thought he was getting away with it. "Of course I saw that," I said.

Mays was another hitter whom I pitched inside because he'd murder the ball if he could straighten his arms. I brought the ball in close to Frank Robinson, as well—there's no telling how many times I hit him in the elbow—although I believe most pitchers tried him outside. The way he crowded the plate, they figured he was waiting to pounce on the inside pitch, but it seemed to me that he beat a hell of a lot of guys who pitched him away. There were very few of the superstar hitters whom I pitched away, an exception being Roberto Clemente. He was completely unorthodox in the batter's box and would rip a pitch high and away—like the one he broke my leg with—but I could get him out low and away.

Bear in mind that when I say I could get somebody out a certain way, or I had luck with him by doing this or that, it wasn't an exact science. The good hitters all had strategies for me, too, and there wasn't a single one of them whom I *knew* I was going to put away every time—unless it was Rusty Staub. Staub was one fellow whom I absolutely figured out. He liked to pull the ball early in the count, then back off and go the other way with two strikes, anticipating breaking balls. So I would pitch him backwards, feeding him my sorry curveballs until he was set up, then blowing a fastball by him inside. Worked every time.

The kind of guys I'm discussing here—the money players—demanded special consideration because they basically couldn't be intimidated, but I always held out hope that I could somehow throw them off their games. I thought for sure I was getting to Pete Rose at one point when I knocked him down and he got up and spit at me. When he got back to the dugout, though, I saw Sparky Anderson walk over and say something to him. I heard later that Sparky, wise man that he was, advised Rose never to show me up.

For a singles and doubles hitter, Rose carried himself with a big man's swagger and could give a pitcher a hard time just through his sheer will to make something happen. He broke through as a prime-time player when he won his first batting title in 1968, checking in at .335 for a season in which only six guys in all the majors hit .300. Never one to sell himself short, Rose declared that he should have been the National League's Most Valuable Player that year.

While respecting his performance and his opinion, I had a different point of view on 1968.

# CHAPTER IX

Drysdale and Marichal were both making a hundred thousand dollars by 1968 and I had reason to believe I was worth as much. In addition to my second World Series MVP award, the 1967 season had brought my third consecutive Gold Glove (which, like so many of my honors, I managed to belittle when I moaned that the Rawlings company had used "a horrible picture" on the face of the trophy by selecting one taken before I had repaired the gap between my front teeth—a comment construed as ingratitude but actually made out of embarrassment) and widespread endorsement as the leading pitcher in the game. I figured, also, that my bargaining power would not be impaired at all by the fact that Bing Devine was back on the job as general manager, with Musial settling into a vice presidency. Devine even made a trip to Omaha to talk salary. Charline and I welcomed him into the new ten-room house we had built on the west side of town after a three-year struggle for a loan and a decent lot (there were plenty of those around, but all of them were situated in white neighborhoods that seemed to be intent upon remaining that way). Although my salary was more than enough to cover the payments for the place we ultimately settled upon, our application was denied by two banks and a

loan company before we were finally able to borrow money from an insurance company.

Charline decorated the house with modern art that I didn't understand.
I was more partial to the oil portrait of the family that Curt Flood painted
and gave to us. It disappointed Charline that I was never particularly interested in contemporary or classical culture—she gravitated toward social
circles in which that sort of thing played a large part and was frustrated
that I was so upwardly immobile—but in my own way I was not entirely
unappreciative of the arts. Crafts that required picking or strumming or
designing or building appealed to me and kept my hands busy in the off-
season. And although I never purported to be an avid reader, in 1968 I
even wrote a book that was released during the summer. It was an autobiography called *From Ghetto To Glory*—a prelude to this one, more or
less—and may I add thankfully that the critics and sportswriters were
generous in their praise of it. They seemed to be impressed by the mala-
dies and hardships of my childhood, and the warm response was both
gratifying and worrisome. I felt unburdened in a way—to have my human
side finally acknowledged—but exposed in another, and uncomfortable
about the repercussions such personal information might have for my
pitching. The veil had been lifted.

Of course, everything has its price, and the royalties from the book
helped close the gap between the salary I had hoped to make for 1968 and
what the Cardinals actually paid me. My contract didn't bring me Mays or
Marichal money exactly, but it was close, and for me it was relative wealth.
I used it to invest in two local real estate companies. While Charline devoted her civil rights energy to the Urban League and the open housing
debate, I preferred activism of a more economic nature.

Investments notwithstanding, I realized that my personal economics
were based mainly upon my earned run index and the won-lost record I
cashed in at the end of every season. The trends in these areas were extremely promising as the spring of 1968 approached, as were the prevailing currents around the league. For whatever reason or reasons, it
seemed that mastery of the pitching art was not quite as elusive as it had
been a decade before. Between 1958 and 1967, the National League ERA
had been reduced from 3.95 to 3.38. Bigger ballparks no doubt had some-

thing to do with it, as did bigger gloves, faster fielders, and bullpen specialists. Pitching was still a far cry from being *easy*, and great hitters lurked in nearly every lineup, but by 1968 I had reached the point that, correctly or not, I expected to dominate every game I started.

My confidence entailed no disrepect for the opposition. On the contrary, there was a feeling among the players that the major-league talent level had attained a peak we wouldn't see again in our careers. Expansion was due to arrive in 1969, diluting each league with an additional two teams (Seattle and Kansas City in the American League, Montreal and San Diego in the National) and fifty players. This, in turn, would engender a divisional setup within the leagues that would split them in half and dramatically redefine pennant races as we knew them. Although nobody could have predicted the extent to which it would be true, it was generally felt that the 1968 season would mark the end of a baseball era and the game would not be the same thereafter.

We knew for certain that the Cardinals would be different after 1968, because Roger Maris announced he would retire at the end of the season. Heading into the spring, though, we could only hope—and trust—that the '68 Cardinals wouldn't be significantly different from the '67 version. The veterans on the squad didn't have to be reminded of the disastrous plunge taken by the 1965 team after the last St. Louis world championship.

Prodded by fresh memories and expecting the best this time around, I was raring to go when we arrived in St. Petersburg, where my first assignment came in the exhibition opener against the Mets. Schoendienst usually honored my request to pitch only against American League teams in the spring, but since it was the opening game and I was eager to crank it up, I went ahead and took the mound in the top of the first. Anyway, the leadoff batter for the Mets was a former American Leaguer, center fielder Tommie Agee.

Many people have described what followed as my way of welcoming Agee into the National League, but that wasn't the case. It was the first pitch of the spring, and it simply got away from me. To compound the problem, Agee had a closed stance that made it hard for him to pick up the ball quickly and get out of its path. The result was that the pitch banged against his helmet and laid him out in the batter's box. Although he was carried off the field on a stretcher, Agee wasn't seriously hurt, thank goodness. I didn't apologize for the scare—that wasn't my style—but the fact is, I had no reason or desire whatsoever to hit Tommie Agee on the first pitch of the spring. I repeat that if I'd wanted to hit him, or anybody, I wouldn't have aimed at the head. It's strange how stories circulate, but the newspapers made quite a to-do about the incident, surmising that it was my bullyish manner of introducing myself to the new kid on the block. What a crock. The story has taken on greater proportions as the years pass, becoming a popular tale to describe what a surly, unforgiving son of a bitch Bob Gibson was on the mound. Not long ago I saw Agee at an old-timers' game in Houston and attempted to explain to him what really happened. He just looked at me. The fable had been retold so many times that even he had a hard time believing the real story.

(As hard-nosed as baseball was in those days, I've never known a pitcher who willfully hit a batter in the head. Without trying to sound unsympathetic—I'm fully aware of the possible consequences—I still say that if a guy gets hit in the head, it's his own fault. A lot of hitters are simply too smug at the plate, going up there with quick reflexes, a plastic helmet, and a dangerously false sense of security. It's much too easy for a hitter to believe that a ball will never touch his head, because he gets a great view of any pitch headed in that direction and to avoid it all he has to do is twitch. The fallacy in this reasoning is that it doesn't account for the element of surprise or shock. I harped at Bill White one night about his disrespect for the inside pitch, and he dismissed my warning, as he usually did, by assuring me he would never be hit in the head. I said, "Yeah, some day, when you least expect it, you're gonna take one in the coconut the way you dive in there." The very next night, he was expecting a curve from Bob Veale, Pittsburgh's enormous lefthander, and walked right into a fastball that hit him so hard, it bent his helmet back against his skull. When he got up and walked—slowly—to first base, I couldn't stop laughing. Bill said, "Yeah, yeah, he got me.")

After the Agee incident, the rest of the spring was comparatively uneventful until we were just about ready to break camp and head north to start the season. We liked the way the club was shaping up and felt pretty good about ourselves as we worked out at Al Lang Field on the morning of Friday, April 4. But the jogging and throwing came to a sudden stop when somebody said something about Dr. Martin Luther King, Jr., being shot. Several of us ran immediately into the clubhouse, where the news was verified on television: A sniper, later identified as James Earl Ray, had killed Dr. King on the balcony of a Memphis motel.

Not two months before that, I'd been in Atlanta for a banquet and walked right past Dr. King in the airport. He'd looked at me as though he recognized me but wasn't sure who I was. I regretted that I hadn't said anything, and I reeled from the impact of the assassination—the cold-blooded murder of the one man in my lifetime who had been able to capture the public's attention about racial injustice, break through some of the age-old social barriers, and raise the spirits and hopes of black people across the country. That evening, some of the players got together at Cepeda's apartment and decided to inform the Cardinal management that we had no intention of opening the season as scheduled the next week. As it turned out, the entire major-league schedule was postponed a day or so as the nation mourned the death of the greatest peacemaker of our times.

> *Everybody on the club was dismayed by what happened to Martin Luther King. It was a very disorienting time in many respects, and that was probably the hardest moment. Bob and I had a very serious discussion in the clubhouse that morning. He was very emotional, and initially he turned his back on me. Probably the last person he wanted to talk to that morning was a white man from Memphis, of all places. But I confronted him on that, as I knew he would have done if the tables had been turned. I told him that I had grown up in an environment of severe prejudice, but if I were any indication, it was possible for people to change their attitudes. He didn't really want to be calmed down and told me in so many words that it was plainly impossible for a white man to completely overcome prejudice. I said that he was taking a very nihilistic attitude and that just because some white people obviously maintained their hatred for blacks and considered them inferior, it was senseless to embrace a viewpoint that would lead nowhere. I found myself in the unfamiliar position of arguing that*

*the races were equal and that we were all the same. It was a soul-*
*searching type of thing, and I believe Bob and I reached a meeting*
*of the minds that morning. That was the kind of talk we often had*
*on the Cardinals.*     —TIM MCCARVER

In addition to the tragic implications Dr. King's murder had for the nation, it also made me keenly aware that there was little of which lunatics
were not capable in the name of racial hatred. I had received death threats
from time to time but never before took them very seriously. One swell
fellow from New York advised me in writing that I could save my own life
by leaving a quarter of a million dollars in a trash can at a subway stop
near Shea Stadium. I laughed at the thought of having a quarter of a million dollars. But that night, after going out to dinner following the
ballgame, I returned to my hotel room and there was a man lurking by my
door. I thought, "Oh, shit." As I walked up, he said, "Are you Bob Gibson?"

"Yes."

"I'm from the FBI."

The anxiety passed quickly when I realized that the man in the hallway
was not a comrade of James Earl Ray—that, in fact, he was there to *protect*
me—but the fact that I *had* anxieties, even below the surface, meant that
I had to deal with them. As disturbed as I was about Dr. King, I knew, also,
that I couldn't let it undermine my pitching. There was a season to play,
and I expected a lot out of it. What I *didn't* expect—in fact, about the last
thing I would have anticipated with the ballclub we had—was winning
only three times in my first ten starts.

We opened, belatedly, against the Braves, and I left for a pinch hitter after seven innings, trailing 1–0 on an unearned run—a sign of things to
come. We rallied to win the game 2–1, the moral being that the club
seemed to score a little better when I wasn't in the game. We also won the
next time I started, 4–3, but again I left after seven innings, before we had
taken the lead. Then Ferguson Jenkins of the Cubs beat me 5–1 and I was
still winless after three starts.

I clicked off three in a row after that, holding the Pirates, Astros, and
Mets to a run each—beating Bob Veale for my first victory and pitching

twelve and eleven innings back-to-back in the latter two, the last coming against Tom Seaver—but then hit the skids. Actually, I gave up as many as three earned runs only once in my next four starts, but lost them all as the Cardinals scored a combined total of three runs. I was 3–5 and extremely out of sorts. My earned run average was 1.32 and I hadn't won in three weeks. After I lost a one-hitter to Drysdale and the Dodgers on the heels of a game in which I shut out the Phillies for nine innings before losing 1–0 to Woodie Fryman on a two-out tenth-inning single by goddamn Bill White, McCarver followed me into the trainer's room and said, "Hoot, I'm really sorry. I know our crappy hitting has gone on for too long . . ." I stopped him in the middle of the apology and snapped, "This is bullshit. I'm tired of listening to these fucking excuses." Then I turned and disappeared into the shower. I don't know why I took out my frustrations on McCarver—I guess he was good for that—but I wouldn't talk to him for hours afterwards.

The team was somehow hanging in through its slump, and to help out a little I took it upon myself at one point to offer Steve Carlton some pitching advice. He said, "How the hell can you help me? You're three and five." Maybe our inability to score runs was making everybody a little testy, but just to play it safe I left Carlton alone after that. He had his own problems, I suppose—mainly with the media. As great a pitcher as he eventually became, it was unfortunate that Carlton's claim to fame became the fact that he steadfastly refused to talk to reporters for so many years. I always felt that he adopted that position because he was unsure of himself with the media and didn't want to say something that might embarrass him when it was broadcast or appeared in print.

The hitters finally picked up the pace a little bit around the end of May, and their revival gave me a lift. After beating the Mets 6–3, I shut out the Astros 4–0 on three hits. At that point, I was a hot pitcher with a .500 record, which left me far short of the standard being set by Drysdale, who had just pitched his sixth straight shutout on a fantastic, record run of 58⅔ consecutive scoreless innings. The last of Big D's shutouts came on June 4, the night of Robert Kennedy's promising triumph—for him and for the civil rights movement—in California's Democratic presidential primary. Kennedy made a point of congratulating Drysdale in his victory speech at the Ambassador Hotel, after which he attempted to wend his way to a waiting car through the hotel service area. He was shot in a passageway to the kitchen and was dead the next day.

For the most part, ballplayers are able to divorce themselves from the events of the real world. Baseball is a self-absorbed sort of lifestyle that affords a certain detachment from many public concerns, but even for those of us in the game, there was no escaping the pervasive realities of 1968—the assassinations, the cities burning, the social revolution. The Cardinals, I'm sure, were more socially conscious than most clubs, and the black players in particular were deeply affected by what went down in 1968. We were angrier than usual, and I think it showed. I know it did in my case.

I was probably pitching the best baseball of my career, but my efforts were obscured, initially, by several things. First of all, anything any ballplayer did on the field that summer seemed relatively insignificant against the political backdrop of the nation, but even in the baseball context my work was not especially noteworthy early in the year. My record was mediocre, Drysdale was hogging the headlines, and in fact I was little different from any number of pitchers who were turning the National League on its ear. Guys like Jenkins of Chicago, Veale and Steve Blass of the Pirates, Marichal and Gaylord Perry of the Giants, Seaver and rookie Jerry Koosman of the Mets—practically all of the guys I was hooking up with—were reeling off shutouts right and left and keeping their ERAs in the restricted neighborhood of two-something. The pitching in the league was so good that I even tried switch-hitting for a while, thinking that if I went up there left-handed, I wouldn't have to deal with all those wicked sliders I was seeing.

I realized all along, though, that my best and only effective antidote to the epidemic of great pitching going around was to outpitch it. There was nothing I could do about the fact that, more often than not, I would continue to match up with the best pitchers the other teams had to offer, and my teammates, as much as they would have liked to, were not in a position to guarantee me any reasonable number of runs. The answer, clearly, was to take a cue from Drysdale and throw some damn shutouts, which was something that appeared to be within my power at the time. My fastball was boring into McCarver's mitt and my sliders were behaving like smart missiles. I was definitely settling into what would be referred to today as a zone.

I really can't say, in retrospect, whether Robert Kennedy's assassination is what got me going or not. Without a doubt, it was an angry point in American history for black people—Dr. King's killing had jolted me; Kennedy's infuriated me—and without a doubt, I pitched better angry. I suspect that the control of my slider had more to do with it than anything, but I can't completely dismiss the fact that nobody gave me any shit whatsoever for about two months after Bobby Kennedy died.

Ironically or not, my shutout of Houston—my first of the year—occurred the following day. The Braves were next in line, and I shut them out, too. The ballclub hadn't exactly blasted out of its hitting slump—which was beginning to look more like a permanent condition—but Briles, Carlton, Washburn, and Hoerner were caught up in the pitching spirit, and as a staff we were easily the best in the league. That was sufficient to get us into first place by early June.

My third shutout, a four-hitter with thirteen strikeouts, came against Gary Nolan and the Reds, and it lowered by ERA to 1.29. I was pitching the best I had ever pitched in a month that wasn't October. Jenkins was the next challenge, and it took another shutout to beat him, 1–0. When I threw a four-hitter at Pittsburgh on June 26, my shutout streak had reached five. With forty-seven consecutive scoreless innings, I was actually closing in on the record Drysdale had established just three weeks before. After everything that had happened in the previous months, it felt wonderful just to go out and kick ass for nine innings every fourth or fifth day (my rest varied from start to start). When a reporter asked me about the pressure involved in maintaining the streak, I said that I felt more pressure every day just being a Negro in a white society.

As fate and the Dodgers would have it, my next assignment was against Drysdale in Los Angeles. There was so much hoopla surrounding the game that the start of it had to be delayed until the congestion cleared at the turnstiles. Another shutout would put me within three innings of surpassing Drysdale, which meant that the Dodgers had the last good chance of stopping me. Their best opportunity came with two outs in the first inning, when Len Gabrielson singled and Tom Haller hit a ground ball that hopped away from Javier and into right field, sending Gabrielson to third. That brought up Ron Fairly, my old nemesis, which prompted Johnny Edwards, our backup catcher, to set up for an outside fastball. I had been throwing bull's-eyes for so long that Edwards was caught off guard when the pitch instead sailed inside, and it bounced off the tip of his mitt when he reached for it, enabling Gabrielson to sprint home and jump on the plate—both fists raised in the air as if he had won the game—with the first run I had given up in four weeks. The call could have gone either way (frankly, I thought it should have been a passed ball since the pitch was not in the dirt and Edwards got his glove on it), but the official scorer at Dodger Stadium ruled it a wild pitch. As a result, the run was earned and my scoreless inning streak was over at 47⅔. If the pitch had instead been ruled a passed ball, the run would have been unearned—that is, not charged to the pitcher—and wouldn't have counted against the streak. I was upset, of course, but in the dugout Flood told me to forget it because if it hadn't been for the wild pitch, we would have found some other way to screw up the record.

The guys helped me out against Drysdale, though, and we beat him 5-1 for my seventh straight victory and the 135th of my career, which moved me ahead of Dizzy Dean and into second place on the Cardinal all-time list behind Jesse Haines. That put me in a better humor, and after the game the reporters flocked around to ask about the run that broke my string. "What do you mean?" I said. "You saw it. The fucker missed the ball." None of the writers wrote anything down in his pad. They all stood quietly, studying me to see if I was kidding or not. Finally I smiled and said, "Hey, that's the way it goes." It wouldn't have been good form to complain about the call, but I disagreed with it and I was also well aware that Drysdale had gotten the benefit of a controversial call during his scoreless inning streak. In a bases-loaded situation against the Giants, he had hit Dickie Dietz with a pitch to apparently force in a run, but the umpire, Harry Wendelstedt, ruled that Dietz hadn't tried to get out of the way (which nullified the hit-batsman) and called him back. Drysdale then retired Dietz to keep the streak intact.

I faced San Francisco in my next start, and after surviving Drysdale I found myself matched up with Marichal, who had already won fifteen games, five more than me. In my own mind, I still needed three more innings to exceed Drysdale's record, and was in serious jeopardy of failing when the Giants loaded the bases with no outs in the first. But I struck out Mays, McCovey, and Hart in succession, and stayed out of trouble the rest of the afternoon as we beat Marichal 3–0 in a game in which Edwards aided the cause by hitting a home run. If the call in Los Angeles had gone the other way, my scoreless inning streak would have reached sixty-five by the end of that game. At the all-star break, my earned run average was 1.06.

Schoendienst, who managed the National League team by virtue of our pennant the year before, elected not to pitch me in the all-star game on two days' rest. Drysdale started, Seaver struck out five batters in two innings, and appropriately for 1968 the game ended 1–0, Mays scoring the only run on a double-play ball hit by McCovey in the first.

The Cardinals were beginning to pull away in the pennant race by that time, and Red gave me an extra day off to start the second half of the season. Fortunately, it didn't break my rhythm. The sliders were still biting, my fastballs were finding the corners—even when they didn't, I was around the plate so much that the umpires were giving me the calls—and I held Houston hitless through the first five innings of my next outing. In the dugout that night, Maxvill happened to notice that my index finger was bleeding from a nail that broke off, and as we batted with a big lead he came over and told me I didn't have to prove anything. I said, "Okay, Maxie." Then I spit on my finger, rubbed it on the dirt, and went out and gave up my second run in seventy-one innings when Rusty Staub (the man I *knew* I could get out) singled and scored on a double that Denis Menke (whom, unlike Staub, I never quite got a handle on) bounced off the right-field chalk after fouling off five pitches. We won 8–1 on a three-hitter.

According to the pitching rotations, I was due to square off with Marichal again the next time out, but when the game started Mike McCormick was on the mound for the Giants. We jumped on him early and led 6–0 in the fourth inning when the game was rained out. Marichal started the next night instead and won his seventeenth. I had to wait four more excruciating days to get back out there, and this time shut out the Mets 2–0 with thirteen strikeouts, lowering my ERA to 1.01.

By that point, the guys in our bullpen had resorted to playing checkers when I pitched. I hadn't been relieved since the end of May, and never all year in the middle of an inning. It was my policy to not place limitations on myself, but since the first of June my work had been closer to perfect than I ever imagined it could be. It seemed that every time I delivered a pitch, I knew exactly where it was going. That was not an ordinary feeling for me. My control was so good that it was almost as if I had no control at all—that I was just a spectator watching my pitches shoot inside and high to keep the batters honest, then outside and low (right in the "cock box," as we called it, referring to the inches between the knee and groin) to put them away. For weeks and weeks I was *always* ahead in the count, which can't be underestimated, and seemed so completely immune from mistakes or from the best efforts of the men I faced that at times my biggest problem might have been keeping my teammates interested.

> *I was almost like a cheerleader when Gibson pitched in 1968. I hardly paid any attention at all unless there was a man on first base and less than two outs. Otherwise, all I did was catch the ball from the catcher after strikeouts.*
> —MIKE SHANNON

There was no problem, though, in keeping the fans interested. Despite the mockery we had made of the pennant race—our record was 49–15 through the middle months of the season and our lead once reached 14½ games—the people poured in when I pitched. I'd frankly never considered myself a gate attraction and hadn't thought of using that as a bargaining chip in contract negotiations, but it became apparent that the Cardinals were getting rich off me. Attendance in St. Louis increased by nearly twenty-five hundred a game when I pitched, and the additional ticket receipts alone would have covered my salary for the season.

By July 25 I had beaten every team in the league except the Phillies, and added them to the list with a five-hit, 5–0 decision over Chris Short that reduced my ERA to 0.96. When Ed Charles of the Mets doubled home Ed Kranepool in the fourth inning of my next start, a 7–1 victory, it concluded a stretch of ninety-five innings in which I had given up only two earned runs (one of them on the wild pitch), resulting in an ERA of 0.19 for the most amazing eight weeks of my life. Ironically, the ninety-five innings could be measured from Charles to Charles, beginning when the Mets' third baseman homered against me in the seventh inning on the second day of June.

When July was in the books, I had become the first man ever to win the National League's Player of the Month award twice in a row. August, however, immediately promised to be a different story. I began it by pitching eleven innings against the Cubs and striking out ten, but allowed four earned runs (more than I had given up, total, in two months) while earning no decision in a game we eventually lost 6–5. Five days later I revisited July by shutting out the Braves, which was required in order to escape with a 1–0 victory against a hot knuckleballer named Phil Niekro, who had come out of nowhere to lead the league in ERA in 1967 and was keeping up the good work.

As it turned out, August wasn't so bad at all. The Giants and everybody else remained far behind us—despite the fact that nobody in our lineup threatened to hit twenty home runs or drive in a hundred runs—and I came up with a couple more shutouts, beating Woodie Fryman and the Phillies 2–0 (evening the score with Fryman for his 1–0 shutout over me in May) and striking out fourteen Pirates as we clobbered Bob Veale, 8–0. The game before that, I had also faced Pittsburgh and fanned fifteen for a season high, but it was not a good night. My fifteen-game winning streak had been aborted by a 6–4 defeat in which Stargell tagged me for a three-run homer (the first I had surrendered in twelve weeks despite the fact that I was relying heavily upon my rising fastball; in a stretch of three games, our infielders had only eight assists) and the Pirates also scored three unearned runs, two in the ninth. My record stood at 18–6 when the streak ended, and my ERA at 0.99. Ten of the fifteen victories had been shutouts.

After blanking Pittsburgh and taking a side trip to New York to celebrate the release of my book, I had a chance to win my twentieth game at Crosley Field in Cincinnati, a bandbox that I regarded as the toughest park on the circuit for pitchers. Besides that, the Reds were the highest

scoring team in the league; but this was 1968. They managed only four singles and Javier won the game for us, 1–0, with a homer in the tenth off Ted
Abernathy, a submarining reliever.

With twenty wins under my belt, I had the slightest of chances to catch
Marichal for the league lead and was eager to take him head-on in my next
start. But for the second time of the three occasions in which we were
scheduled against each other that season, he didn't answer the bell. It was
a twilight doubleheader and Herman Franks said it was too hot for
Marichal to pitch the first game. I found this to be curious, considering
that he was from the Dominican Republic and I was from Omaha, but
wasn't too upset about it until I lost 3–2 and he won the nightcap 8–7.

The club gave me a few more runs to work with the next time and I
beat the Dodgers 5–4, the only game all season in which I gave up as
many as four runs and won. By that time, I had conditioned myself not to
expect more than a run or two, at the most. There had been moments during the summer when our offense had shown some signs of life, and in
fact, believe it or not, we led the league in batting average and tied for
fourth in runs, but for whatever reason—the fact that I usually drew the
ace of the other team (aside from Marichal) probably had something to do
with it—we simply didn't score as well when I pitched. In games that
Briles, Carlton, Washburn, Jaster or anybody else started, the club averaged 3.8 runs. In games that I started, we averaged 2.8—a full run less.
There were many, many times when I could have put that run to good
use—like the game at Candlestick Park that followed my victory against
the Dodgers.

Gaylord Perry was San Francisco's pitcher that night, and we couldn't
do a thing with him. I mean, not a thing. I was pretty sharp, too, and for
that matter, so was the home-plate umpire, Harry Wendelstedt, who distinguished himself with what I consider to be the best job of calling balls and
strikes that I ever witnessed. In my opinion, Harry didn't miss a pitch all
night, and I told him so afterwards. That wasn't an easy thing for me to
do—not only because I was reluctant to compliment an umpire, as a rule,
but mostly because I was not in a sociable mood when the game ended.
Perry had pitched a no-hitter and a little guy named Ron Hunt had homered off the goddamn foul pole to beat me 1–0.

Wendelstedt's good work may have had some subtle influence on the extraordinary pitching that night, but I suspect, on the other hand, that the good pitching had a bigger effect on his umpiring. Wendelstedt wasn't behind the plate the next day when Ray Washburn duplicated Perry's performance, completing the only back-to-back no-hitters in baseball history. Although the pennant race was effectively over by then (the Giants would finish second for the fourth year in a row), those two unforgettable games may have said more about the 1968 season than anything.

While others in my profession were making history—in addition to the feats of Drysdale, Perry, and Washburn, Detroit's Denny McLain was creating a commotion in the American League with his celebrated pursuit of thirty victories—my mark on the Year of the Pitcher would be made if I could pitch three hundred innings, which I would do if I finished my last two starts, and keep my earned run average under 1.14, the record for three hundred or more innings set by Walter Johnson in 1913. Earned run averages don't lend themselves to clean comparisons between eras, and the all-time record, regardless of conditions, is the 0.86 by Tim Keefe of Troy (the fact that Troy, N.Y., was even in the National League tells you something) in 1880, when pitchers threw underhanded from forty-five feet and were allowed eight balls before walking a batter. Since 1900, when the pitching guidelines began to approximate those that we know now, the lowest ERA is the 0.96 recorded by Dutch Leonard of the Red Sox in 1914. Between 1920 (the end of the dead ball era) and 1968—the period that was most pertinent to my case—the ERA to beat was the 1.64 of the Yankees' Spud Chandler in 1943, when many of the best hitters were off fighting World War II. Meanwhile, the National League standard was considered to be the 1.22 of the Phillies' Grover Cleveland Alexander in 1915, and the really important record—the one that all the reporters said would secure my place in history if I could break it—was Johnson's for three hundred innings. Or so I was told, anyway.

After the Dodgers beat me 3–2 on my second-to-last start, my ERA stood at 1.16. I was a lock to wipe out Chandler's record, but I didn't put much stock in that one because pitching statistics up and down the line were distorted in 1968, and in fact Luis Tiant of the Indians was also in the process of bettering Chandler with a 1.60 ERA. The record I wanted was

Johnson's, and to get it I would have to shut out Houston in my last start of the regular season.

The Astros—Denis Menke included—cooperated, restricting themselves to six hits and turning none of them into runs. My final earned run average figured out at 1.12, which, for practical purposes, most baseball authorities have adopted as the lowest in baseball history, Keefe and Leonard notwithstanding. The shutout was my thirteenth of the season, which tied me for second all-time (with Jack Coombs of the Athletics, 1910) behind Alexander, who threw sixteen in '16. (Incidentally, that gave Nebraska a sweep of the top two spots, Old Pete having hailed from a tiny place in the middle of the state called Elba.) My final won-loss record was 22–9, and I still can't believe I lost nine games that year. Some stat guy calculated that if we had scored four runs every time I started, I would have been 31–2, and if we had just scored three every time, I would have finished 27–5. If the Cardinals had produced runs for me at the same rate they did for our other pitchers—that is, if they had scored one more run every time I pitched (in the process averaging 3.8 per game instead of 2.8)—I would have been 24–4. I didn't have these statistics at my disposal when the 1968 season ended, but rest assured that my teammates got the general idea. We didn't conceal our feelings on the Cardinals. After a while, my lust for runs became sort of a running joke.

> *There was one game we were winning about 8–0 with two outs in the fifth when our pitcher—I forget who it was—got hit by a line drive and had to come out. Of course, the winning pitcher in a game like that is the one who finishes the fifth inning. Red started to look around for somebody to put in and we all had to laugh because there was Gibson, who had just pitched ten innings the day before, right in Red's face going, "Gee, Red, you know I'm feeling really good today!"* —MIKE SHANNON

One of the 1968 statistics I'm proudest of is the fact that I completed twenty-eight of my thirty-four starts and only twice failed to last until the eighth inning. Beginning late in 1967 and ending early in 1969, I went fifty-six starts without being relieved in mid-inning—a feat that would be virtually impossible today, when so many relief pitchers are paid to come in and get one damn batter out.

The 1.12 is the number that seems to have impressed a lot of people over the years, but at the time I wasn't that impressed myself. It seemed to me that, for all the great players around, nobody really *hit* that year. There were only five guys in the National League who averaged .300 or better (Flood was one of them), and only one—Carl Yastrzemski at .301—who did it in the American. Several pitchers came in with ERAs under 2.00 (most of them in the American League), and two won more games than I did—Marichal, with twenty-six, and McLain, whose final tally of thirty-one wins remains the most since Lefty Grove in 1931. As the first thirty-game winner since Dizzy Dean in 1934, McLain received much more attention than I did during the season. At the same time, though, I truly believed that nobody *pitched* better than I did in 1968, and the passage of time has thrown a favorable light upon the numbers. In recent years, I've read articles in which the case has been made that my season was the best a pitcher ever had. I'm not the proper authority to make that call and I don't know what other pitchers from other years bring to the table, but I will say this much: I had my shit together in 1968.

In the voting for Most Valuable Player in the National League, I outpointed Rose 242–205, although I suspect the outcome might have been different if we hadn't won the pennant by nine games. Our command of the league was reflected by the fact that four of the top seven vote-getters were from the Cardinals, the others being Flood, Brock (who led the league with 62 stolen bases), and Shannon (who, in a revealing commentary on our power—we didn't have any—led the team in RBIs with a mere 79).

Cepeda was not nearly as productive in 1968 as he had been the year before, but his presence and enthusiasm were still vital to our ballclub. Those things were just as important to us, anyway, because the Cardinals went about winning with execution and brains and an abiding belief in ourselves. I've often talked about this over the years with Flood and McCarver and Shannon, and we all agree that we won mainly because we had a special group of guys and a collective spirit that rubbed off. That was true of the '68 team in much the same way that it had been for the '67 team and the '64 team, although the players were not the same in every case, man for man. Flood and Brock and McCarver and Shannon and I were on hand all those years, but among other significant changes White and Boyer had departed and Maris and Cepeda were in their places—in the clubhouse, that is, if not the field.

It was rare that a teammate came along who didn't buy into the attitude that made the Cardinals special, but there were a few. I remember, after having some drinks on the flight back to St. Louis after we had clinched the pennant in 1968, getting into an argument with Phil Gagliano, a reserve infielder who like McCarver came from Memphis but unlike McCarver never grew out of the old racial notions he had been raised on. The more we drank that night, the more Gagliano insisted that white people were better than black people. I said, "In what way are you better than me? Are you more educated? Are you a more decent human being? Are you a better ballplayer? Hell, I could use you as a tax write-off." I suppose I'm not a forgiving person. When Gagliano was in the hospital with an illness the next year, I was the only guy on the club who didn't visit him.

For the most part, though, the '68 Cardinals respected and cared for each other in the tradition that had been established when Boyer and White and Musial were with us, and there were guys on that team—any number of them—for whom I would have cut off my right arm. But not until after the World Series.

I had nothing against Denny McLain personally. I'm sure he must have been a fine pitcher to win thirty-one games, and as an amateur musician myself I could appreciate his love for and skill at the Hammond organ. I thought it was a little strange that he drank cases of Pepsi-Cola every day and stranger yet that the Tigers allowed him to fly his own plane around the country between starts, but I had to admire the job he had done of marketing himself, appearing during the season on the *The Ed Sullivan Show* and Steve Allen's and Bob Hope's and the covers of *Time* and *Sports Illustrated*. Hell, if a pitcher could do all of that and still win thirty-one games, more power to him.

My only real problem with McLain was what he said before the World

Series started. It was probably something he regretted as soon as the
words left his mouth (he later said he made the remark under the influence of champagne and happiness), but the quote made the rounds and as
a result I couldn't ignore it. He said he didn't want to beat the Cardinals;
he wanted to humiliate us.

My reaction was the same as it always was going into a World Series:
Fine. Now watch this.

For the Cardinals, the story line was all too familiar. If it wasn't McLain
and the fence-bangers behind him, it was Mantle and the mighty Yankees
or Yaz and the Miracle Red Sox. Once again, we entered the World Series
as the *other team*, more or less—this time, despite the fact that we were
world champions and had made a shambles of the National League. Our
pitching was easily the best and deepest in the game, and the two guys at
the top of our batting order—Brock and Flood—could work the bases like
no other pair in baseball. Admittedly, we were lacking in the power department, pointed up by the fact that Cepeda, our only real slugger, led the
club with sixteen home runs and managed only seventy-three RBIs, and it
was this shortcoming that made us seem feeble in the media comparisons
with Detroit. The Tigers had a second baseman, Dick McAuliffe, with as
many home runs as Cepeda, and a gang of big guys who produced runs
in a manner of which we were not capable. Willie Horton, a burly left
fielder, had hit more than twice as many home runs (thirty-six) as our top
guy, and three others (Norm Cash, twenty-five homers; Bill Freehan,
twenty-five; and Jim Northrup, twenty-one) would have qualified as
cleanup hitters on the Cardinals. On top of all that muscle, Detroit's Hall
of Fame outfielder, Al Kaline, was available for the World Series after
spending much of the season on the disabled list.

To create a place for Kaline in the lineup, Detroit manager Mayo Smith
had made a controversial decision to move center fielder Mickey Stanley
to shortstop, a maneuver that weakened the Tigers defensively but magni-
fied their advantage in power. With Kaline as a part-time player, Detroit
had still blown away the American League by a dozen games, winning 103
as opposed to our 97. It was not only the hot team, but in a way the hot
town also, with gold records stacking up to the ceiling in the Motown recording studios. The whole city seemed determined to do something on a

scale big and grand enough to enable it to finally turn the page on the dev-astating riot that had ripped the place apart the summer before. We knew we were up against powerful forces.

For that reason, I was glad the series opened in St. Louis, where we could just concentrate on beating the Tigers—or so I thought. The day of the first game there was a civil rights rally of some sort under the arch, which was a fairly common thing in those times and no particular concern of mine until I arrived at the stadium and a television reporter inquired if he could ask me a couple of questions. I said, "Sure," presuming he was going to talk about Horton or Cash or McLain. Instead, he said, "What do you think of the black people demonstrating under the arch?" I stared at him for a second and said, "I don't give a fuck. I've got a ballgame to pitch." I don't believe the interview made the air.

Naturally, I had my own thoughts about race relations, and the guys on the ballclub knew in no uncertain terms what they were, but I didn't con-sider the pitcher's mound to be a political platform. In the order of prior-ities, I regarded myself as a ballplayer with a personal point of view, not an activist with a fastball. My idea of clubhouse ideology was the button I stuck over my locker before the series. It said: I'M NOT PREJUDICED. I HATE EVERYBODY.

The buildup before the first game not surprisingly centered around McLain and me. Although I was careful not to say it publicly, I believed deep down that I had the advantage against him because, for one thing, I knew a lot more about him than he knew about me (unless he had read my book, which I doubted, considering his schedule), and besides that, I didn't think *any* pitcher could beat me in the World Series. With all re-spect for his thirty-one victories—Lord knows I would have gladly traded my ERA record for nine more wins—I sure as hell didn't think Denny McLain could do it. It seemed to me that he had too many things on his mind to be able to summon up the kind of special, concentrated perfor-mance required to win—or at least to beat me—in the World Series. Even as he was clicking off all those victories during the regular season, McLain was as much a showman as a competitor. The biggest difference between us might have been illustrated by his reported confrontation with Mickey Mantle in Mantle's last at bat at Tiger Stadium before his retirement. In a very noble, theatric gesture, McLain had allegedly grooved a fastball for Mantle to blast out of the ballpark as a symbolic farewell, a home run that allowed Mantle to pass Jimmie Foxx for third place on the all-time list. There was something to be said for McLain's stage presence, if indeed he invited Mantle to take him deep, but I would have dropped my pants on the mound before I would have deferred to an opposing player that way. My method of showing respect for a guy like Mantle would have been to reach back for something extra with which to blow his ass away, if I could. But I guess that's why McLain was on the cover of *Time* and I was still borrowing money from insurance policies.

There was one other thing about McLain that put confidence in the back of my mind. Around July, when his push toward thirty wins was in high gear and dominating the national media, Roger Maris had said that McLain was not the guy on the Tigers we would have to worry about when we got to the World Series. Maris, of course, was familiar with the pitchers in the American League, and he was convinced that we would beat McLain but should be more concerned with Detroit's number two starter, a roundish lefthander named Mickey Lolich. Lefthanders in general gave us trouble, and Lolich had been hot late in the season with a good slider that seemed to get better the more he pitched.

McLain managed to hold us down for the first three innings of game one, but I still liked our chances. I found my groove early, striking out the side in the second inning on eleven pitches. With the competitive glare of the World Series, the personal challenge from McLain (humiliate, my ass), and the way the Tigers, like the Red Sox and Yankees before them, seemed to go after my sliders as if they were fastballs, I was in my element and working fast.

In the fourth, we put together some walks, singles, and stolen bases—a Cardinal kind of rally—for three runs, and in the top of the sixth, with the situation unchanged, Smith lifted McLain for a pinch hitter. By the time Brock homered in the seventh, the game, although not secure, was pretty much in hand. When the Tigers weren't striking out, they were hitting the ball harmlessly in the air. Shannon never once touched it at third—off the bat, anyway. Going into the ninth, it was still 4–0 and I had fourteen strike-outs, one short of the World Series record Sandy Koufax had set against the Yankees in 1963. I was not aware of that in the least, however, and scarcely cared. I just wanted the thing that McLain had gotten thirty-one times during the season.

Stanley led off the ninth with a single, Detroit's fifth hit, and that set me up against the heart of the Tigers' lineup—Kaline, Cash, and Horton. After Kaline went down swinging on a fastball, McCarver, for some peculiar reason—I couldn't imagine why in the hell he would do such a thing at such a moment—lumbered out to the mound pointing at something over my head. As usual, I tried not to pay any attention to him, and yelled, "Give me the goddamn ball!" I was in a rhythm and the only thing he was doing was breaking it. But he kept pointing and shouting something, and the crowd—the biggest ever to watch a sporting event in St. Louis at the time—was making a hell of a racket, so finally I had no choice but to turn around and see a message on the scoreboard that said I had tied Koufax's record. Still aggravated at the delay, I touched my cap, pawed at the dirt for a second, and screamed at McCarver once again to give me the goddamn baseball. Without wasting any more time, I then struck out Cash on a curve and on a two-and-two count to Horton threw a slider across the inside corner that he just looked at.

> *I can still see that last slider heading right for Horton's ribs and breaking over the plate. I bet he still thinks the ball hit him. Talk about a batter shuddering . . .*
> —TIM MCCARVER

I caused a little stir after the game when a writer asked me if I was surprised at my performance and I said I was never surprised at anything I did. I was showing a little attitude, making an investment in my next start, but what I said was essentially true. What *did* surprise me about that game was the way the Tigers talked of it afterwards.

> *Gibson was the best I ever saw in one game. He struck me out on the final pitch of the game because I never saw that pitch. Based*

*on what I saw from him—or* didn't *see—that day, if I had to*
*choose a pitcher for all time who had the best hard stuff, it would*
*be Bob Gibson.*    —WILLIE HORTON

I was unaccustomed to such lavish respect coming from the mouths of
my opponents. McLain said he was awed, Cash called me Superman, and
Kaline, the veteran of sixteen seasons, said, "I've never seen anyone pitch
like that before. Today he was the best I've ever seen. If he continues to
pitch like that, we can't beat him." We didn't talk like that in the National
League. Mike Shannon has told me he frequently runs into players from
that Tiger team, and they almost compulsively start talking about the first
game of the '68 World Series. I read a quote recently from Jim Northrup
where he commented that he had faced Nolan Ryan when Ryan pitched
no-hitters, but he had never been in a game in which a team—especially
a team of fastball hitters, which is what the Tigers were—was so completely overmatched. He said, "There wasn't any human being alive who
could have hit him that day." It warms my heart to hear that.

Horton and Cash were apparently not so overwhelmed that it threw
them off their games, however, because the next day they both hit home
runs against Nelson Briles. So, incredibly enough, did Mickey Lolich. It
was the first home run he had ever hit in the major leagues, suggesting
that Lolich might be attaining a higher level for the World Series. He had
been 10–2 during the last two months of the regular season, and when he
beat us 8–1 in the second game we knew that Maris had been right.

The series switched to TIGERTOWN, USA (as the billboards proclaimed)
for the third game, and I guess our guys figured that as long as they were
in Detroit they ought to play like the Tigers played. Kaline cracked a two-
run homer against Washburn in the third, but McCarver topped him with
a three-run shot in the fifth and Cepeda did the same in the seventh for a
7–3 victory.

I even hit a home run in the fourth game, and so did Brock. His was on
the second pitch of the day from McLain, who didn't throw many more.
We had little trouble with him and were ahead 4–0 in the third when rain
held us up for the second time. We had waited more than half an hour to
start the game, and this time I ate ice cream as we sat around the club-

house for more than an hour. My mood, which was marginal to begin with, got edgier with each minute that passed. The night before, I had been awakened at 2:00 A.M. by people pounding on the door yelling "Telegram!" Then the phone rang and somebody asked, "Is Denny McLain there?" Between the fans and the rain, I was in a pretty good frame of mind for pitching by the time the game resumed.

By then, McLain was gone—they said a sore shoulder had something to do with it (the arthritis in my elbow didn't feel too damn good, either, but a 4–0 lead beats the hell out of cortisone)—and Joe Sparma was in his place. Sparma was the guy off whom I connected in the fourth, becoming the first pitcher ever to hit two homers in the postseason (including Babe Ruth, who was a great World Series pitcher for the Red Sox in 1916 and 1918). Detroit's only run came on a homer by Northrup in the bottom of the fourth. I wasn't quite as sharp as I had been in game one, but ten of the Tigers went down on strikes and only two of them reached base after the fourth. The victory, 10–1, was my seventh straight in World Series competition, which was (and remains) a record—one of which I'm every bit as proud as the ERA record.

With the ringing victory in game four, we were up three games to one and looking good. We looked even better when Cepeda hit a three-run homer against Lolich in the first inning of game five (which was preceded by Jose Feliciano's controversial blues version of the national anthem, which I sort of liked but many people thought was shamefully disrespectful). With Briles on the mound and pitching well, we were within spitting distance of our third world championship in five years. The Tigers came back with two runs in the fourth (the second coming when Northrup's grounder struck a pebble and bounded over Javier's head), but we were rallying again in the fifth when Brock—who was single-handedly wrecking Detroit's pitching staff, clubbing the ball all over the park while tying his own World Series stolen base record from the year before as well as Eddie Collins's career record for Series steals—inexplicably elected not to slide while trying to score from second on a single to left by Javier. Horton's throw arrived at home plate just as Brock did, and Bill Freehan quickly slammed his glove into Lou's hip as Doug Harvey (who, of course, never made a mistake) called him out with a flair. In the column I was writing during the series for the New York *Daily News*, I defended Brock, noting that often, if the catcher has home plate effectively blocked, a runner can't reach it by sliding. I'm still reluctant to second-guess the greatest baserunner in Cardinal history on an instinct play such as that one, but in my heart I wish Lou had slid. Unfortunately, he's probably still remembered as much for that play as for his 3,023 hits and his 938 stolen bases and the heroics he produced routinely in that World Series and others. When I was asked to introduce Brock not long ago at an old-timers' game, I had all his records and accomplishments enumerated on a sheet in front of me, but instead of regurgitating the numbers I simply said, "And here's the guy who didn't slide." Everybody knew exactly who I was talking about. Lou takes that sort of thing in pretty good humor, but until the day he dies he will swear that he was right not to slide.

We were clinging to the 3–2 lead in the bottom of the seventh when Lolich, still operating in another dimension despite our early runs, singled with one out. Hoerner replaced Briles at that point, but McAuliffe singled, Stanley walked, and Kaline produced perhaps the biggest moment of his Hall of Fame career, a two-run single that gave Detroit a 4–3 lead. Cash drove in another run with a single, and Lolich kept us frustrated the rest of the way. We had two runners on base with one out in the ninth, but Lolich struck out Maris, who was pinch-hitting, and fielded Brock's slow roller for the final out.

I was surprised that Red had seen fit to start a seldom-used right-handed hitter, Ron Davis, in right field rather than Maris for the fifth game. What stands out in my memory, however, is the image of Davis after hearing he would be in the lineup. Instead of celebrating the opportunity to start a World Series game, he sat solemnly in front of his locker with his head hung low, as if he dreaded the assignment. Perhaps he was only psyching himself up in his own way, but at the time I didn't think so. On the contrary, I was concerned that he seemed apprehensive about taking the field. I don't mention this now for the purpose of blaming what happened on Ron Davis, but because, in retrospect, it might be that Davis's reaction was symptomatic of an attitude that was overtaking the ballclub. Maybe, with two world championships under our belt and a third there for the taking, we adopted the approach that the 1968 series was ours to *lose*, not to win.

That's certainly the way we played in game six, back in St. Louis. Mayo Smith had decided that Lolich would pitch the seventh game, if there was one, which freed up McLain—rested and ready after an abbreviated workout in game four and a shot of cortisone—to start the sixth game. We reached him for nine hits but only one run this time. He proved to be a much better pitcher with a lead to work with—especially one the size that the Tigers built for him. They scored twice in the second and then ten damn times in the third, four of them on a grand slam by Northrup. We went through seven pitchers and they whipped us good, 13–1.

It was down to me and Lolich in game seven. I thrived on this sort of situation—to me, it was the whole reason for being an athlete—and there was no sense of panic on the club even after the disasters of games five and six. In fact, McCarver recently commented that, after thinking about the 1968 series for twenty-five years, he has come to believe that the Cardinals may have been overconfident in the knowledge that no matter what happened in games five and six, I would be on the mound for game seven. It's a dangerous thing to let another team gain momentum, and whatever our level of confidence, Lolich and the Tigers had given us plenty of cause to respect them in a one-game showdown.

Through the early innings of the seventh game, Lolich eluded trouble with smarts and guts. He was not a finely tuned athlete (the fact that he now runs a doughnut shop is not inappropriate) and I had no doubt that he was dog-tired after pitching nine innings three days earlier. I firmly believed that if I could hold the Tigers in check for a while, we would get to Lolich by the sixth or seventh. In the second inning I broke Koufax's series record with my thirty-second strikeout, and by the sixth had retired twenty of the twenty-one batters I had faced. Things were going pretty much as planned, but it was high time to do something about Lolich.

He set us down again in the sixth, and there was still no score in the top of the seventh. I had to navigate one more time through the fat part of Detroit's lineup and with two outs in the seventh was very careful not to give Norm Cash a pitch he could pull out of the park. Instead, he singled to right. Horton was another power hitter whom I wanted to keep in the stadium, and he bounced a single to left. That meant I had to retire Northrup, who had given me more trouble than any other Tiger. Knowing that the first pitch would be a strike, he went after it and hit it hard to center field. As soon as the ball left the bat, I was confident that Flood would track it down, as he had done on so many similar occasions over the years. This time, though, Curt's first step was toward the infield, and when he realized he had underestimated the hit, he turned sharply and for a split second lost his footing on the wet grass. By then, it was too late to catch up with the ball, which bounced to the wall for a triple. The two runs that scored seemed to me like two thousand. Freehan followed with a double to make it three.

As we returned to the dugout, each of us struggling inside to keep our spirits alive, Flood stepped in next to me and said, "I'm sorry. It was my fault." I said, "Like hell. It was nobody's fault." What is often forgotten about that play is the fact that Northrup hit the damn ball four hundred feet.

I remain grateful to Schoendienst for sticking with me. The obvious thing would have been to pinch-hit for me in the eighth inning, and Red's decision to leave me in the game had more to do with consideration than strategy, which is a rare thing in baseball. The Tigers scored another run in the ninth on singles and in the bottom of the inning Shannon homered with two outs to put us on the board, at least, but one batter later Lolich had beaten me. Regardless of what happened in the seventh, he was the better pitcher that day. That's not an attempt to be gracious; it's just a fact that I have no trouble living with.

Naturally, the reporters in the clubhouse after the game wanted to know, first off, if I thought Flood should have caught Northrup's ball. I answered that I thought he was *going* to catch it because he was Curt Flood, but that's not the same as saying he *should* have caught it. Before the game, I'd walked out to center field and noticed how difficult it was to pick out the ball in all the white shirts behind the screen. "If Curt Flood can't catch that ball," I said, "nobody can. I'm certainly not going to stand here and blame the best center fielder in the business. Why couldn't we score any runs off that lefthander? That's the reason we lost." I also reminded the writers of all the games Flood had saved over the years for me and every other pitcher on the staff. Nevertheless, in the papers the next morning my buddy took a lot of heat that he shouldn't have had to take.

A week later, I was in an airport somewhere when an old lady recognized me and walked up to say something. I assumed she was going to ask for an autograph or maybe congratulate me for my season or my World Series records. Instead, she asked me if I still spoke to Curt Flood. I said, "Lady, how can you ask that?"

The irritating absurdity of her question—and the most regrettable aspect of the fact that Flood is still held accountable by many people for what happened in the seventh game—lies in the reality that Curt Flood was more than my best friend on the ballclub. To me, he personified what the Cardinals were all about. As a man and teammate, he was smart, funny, sensitive, and most of all unique. As a ballplayer, he was resourceful, dedicated, and very, very good. Hell, the little guy was us, through and through.

# CHAPTER X

Things were never the same again.

As soon as the 1968 season was over, the great thinkers of baseball, in their infinite wisdom, started screwing around with the game on the premise that the only way to fix it—the implication being that good pitching, as demonstrated so conspicuously in 1968, was inherently a *problem*—was to manipulate conditions in a way that would offer new hope to hitters. Some have called these changes the Gibson Rules in light of the fact that it was my 1.12 ERA that caused so much of the panic. I respectfully decline the honor, thank you. I will accept no responsibility for what baseball did to itself.

The most publicized change was the lowering of the pitcher's mound from fifteen inches to ten, which represented the first major alteration in the physical dimensions of baseball since 1921, when it was still adjusting to Ruth. Among all the modifications, though, that one probably had the least effect. It affected *me* the least, anyway, because, unlike other pitchers, I relied very little on an overhanded curveball. Those who did, such as Nelson Briles, found that they were less able to bring down the curveball from on high and drop it vertically through most of a batter's latitudes. My fast slider wasn't bothered much.

My control, on the other hand, was bothered plenty, but not by the height of the mound. They shrank the damn strike zone. In 1969, I would walk half again as many batters per inning as I had the two previous seasons, and I can promise that my location wasn't that different. I had been a high-strike pitcher, and suddenly there was no such thing as a high strike. Technically, the upper limit of the strike zone was lowered from the armpit (originally, it was the shoulder) to around the letters, but the umpires seldom called a strike at the letters. After a while, they never did. The strike zone hasn't officially been changed since 1969, but unofficially it has been much abused. These days, a pitcher is lucky to get a call at the navel.

Although an adjustment at one extremity would have more than sufficiently changed the parameters of the strike zone, baseball went a step further by also pulling it up over the bottom of the knee, thereby managing to simultaneously take away the northernmost and southernmost pitcher's pitches. Even this was apparently not enough to restore the balance, however. A pitcher might still have been able to work inside-out, as I had traditionally done, but the corners of the plate were also more conservatively defined after 1968. The strike was under siege from all sides.

Having lowered the mound and made a mockery of the strike zone, baseball had one more finger to cut off in the systematic dismemberment of its pitchers. Worst of all the changes, in my estimation, was the way in which umpires began warning us for any delivery with an inside agenda. You can imagine where I fit into that scheme. The commissioner's office was reaching straight into my pocket. I complained about all the revised rules—not to mention the new and improved (batter-friendly) ball we had to toss up there—to Bob Broeg, the *Post-Dispatch* sports editor, and he said, "Goddamn it, Gibby, you're changing the game. You're making it like hockey. It isn't fun anymore." My point of view was somewhat different.

I suppose everybody has his own definition of "the good old days." For me, they ended when the curtain was drawn on 1968. Until then, pitchers and hitters competed fearfully in a tradition-rich environment of mutual ill will, and ballplayers in general had their manhood intact. But baseball wasn't content with that stimulating arrangement. Nobody in baseball, it seemed, was content with the way things were.

Obviously the Cardinals weren't. Among the regrettable turns that baseball took around that time, there was the unpleasant business of what the Cardinals were starting to do to themselves.

We could see it coming at the end of '68. After our lead in the pennant race had maxed out at fourteen or fifteen games, we inevitably dropped a few, which brought the Giants within nine at the end. There was never any doubt whatsoever about whether we would win the thing, but for some reason it became fashionable in the St. Louis media to refer to us as "fat cats." Naturally, when we squandered the two-game lead and lost the World Series, the writers and wise guys declared that they could see it coming all along—that we had become too complacent, too comfortable, too concerned with money and *clothes*, believe it or not.

This theme was helped along by the fact that the major-league players' union, just starting to emerge as a viable bargaining agent, was recommending that we go out on strike during spring training of 1969. As player representative of the Cardinals, I was interviewed about the potential strike by Johnny Carson on *The Tonight Show*, effectively establishing me (who, after coming to new terms with Bing Devine, was making the highest salary on the club at $125,000) as the fattest of the Cardinal cats.

It was curious to me and the other players that there didn't seem to be much parallel sentiment concerning the greed of the owners, despite the fact that they had just signed a new television contract that raised their network revenues from half a million dollars to seventeen million. At the same time, the owners were attempting to reduce the players' percentage of the TV money. All we wanted was the same old percentage we had been getting for years.

This is what I explained on the Carson show. It is also what apparently ticked off Gussie Busch. Not long after I had returned to St. Petersburg from New York, Mr. Busch called a public team meeting at the training compound. It was unusual for players to meet with the owner, and unprecedented—not to mention discomfiting—to do it with reporters in at-

tendance. Busch mounted the soapbox and lectured us on the inflated salaries we were making and the public responsibilities that went along with
the territory. He even made a reference to players talking about the owners on national television. When he was finished, he handed out copies of
his speech to the press. It was all very strange. The writers immediately
asked us what we made of the meeting, but we didn't really know yet.

We had a better idea of how to interpret Busch's message on March 17,
when the Cardinals traded our spiritual leader, Orlando Cepeda. It wasn't
the *deal* that jolted us so much—in return we received Joe Torre from the
Braves, a hitter with excellent credentials—but the very idea that management was messing in a major way with a club that had run away with two
straight pennants. Trading Cepeda signaled to us, loud and clear, that
things would no longer be the same around the Cardinal clubhouse. The
front office apparently had very little regard for what the players considered to be the special character of the ballclub.

It turned out that Joe Torre became one of my best friends in the
world—he still is—and he produced extremely well for us, but it was
nonetheless impossible not to miss a guy like Cepeda. I believe strongly
that Cha-Cha ought to be in the Hall of Fame because his numbers, which
he compiled despite knees of spaghetti, put him in the ballpark, and they
represented only a small part of his value as a teammate. Nobody could
keep a ballclub loose like Cepeda. I'll always see him up on that money
trunk, leading cheers in the clubhouse, but my last memory of Cepeda as
a Cardinal was made during a tour of Japan the team took after the 1968
season. We were at a cabaret in Sapporo, the kind of place where the gei-
sha girls would sit with the men whether or not their wives were there,
which many of ours were. Orlando had gone off to the bathroom, and a
minute later he came running back, his eyes as big as compact discs, mo-
tioning for us to come and see something. Half the ballclub followed him,
and when we got to the bathroom there was a Japanese woman squatting
on the stool next to Cha-Cha's. Naturally, we couldn't witness this specta-
cle in polite silence. It was not a proud moment for the Cardinals, but it
was an unforgettable one.

Cepeda was the only starting player to be traded that season (Maris, don't forget, had retired after the 1968 World Series), but we all sensed that a breakup was coming—or would come, if we didn't win at least another pennant. Of course, we expected to do that.

Actually, it figured to be easier than usual because the leagues had split into divisions for the 1969 season. In order to take advantage of our rivalry with the Cubs and to better balance the divisions, we were placed in the East along with Chicago, the Mets, the Phillies, the Pirates, and the expansion Montreal Expos. Of that group, it seemed that only the Cubs had a legitimate chance of stopping us.

One of the teams that we hadn't counted on stopping us was us. It was a Murphy's Law kind of season for the Cardinals, beginning in spring training, when our new right fielder, former Cincinnati star Vada Pinson, whom we had acquired for Bobby Tolan and on whom we were heavily depending for offensive spunk and veteran leadership, caught his foot under a fence in Bradenton and broke his ankle. (In Cincinnati, meanwhile, Tolan produced precisely the kind of numbers we had hoped for from Pinson, eventually interrupting Brock's string of four straight stolen base titles.)

Pinson's injury put a crimp in our offense, but that alone did not justify our inability to score runs. Everywhere else in the league, hitting was up in 1969—way up. The other nine teams improved their scoring by an average of 139 runs from the Year of the Pitcher. We improved ours by twelve. I was pitching well—not as well as 1968, of course, but damn well—and so was Carlton, but at the plate the Cardinals were still stuck in 1968.

*On days when he wasn't pitching, Gibson used to sit on the bench and we'd fall behind 3–0 or so and he'd leave saying, "I'm sick of you guys! I'm out of here!" He'd go sit in the clubhouse for a few innings, but if we happened to score two or three runs, he'd be right back there yelling, "Yeah, yeah, let's go!"*
—JOE TORRE

Torre (in addition to being so damn congenial that it really pissed me off) came up big for us in his first year with the club, driving in 101 runs, but nobody else drove in seventy. On the whole, our offense was so lame (we only outscored the Expos by thirteen runs) that I started stealing bases in 1969 just to get something going. I had five that year, the most in my career—not bad for a thirty-three-year-old man, and only forty-eight behind Brock, who led the league.

On one of my slides, though, I jammed my knee, which in turn put more stress on my shoulder, which ached for reasons that may have had to do with the new mound elevation. Everything on me seemed to hurt in 1969—partly because of the condition of my body and partly because we were so damn far out of the race most of the year. Victory is one of the best painkillers I've ever come across, and we'd been taking large doses of it in recent seasons. Bob Bauman, our trainer, said around 1969 that "there were times in the last couple of years you wouldn't have given two cents for Gibson's arm. He has the highest threshold of pain I've ever seen in an athlete." The fear of Josh had a lot to do with it, too.

The most consistently troublesome health problem I had in the late sixties was an arthritic elbow not unlike Sandy Koufax's. He once commented that my elbow was probably as bad as his, but I don't think it was. I do think, though, that I was more determined to stay on the mound than any other pitcher. In fact, I went well over a season (from late 1967 to early 1969) without being taken out of a game in mid-inning, the streak finally ending when Ferguson Jenkins and I went the tenth inning of a game tied 1–1 and Billy Williams and Ron Santo did me in with a tiebreaking double and a single.

I hated losing to the Cubs—mostly because Ernie Banks was always mouthing off about it when we did. They were the hot team for the first half of the season, but when New York made a run at them I said publicly that if we couldn't win the pennant, I hoped the Mets would. There didn't seem to be much chance of that—the Mets had never won *anything*, and in fact had never been higher than ninth place in the standings—but there was something inexplicable about their 1969 team. Near the end of June, we played them a Sunday doubleheader at Shea Stadium, and a team record fifty-eight thousand people showed up. In the first game we were beaten by a rookie pitcher named Gary Gentry, the third outstanding rookie they had added to their staff in three years, following Tom Seaver and Jerry Koosman. Koosman and our big young righthander, Mike

Torrez, hooked up in a 1–0 second game that the Mets secured when a reserve outfielder named Rod Gaspar threw out Brock at the plate in the eighth inning. Their Rod Gaspars kept winning games for them, and there was a general feeling that somehow the Mets might have to be reckoned with before the season was out.

Even so, the Cubs were still about five games ahead of them at the all-star break and we were close enough to hold out hope for the second half of the season. I made the all-star team again—although I wasn't quite in 1968 form, I was proud of my work and resented the comparisons to the year before—and Carlton was pitching so well that Red Schoendienst named him the National League's starting pitcher. The game was held in Washington that year, and was preceded by a reception and dinner at the White House, where I met Jackie Robinson for the first time while he and I were waiting in a long line to shake hands with President Nixon and Vice President Spiro Agnew, both of whom Robinson had strongly criticized during the 1968 campaign. After a while, we both agreed that we could make better use of our time and stepped out of the line. At the dinner, Jackie and I found ourselves on either side of Attorney General John Mitchell and managed to engage him in a discussion on race relations. Mitchell told us to rest assured that the administration was "developing a policy" to deal with the urban unrest that was overtaking the country, but said that the plan was mostly undercover and they didn't want people to know that the government was operating in the cities. I told him that sounded like bullshit. Jackie and I further argued that whatever policy the Republicans had in mind for the cities no doubt had more to do with protecting the white interests than with helping the people in the black neighborhoods, but I don't think we got the point across.

Sometimes it seems as though the only place a ballplayer can make a point is on the ball field, which the National League team did in the All-Star Game with comparative ease. By the time I pitched the fourth inning, following Carlton's three, Willie McCovey had already homered twice and Johnny Bench once to reinforce our dominance over the American League all-stars. The victory, by the score of 9–3, was our seventh in a row.

We were due to renew the season by playing the Giants in St. Louis and as a result I traveled back with McCovey and Willie Mays. I really hadn't mellowed much on my policy of staying away from players on opposing teams, but I had been playing all-star games with Mays and McCovey for most of the decade and by this time it seemed sort of silly to pretend like we didn't know each other. So I was sitting with them at the airport lounge in Washington when a fan walked over and offered to buy drinks for our table. Mays said no, but the fan persisted, as fans tend to do when they are trying to impress their friends. When the guy was back at his own table he was still offering to buy us drinks, so finally Mays looked quietly at Willie and me and said, "I gotta show him." He then called for the waiter and ordered two bottles of Dom Pérignon. When the guy received the bill, he was shocked. But at least he was able to sound like a big shot when he told everybody he bought two bottles of Dom Pérignon for Willie Mays, Willie McCovey, and Bob Gibson.

For the Cardinals, the second half of the season was painfully similar to the first. We could make no headway on the Cubs, who were having a memorable summer, but the Mets, on the other hand, kept hanging around on good pitching and who-knows-what. The strange part of it was that *our* pitching was actually better than the Mets'. As a staff, we led the league in earned run average on the basis of Carlton's (2.17) and mine (2.18), which were second and third in the individual rankings behind Marichal (2.10). But Carlton remained short of twenty victories and I had to put on my customary late-season surge to get close. The Mets, meanwhile, outscored us by nearly forty runs despite the fact that they had no players with eighty RBIs, only one (Tommie Agee) with as many as fifteen home runs, only one (Cleon Jones) with a .300 average, and only two (Agee and Jones) with more than 400 at bats.

Midway through the second half of the season I became the third pitcher (Walter Johnson and Rube Waddell being the others) to strike out two hundred batters in seven different years. My total was no doubt enhanced by the fact that I pitched into extra innings nine times in 1969, accounting for my career high of 314 innings pitched. It amuses me these days when I hear a 225-inning pitcher referred to as a "workhorse."

But I lost six of those nine extra-inning games, and consequently had to chase twenty victories down to the wire. Red said that it was in the interest of maximizing my starts in pursuit of twenty wins that he pitched me on

three days' rest against the Cubs in the final game of a mid-September series. By then, the Mets had overtaken Chicago in an incredible rush, and
despite Red's efforts at political correctness in the pennant race, I was less
gracious when it came to explaining the situation, making it known that I
was pitching against the Cubs because I wanted to beat them. My opponent was Ken Holtzman, and he fell 2–1. If I had waited to take my regular
turn, I would have pitched the next day against the Mets.

Instead, Carlton stepped up to take my turn against the Mets and set a
major-league record at the time by striking out nineteen of them, breaking
a mark set by Bob Feller, Sandy Koufax, and Don Wilson. It was one of the
most remarkable evenings of baseball I ever witnessed. Carlton was overpowering with both his fastball and slider, and nobody could touch him
with the exception of a burly outfielder named Ron Swoboda. Early in the
game, Swoboda hit a two-run homer, and late in the game, after we had
taken a 3–2 lead, he hit another one in the same spot to beat Carlton 4–3.
If the Mets could win that night, they could win any night.

We saw a lot of New York in the final weeks of the season. More often
than not, I hooked up with Tom Seaver, who won twenty-five games and
the Cy Young award that season. In St. Louis, I beat him 3–1 after working
out of a bases-loaded jam in the ninth, but in our last series at Shea Stadium he returned the favor. The Mets clinched the pennant that week by
sweeping us three games, beating me, Briles, and Carlton. Donn
Clendenon hit a three-run homer and Ed Charles a two-run homer against
Carlton in the first inning of the clincher, and their rookie, Gary Gentry,
shut us out. The Mets ended up winning the pennant by eight games. We
were impressed and not at all surprised when they blew past the Braves in
the playoffs and the Orioles in the World Series. Like Neil Armstrong and
the *Apollo 11* crew that walked on the moon that summer—and like Joe
Namath and the New York Jets that winter—the Mets were on a mission.

My personal mission, as always, was to win twenty games, and to do so
I had to get number twenty—and avoid my fourteenth defeat—on the last
game of the season, by which time we were thirteen games out of first
place. I gave up an unearned run early in the afternoon and, despite everybody's eagerness to get the damn season over with, pressed on with a 1–1
game into the twelfth inning, when we finally busted through on a bases-

loaded walk. It was my fourth season with twenty wins and no doubt the most difficult. With his outstanding 2.17 ERA, Carlton could win only seventeen games.

Our fourth-place finish in the six-team division (we beat out only the Phillies and the expansion Expos) naturally rallied our critics, who were persuaded that the club ought to be broken up. This was a point of view that the Cardinal management—specifically, August Busch, who deeply begrudged the comparatively high salaries many of us were making—was more than happy to accommodate.

The big deal came down before the World Series even started. It involved Flood, who had fallen under .300 in 1969 for only the second time in seven seasons; McCarver, who, although his arm was beginning to weaken, had been a stalwart catcher for the same period of time; Joe Hoerner, our top reliever; and a utility outfielder named Byron Browne. They were traded to the Phillies for Dick Allen, whose bat I regarded as perhaps the most vicious in baseball; Cookie Rojas, a second baseman who could hit a little; and a journeyman right-handed pitcher named Jerry Johnson. I was enthusiastic about the idea of acquiring Allen—Lord knows how much we needed his power—was happy to have Rojas on our side, and was sickened by the thought of Flood and McCarver leaving us. Those two guys struck right at the heart of what the Cardinals had been all about for the past decade. I loved the Cardinals, was proud to be one, and recognized that Curt Flood and Tim McCarver were two of the biggest reasons why. With them gone, being a Cardinal would never mean quite the same thing.

Depressed as I was over the trade, however, I understood that it was a fact of life in baseball. I'd always dreaded being traded myself, especially early in my career—the Solly Hemus years—when I was frequently rumored to be involved in one deal or another, often with Joe Cunningham. But there was nothing a player could do about it. Baseball's reserve clause made him the property of the ballclub to which he was under contract, and every contract contained a clause stipulating that the employer had the right to transfer it to another franchise.

I talked often with Flood after the deal was made. He was extremely upset about it for many reasons. He had started a couple of successful businesses in St. Louis, an art studio and a photography studio serving high schools, and also operated a nightclub. In addition, he had many friends in town, not the least of whom were his teammates. At the age of thirty-one, and as a twelve-year veteran of the ballclub, he simply didn't want to go anywhere else. That was understandable, of course, but what I *didn't* understand at first were remarks Curt was making about *not accepting* the trade. I didn't see that as an option, but Curt did. He believed that it was his constitutional right as an American citizen to resist any attempt to treat him as anything less.

In a Christmas Eve letter to baseball's new commissioner, Bowie Kuhn, Curt wrote exactly that. By so doing, he announced to baseball that he was not going to Philadelphia no matter what the Phillies and Cardinals thought. He also informed the commissioner that he was not a piece of property to be bought, sold, and traded. Kuhn wrote him back, asking what his specific grievance was. Apparently, being treated like a side of beef was not something that baseball perceived as a problem.

Although I had many questions about Curt's course of action, I knew exactly where he was coming from and I suspected I knew exactly where he was headed. I knew that there would be no changing his mind once he had made it up, but privately I thought to myself, "Jesus, Curt, what are you doing?"

The next step was inevitable. My best friend in baseball sued the game.

> *When I look back on the person I was in 1969, I know that person had to do what he did. When I look back on that man, I see someone who was a child of the sixties. I spent most of my early years in the Oakland-Berkeley area, and there was an incredible amount going on. Huey Newton, the Black Panthers, Vietnam. The assassinations. It was all a critical part of my life.*
>
> *You have to do what you feel is right for you. I can look my God in the eye, and can look at some of the things that happened as the closed thinking of the time. One of the ways, for instance, that management would bind players to them in those years would be through personal loans and advances on next season's salaries. What I mean is that players would come in to the owners after the*

*season had ended and need money. The owner would say, Okay,*
*and begin advancing the player money from next season's salary.*
*By the time the following season began, that player would be in-*
*debted, literally, to that owner. I always likened it to a plantation*
*owner, allowing his players to play for him in the same way that*
*the plantation owner allowed the sharecropper to work his land*
*while at the same time keeping him deep in debt and constantly*
*beholden. I couldn't stand to be treated that way. When I was*
*traded, it drove me up a wall.*

—CURT FLOOD

In the suit, Flood asked for changes in baseball's reserve clause and $1.4 million in damages. From talking to his lawyers and the new head of the players' union, Marvin Miller, he knew that his chances to win the suit were remote, but nothing could deter Curt. By the time players reported to spring training in 1970, it was obvious that he would not be playing ball that year. To compensate his loss to the Phillies, the Cardinals sent them Willie Montanez, a promising young first baseman. Meanwhile, as Flood's suit made the judicial circuit, Curt waited it out in Copenhagen, Denmark. I received long, philosophical letters from him every now and then. I missed him.

At the ballpark, I missed Flood in center field, where his remarkable catches would often bring his cynical teammates to the top step of the dugout in applause. But I also missed his discussions about the latest works of James Baldwin, and I missed his plays on words. (When, for instance, he took his place in the outfield between Stan Musial and Minnie Minoso, he referred to the alignment as Old Taylor and Ancient Age with a little Squirt for a chaser.) I especially missed him as a roommate. By that time, Curt and I understood each other so well that we no longer had to talk to communicate, as illustrated by the time a television evangelist was carrying on one Sunday morning as we were getting our things together to leave for the ballpark and suddenly the preacher said, "If you believe, place your hands on the TV!" Without uttering a word or even breaking stride, Curt and I both walked over to the television, placed our hands on it, then turned and left the room.

(In the interest of agitating my friend, and since he has been so thoughtful to pass along his observations about sharing accommodations with me on the road, I ought to also mention the time we checked into a hotel on the same day that the Cincinnati Reds checked out. While we were putting our things away, Flood picked up a little directory that was lying on the bureau and as he started to flip through it he let out a yell. "Hey! he screamed. "Somebody's got my phone book!" It seemed that one of our acquaintances on the Reds had an amazing number of friends and associates in common with my roomie.)

As close as Curt and I were, we generally went our separate ways at night, but if I shopped or lunched on the road before a ballgame, it was often with him, and it was often eventful. We were eating at a little place across from the Warwick Hotel in Philadelphia one bright afternoon when Curt suddenly leaned forward and whispered, "The guy in the next booth thinks you're Ray Charles." I happened to be wearing sunglasses, and we couldn't resist playing out the scene. When we finished our sandwiches, I stood up and stumbled around a little while Curt found my wallet for me, then took my arm to lead me out. As we left, we could hear one of the guys telling the other, "See, I told you it was Ray Charles!"

As his legal battle thrashed on toward the Supreme Court, Flood returned from Copenhagen in 1971 to accept an offer to play with the Washington Senators. Following a year away from baseball, however, neither his heart nor his reflexes served him in the tradition to which he was accustomed, and he gave up the charade after about a dozen regrettable games. (It couldn't be easy to play under those conditions. Curt showed up at his locker one day to find a black funeral wreath placed inside it—a scary thing, considering that whoever put it there must have had free access to the clubhouse and lockers.) If Flood's actions had been about money, he certainly would have played out his $110,000 contract with the Senators, but it was strictly a principle thing with Curt. That's what made his eventual defeat so disappointing.

When the Supreme Court decision was rendered in 1972, it expressed sympathy for Flood's cause to the extent that it recognized baseball's reserve clause as an aberration in the American system, but it stopped short of overturning it, and in fact upheld the antitrust exemption that baseball had been granted. With that, Curt was effectively out of options and out of luck. To get away—far away—he moved to Barcelona and then the Mediterranean island of Majorca, where he bought a red Porsche and a little tavern called the Rustic Inn. He kept the inn five years, until the civil police busted in one day and ripped his liquor license off the wall. Flood resettled in Andorra for a while and finally returned to the States to find that free agency was a fact of life in the major leagues. Pitchers Andy Messersmith and Dave McNally had again challenged the reserve clause and in 1976 a federal arbitrator, Peter Seitz, finally upheld the players' individual bargaining rights. The age of million-dollar contracts had dawned in the absence of the man who had carried the battle on his back and borne the wounds in his soul.

> *I look back on what I did as a contribution. I look back on what I did and realize that I derived a personal gain, too. I receive a pension from major-league baseball. I don't sweep the clubhouse for a living, and I'm happy. I know what we did then contributed to the development of one of the strongest labor unions in the entire society. I'm satisfied that the players' association has become as powerful as it has, but I have to note also that its calculated self-serving attitude is alarming. They have no sense of history whatsoever.* —CURT FLOOD

Because he is a talented and resourceful man, Flood has done fine in his life after baseball. Not as fine, though, as so many of the multimillion-dollar modern outfielders who couldn't carry his glove. Curt has too much dignity to say it outright, but the fact is that the modern player has gotten fat from the efforts of Curt Flood and has returned him no gratitude or any other form of appreciation. I've often thought of what an appropriate and decent thing it would be if every player in the major leagues turned over 1 percent of his paycheck just one time to Curt Flood. They certainly owe him that much and more. Failing that, which I know is implausible, I can't understand for the life of me why Flood has not been offered a job with the players' association. As far as I'm concerned, he *invented* the players' association.

———

By 1970, only Brock, Javier, and Maxvill remained as regulars from the Cardinal teams that had won three pennants and two world championships. We were a different bunch almost entirely and the record showed that we desperately missed the old guys.

In a way, this is an odd case to make, because we *scored* a lot more with the 1970 lineup. Torre continued to be an excellent addition, driving in a hundred runs for the second year in a row, and I truly loved having Dick Allen on our side. It seemed like nearly every time he hit a home run—and he hit thirty-four of them, a massive total for our ballclub—it won a game for me, 2–1.

> *Opening Day that year, against Montreal, I hit a home run to tie*
> *the game in the eighth and Gibson beat them 7–2 when we rallied*
> *in the ninth. He struck out the side in the bottom of the eighth and*
> *I don't think they even got a foul ball. It was amazing.*
> —DICK ALLEN

But as a team we just couldn't seem to get it together. In fact, despite all the new offense, we actually finished with a worse record than we had in 1969, falling ten games under .500 and thirteen behind the division champion Pirates. We were so bad that I was booed during a game in which the Giants scored nine runs against me in the first inning. It was the first time I had ever been booed in St. Louis, where, I thought, the fans were too sophisticated for that sort of thing. A player expected it in New York or Philadelphia, but St. Louis fans seem to be better educated in the fine points of the game and usually understand when a player is giving his best effort. I tipped my hat to the boos and they changed to cheers, but that didn't wash the echo out of my ears. It stung badly.

As I look back on it now, it seems that our deterioration as a ballclub traced back to the fact that the Cardinals, as an organization, were simply not willing or prepared to keep up with the times. Our problems started during the player strike of 1969—the meeting with Gussie Busch is as defining a moment as any—and deepened as the players gained more and more independence. The unfortunate aspect of it, to me, is the fact that we were a group of guys who could *handle* independence. Long before independence had become the fashion in baseball, the Cardinals—guys like White and McCarver and Flood and myself—had made an art of it. I've tried to understand the club's position, and to an extent I can: Going back to the first time Branch Rickey ran the club, the St. Louis organization had developed a tradition of trading players who were just beginning to decline, a practice that in general had proven to be successful. The point could certainly be made that McCarver and Flood had begun to decline, but still and all I won't surrender the belief—and they won't—that we had at least one more pennant in us.

> *I think, to a man, all of us who were on that Cardinal team were very disappointed that we weren't given an opportunity to come back and play for the championship again in 1970. It was a dissolution of a team overnight. If you take it another two years down the line and look at what happened when the Cardinals traded Steve Carlton, you can see that Mr. Busch stood on principle, and in the long term he was thousand-dollars wise and million-dollars foolish. There's no good estimate of how many millions of dollars he lost because he traded Carlton away. The truth of the story is that we won three National League championships in five years. We won two World Series. We were a group with tremendous professional pride. And all of that was broken up.*
> —TIM MCCARVER

The Cardinal management, on the other hand, could easily argue that our dropoff in 1970 was a matter of the club being betrayed by its pitchers. After the customary slow start (at one point, after the Giants debacle, my ERA was over 5.00 and people were starting to whisper that I might be at the end of the trail), I had a big year, leading the league with twenty-three wins and claiming my second Cy Young award, but the staff in general took the summer off. Carlton led the league in losses with nineteen,

Briles's earned run average (the lowered mound made things very difficult for him) was over 6.00, and nobody in our bullpen had ten saves. For a change, our offense was actually better than our defense in 1970.

I suppose that Bing Devine and everybody else in the organization had grown tired of watching the Cardinals hit with Nerf bats, and we were remade with a premium on muscle. In the absence of McCarver, Torre shared the catching that year with a highly regarded switch-hitting rookie from Michigan, Ted Simmons. When he wasn't catching, Torre played third, and when Torre was catching, Allen held down third, switching between there and first base, which he shared with Joe Hague. I didn't care where Allen played as long as he played. Because of various injuries, he came to bat only 459 times that year, but his thirty-four homers were the most anybody ever hit for the Cardinals as long as I was with them.

I didn't care, either, where Allen went when the ballgame was over, but everybody else in town seemed to be preoccupied with his social habits. That was a tradition St. Louis apparently inherited from Philadelphia, where nobody had been willing to leave him the hell alone. When he came over to the Cardinals, I made it my job to keep the press off his ass. (If anybody was going to rag on Allen, I wanted to be the one to do it. When I saw a clipping, for instance, that listed him and Torre among the five most overrated players in the game, I taped copies to both of their lockers with the message, "Two out of five ain't bad.") If I saw a couple of writers heading in Allen's direction (they preferred not to approach him *alone*), I'd start agitating them so they'd come over and give me a hard time instead of him. For whatever reason, Dick Allen was the kind of guy in whose affairs everyone was inclined to meddle. He wasn't your all-American boy, by any means, and he did some things—mainly drinking—that people frowned on, but I maintain that if he had been white, he would have been considered merely a free spirit. As a black man who did as he pleased and guarded his privacy, he was instead regarded as a troublemaker. I'm not here to vouch for Dick Allen's character because I frankly didn't know what he did with his free time and I didn't want to know. I didn't try to run with him because I knew I couldn't keep up. But as a teammate, I can honestly say that I was crazy about the guy. He swung that big ol' forty-two-ounce bat like nobody I'd ever played with, and when he lit into a fastball, shit happened. That's all I cared about. He was the only thing that made the loss of Curt Flood a little easier to stomach.

Replacing Flood in the outfield was a different matter. A Cuban named Jose Cardenal did a decent job of it for a season and ultimately a talented Puerto Rican named Jose Cruz got a chance to win the center-field job, but Brock never again had a man of Flood's caliber at his side and the Cardinal outfield has never, to this day, regained the stability it had in the sixties. There have been too many Vic Davalillos.

This is not a knock on Davalillo, because he was a skillful veteran, a popular teammate, and in 1970 the best pinch hitter in the National League. He was not, however, a stabilizing influence on the ballclub. To wit, there was the day in Chicago when his friends had to bring him directly to the ballpark after a long night of festivities. When we saw the condition Davalillo was in, we dressed him, pulled him up the dugout steps (toes dragging all the way), and took him to the bullpen where we could cover him with warm-up jackets. He sat there not bothering anybody, but then, late in the game, a situation developed where Red needed his best pinch hitter. He told Dick Sisler to send for Davalillo, and Sisler, who unlike Red knew the situation, stammered, "N-n-o, Red, you you you don't want Davalillo. You you you want Rojas?"

"No, I want Davalillo!"

"You you you want Taylor?"

"No, goddamn it, I want Davalillo!"

Well, Davalillo, who was a left-handed hitter, had a habit of picking up his right foot when he swung the bat, and when he picked up his foot to swing at the first pitch that day a strong gust of wind came up and blew him right on his ass. As he was lying there in the batter's box, Sisler turned to Red and said, "I t-t-told you you didn't want Davalillo."

Replacing McCarver wasn't much easier. I suppose I'd been spoiled over the years by his understanding of the game and of my pitching methods (God, I hope he doesn't read that!), and when Simmons took his place behind the plate it was like the first day of school all over again. He had no clue about what I was trying to accomplish out there. I had to shake him off the first five or six pitches. Finally he called time, ran out to the mound, and said, "Are you trying to give me a hard time?" I said, "Ted,

I'm trying to win the ballgame. You're just sitting back there putting fingers down." He was calling a game the way you would in Little League— strike one fastball, strike two fastball, strike three curveball. I don't think he even knew about my slider, which was my best pitch. It seemed to me that Simmons was preoccupied with getting his base hits—which, I should add, has its place. I certainly appreciated offense.

McCarver, meanwhile, was continuing to have difficulty with his throwing in Philadelphia, and naturally Brock took generous advantage of him when we played the Phillies. They ended up fighting at home plate one time, and after the game I did something I *never* did—I wrote Tim a nice note. It was against my policy, but I knew that he was having enough problems without feeling forsaken and despised by his former friends and teammates. Besides, my cover had already been blown with him.

The Phillies had not prospered any more than we had from the big trade, and in one game against them in 1970 I struck out sixteen batters, my highest total ever except for the first game of the '68 series. In spite of my slow start (the early reports of my decline actually made me wonder for a while), I was still throwing damn hard, as evidenced by the fact that my 274 strikeouts were the most, by just a few, that I ever recorded in one season. Cito Gaston, now the manager of the Toronto Blue Jays but back then an outfielder for the San Diego Padres, has said that the fastest pitches he has ever seen were the ten with which I struck out the side against the Padres in 1970 after loading the bases with no outs. (The year before, I once fanned the side on nine pitches.) Also in 1970, I surpassed Johnson and Waddell to become the first pitcher to strike out two hundred batters in eight seasons, won my sixth straight Gold Glove award, and, in a feat about which I'm fond of boasting (you know that pitchers love most to talk about their prowess with the stick), checked in with a .303 batting average to become the last pitcher to hit .300 and win twenty games in the same season. Grateful for the unaccustomed offensive support provided by Allen, Torre, Brock, and Cardenal (there were still occasional lapses, as when I lost successive three-hitters), I won twenty-one of my last twenty-five decisions to finish 1970 with the best won-loss percentage in the league and of my career, a .767 mark based on a record of 23–7. It turned out that my victory total represented more than 30 percent of the team's seventy-six. In the calculated undoing of the Cardinals, I had at least managed to keep my bargaining power intact.

As a result, my $150,000 salary for 1971 was the highest ever paid to a pitcher. I also supplemented that with a little broadcasting—I did some college basketball games with Marty Glickman on WPIX in New York, announced the 1970 and 1971 National League playoffs, and had my own television and radio shows for WOW in Omaha. In addition, I filmed a commercial (my only national endorsement) in which I tried to throw a ball through a sheet of Plexiglas, and escalated my interest in radio by purchasing station KOWH. Actually, the Omaha black community owned the station because we went door-to-door raising money for it, but I was the principal shareholder and the guy whose ass was in the sling if we didn't make a go of it.

My boyhood friend Rodney Wead had convinced me that the way for a black community to take possession of its economic destiny was through ownership of local institutions such as radio stations and banks. That's easier said than done, however. When we attempted to start up KOWH, we didn't have the financial luxury of two or three wealthy investors, as most radio stations do, so we had to extract the money from the people who would be listening to the station—if we could get a license. That, too, was a sticky proposition because the FCC stipulated that in order to serve a specific market within a metropolitan area, the station had to represent at least nineteen percent of the people in that area. Omaha's black population was only twelve percent of the city. On the other hand, the fifty-five thousand people in Omaha's black community, if incorporated, would constitute the third largest city in Nebraska behind Omaha and Lincoln. We pushed hard on those buttons and when our applications were completed we hand-carried them to Washington. At the FCC, we presented our case in front of a panel of six officials, all of whom seemed to be completely disinterested except for the one female member. Picking up on that, I directed my conversation toward her. When the license came through, I had to wonder whether her opinion was the thing that made the difference.

Our problems were a long way from over, however. I don't think I understood the full meaning of the word *bigotry* until I tried to sell advertising time for KOWH. Almost none of the established businesses would buy from us, and they searched hard for reasons not to. An owner of a large local tire company even told me flat out that it would be a waste of time and money to advertise in the black community—as if black people didn't drive cars.

At one point while we were scrounging for sponsors, I became aware that ten thousand dollars had been designated by Coca-Cola for advertising in Omaha's black media. The Coca-Cola account was administered through an ad agency run by a man who had been my junior varsity basketball coach at Technical High. All things considered, I figured we were in good shape for the account until I learned that instead of awarding it to us, my old coach had spent his ten thousand dollars with a white guy who had just gotten out of jail and started up a black newspaper in town. Three months later, the black paper was out of business and the ex-con was back in prison. Meanwhile, the radio station stayed afloat but my personal liability expanded to proportions that were beyond my means.

Although my preference would have been to make a little money with the radio station, I hadn't been depending on it for my future after baseball. I felt I had the luxury of taking risks with community-oriented enterprises because I was staking my business livelihood on the prospect of receiving an Anheuser-Busch distributorship from the Cardinals, as Roger Maris had when he retired after just two years with the ballclub. I'd had conversations with August Busch to that effect and had been led to believe that things would work out. Judging from Musial and Maris, it seemed to me that the Cardinals had a good record of taking care of players who had served them well in uniform.

In the meantime, there were a few more perks to enjoy (and, of course, ballgames to win), before I hung up number 45. It seemed that nearly every off-season offered an overseas trip with one special group or another. One year I was a last-minute replacement for Satchel Paige on a tour of U.S. Air Force bases in Germany and Holland. Johnny Bench and umpire Tom Gorman were also along on that trip, from which the enduring memory is a girlie show we attended in Hamburg. We were sitting in the first row and it was a wild performance—every bit of what we bargained for. Right in the middle of the show I happened to look over at Tom Gorman next to me, and he was sound asleep, snoring. I recall thinking, "Man, I hope I never get to be like that."

Another winter I joined Graig Nettles of Cleveland (at the time), the Mets' Danny Frisella, and their traveling secretary, Arthur Richman, for a tour of military hospitals in the Far East and Pacific. Early in the trip Nettles made a gratuitous anti-Semitic remark to me about Richman, who was Jewish, and, although he probably figured it was innocent, his language slapped me across the face. I always figured that if a guy made any sort of ethnic slur about anybody, even confiding it to me, there was no reason to believe he wouldn't make the same kind of comment about me behind my back. So I advised Nettles to keep his distance from me for the balance of the trip, and, for good measure, warned that if he ever stepped into the batter's box when I was pitching, it would be a good idea not to get too comfortable. I expect that Nettles changed his attitude over the years, and I can almost guarantee that he has long forgotten the incident, but I have an elephant's memory about things like that.

The winter trips provided welcome relaxation after the season, the only problem being that I never knew what would happen to the Cardinals while I was gone. For example, as soon as I'd had time—one year, exactly—to become attached to Dick Allen, the Cardinals up and traded him to the Dodgers for essentially Ted Sizemore, a second baseman. Sizemore, whose arrival sadly portended that the end was near for Julian Javier, was a nice player, but there weren't many other Dick Allens around, if any. We would never again have a power hitter like him.

By the same token, though, Joe Torre had a season in 1971 like none I'd ever been around. Everything the man hit that year, he hit hard. Torre was anything but a speed merchant, and for him to win the batting title at .363 meant that he was putting dents in the ball. He also took the RBI crown with 137, which made me proud to be his friend. Romping in front of Joe, Brock led the league in runs with 126 and stolen bases again.

I only wished, as I perpetually did, that more of those runs had come when I was pitching. I kept my earned run average around 3.00 for most of the season but nonetheless managed to lose nearly as often as I won. The pattern started in the opener, when the Cubs' Billy Williams, my number one nemesis, beat me 2–1 with a tenth-inning homer at Wrigley Field.

Somehow, though—hell, *Torre* was how, along with some complementary if erratic hitting from Brock, Simmons, and outfielder Matty Alou, whom we had acquired from Pittsburgh for Nelson Briles—we hung around first place early in 1971 until I pulled a thigh muscle at the end of May. We slumped badly after that, winning only eight games in the month of June and falling from first to fourth while I was on the disabled list— which I didn't need to be on. I was angry the whole time because the Cardinals hadn't consulted me before placing me on the DL, and the thigh had healed after just a few days. All of our losing only made things worse. I remember sitting solemnly in front of my locker after one particularly excruciating defeat to the Pirates, trying to come to grips with our fate, and catching Brock's eye as I looked around the clubhouse. In that passing glance, it was apparent to me that he, and perhaps he alone, was going through the same thing that I was. With all the turnover we'd had on the club, the passion for winning seemed to have slipped out the door along with our old friends.

As the end of June approached, I had won only five games on the season and was champing at the bit to get back out there. But when I finally did, it was like starting the season over, and I was always a slow starter. I'd also been having knee problems after wrenching my left one during spring training, and the result was that since becoming a regular starter I'd never gone so far into the season with so few victories. Weeks after being reactivated, I was still in a foul mood. During a game at San Diego, I vented my frustrations by standing in the tunnel behind home plate and agitating the home-plate umpire, Ken Burkhart, who was not shy about returning my compliments. After leaving San Diego, we traveled to Montreal and again had Burkhart's crew. One game there was delayed by a power outage, during which Burkhart walked toward our dugout to inform Red of what was happening. As he approached, Ken Boyer, who was back with us as a coach, said to Burkhart, "What are you coming over here for, to kick out Gibson?" The light went on in Burkhart's head, and he answered, "Yeah, goddamn it, that's not a bad idea." When I protested, he had all the excuse he needed, and I was gone before I'd said ten words.

I tried not to restrict my insults to the umpires, however. I saved some of my best for guys who weren't hitting, like our veteran reserve infielder, Dick Schofield. It happened that Schofield was one of the great red asses of all time—that being the baseball term for a guy who's always bitching about something or other—although I have to admit I admired his wardrobe (which has nothing to do with this story). Every time he would make an out, Schofield would get pissed off and throw something, which accounted for a considerable amount of debris flying around our dugout. So one day, after he had popped out and performed another of his tirades, I repaired to the clubhouse and came back with a media guide. Turning to Schofield's page and showing it to him, I said, "You know, Dick, there's something I don't understand. It says here that you're a lifetime .230 hitter. Why does it surprise you so much when you make an out?" I believe he genuinely wanted to hurt me at that moment.

Actually, it was probably not the best form for me to call attention to the shortcomings of my teammates at that point, because I had very little to show for the season myself. When I still wasn't winning in early July, the reports of my demise resurfaced. I finally silenced those by throwing back-to-back shutouts at the Phillies and Mets and winning ten of my last thirteen decisions to finish the season 16–13.

By August we had managed to scramble back to the edge of the pennant race, passing the Cubs and Mets and setting our sights on the Pirates, who were still well ahead. On August 4, I won the two-hundredth game of my career, which left us eight behind Pittsburgh, a margin that would probably be insurmountable unless we could cut off a big chunk of it during a four-game series at Three Rivers Stadium in mid-August. We won the first two games of the series, and my start came on Saturday, August 14. As I left the hotel that day to go to the ballpark, a kid in a Cardinal cap and T-shirt walked up and asked, "Are you going to shut out the Pirates tonight?" Naturally, I said, "Yes." For that to happen, however, I would have to be a different pitcher than the one I had been the last time out, when the Dodgers routed me at Busch Stadium.

We were apparently in store for a big Saturday night in Pittsburgh, scoring five runs in the first inning. Leads like that were so rare that they made me giddy, and for some reason—probably because the victory itself was not a major concern—I started thinking immediately about a no-hitter. I'd always resigned myself to the likelihood that I would never throw a no-hitter because I was a high-ball pitcher and somebody was bound to get hold of one during the course of a game. Besides that, a no-hitter, without exception, requires a degree of good luck, with which I was not particularly well supplied. I might have been more discouraged had I known that nobody had pitched a no-hitter in Pittsburgh in more than sixty years—never at Three Rivers or its predecessor, Forbes Field, which had the worst lighting in the league.

I was throwing hard—not the hardest I'd ever thrown, but close—and the Pirates were still hitless through the first few innings. Of course, in keeping with baseball custom, nobody in our dugout said anything to me about the no-hitter, but I wouldn't have given a shit. I did hear, though, that Ted Sizemore, who was playing left field that night, told the other guys that he had also had a rare start in left field on the night in which Bill Singer of the Dodgers had pitched a no-hitter the year before. That and about eighty-one consecutive strikes were sure to do it for me.

As it was, my control was effective but not perfect that night. I walked three batters and one more reached on a wild third strike, but through the middle innings Pittsburgh was still without a hit. It probably helped that Roberto Clemente was not in the lineup, but the Pirates had no shortage of hitters—we used to joke that when they traveled, the players took one plane and their bats rode on another—and I was pretty much having my way with them. Al Oliver, a very difficult left-handed out, said later that it was the first game in his career that he felt overpowered by a pitcher and unable to get his bat around in time.

Even so, the Pirates made some serious bids at base hits. In the seventh inning Milt May, the Pittsburgh catcher, hit a long fly to left field that Jose Cruz ran down and caught with a leap, much to my relief. We were on our way to winning 11–0, and as a result the no-hitter had by then become my mission. My most anxious moment, however, came in the eighth, when Dave Cash hit a high hopper toward third, where Torre lost it momentarily in the lights. Torre confided afterwards that he was praying the ball would hit him in the head so it would be an obvious error, but he managed to relocate it at the last second and make a strong throw to beat Cash by a step.

By the ninth I was so nervous my knees were actually knocking. It would have been apparent to anybody who knew me as a pitcher that I was doing everything in my power to finish off the no-hitter, even throwing breaking balls on three-and-two counts in spite of the big lead. Without a no-hitter going, I'd have been pouring in fastballs and trying to get the hell out of there; but I'd never had a chance like this and knew damn well that I'd never get another one.

My old buddy Vic Davalillo led off the bottom of the ninth and obliged me with an easy grounder to Maxvill at short. Oliver then bounced to Ted Kubiak at second, but the big man, Willie Stargell, still remained. I'd already rung up Stargell for three of my nine strikeouts, but that only made him more dangerous. It was ironic—and a lesson I couldn't ignore—that because he was such a congenial fellow I had allowed myself to make an exception of Stargell and become friends with him over the years, and now he alone stood between me and something I wanted very, very badly. Putting that out of my mind and cutting to the chase, I got two quick strikes on Willie, then slipped a slider over the outside corner. Harry Wendelstedt's right hand went up, and with that I had something I never thought I'd get.

It was only the second Cardinal no-hitter in thirty years, the other being Ray Washburn's in 1968, and I intended to celebrate the occasion to its fullest. I went out for a while with Brock and former Cardinal pitcher Brooks Lawrence, who was there as a broadcaster, then excused myself in order to call everybody I knew and tell them about my night. Nobody was home. I was bursting with my news and nobody would answer the damn telephone. I received a lasting congratulations a few weeks later, however, when the Cardinals (I think my teammates were responsible, although I was never told) gave me a commemorative diamond ring with 45 on it. I still wear it.

The no-hitter and our subsequent victory on Sunday brought us within four games of the Pirates, but that was as close as we got. Torre earned the MVP award and Carlton won twenty games for the first time and our ninety wins would have tied the Giants for first in the National League West, but we proved to be no match for Pittsburgh. Hard as it was to admit, there was no disguising the fact that the Cardinals, without a pennant for three years now, had become just another decent ballclub.

The Cardinal organization, however, seemed intent upon ensuring that, come hell or high water, we would *not* be just another decent ballclub. The

method for doing this was to trade away most of our pitching. During the
1971 season the front office had peddled lefthander Fred Norman, who
would go on to win more than a hundred games thereafter, and the huge
young righthander, Mike Torrez, who had more than 150 victories left in
him. Then, as the players were banding together for a labor walkout before the 1972 season, Gussie Busch shook up the joint but good. Largely
to make a point that he would not accommodate any up-and-comer whose
performance and negotiating posture demanded a level of wealth apparently unbecoming a junior employee, he unexpectedly traded Steve Carlton to the Phillies for a righthander named Rick Wise. Wise was a reliable
pitcher, but Carlton was obviously a great one and delivering him to Philadelphia was a matter of depositing another two hundred–something victories into the account of one of our division rivals. Before the strike was
settled—the 1972 season was shortened by six or seven games—the Cardinals also packaged off a promising lefthander from St. Louis, Jerry
Reuss, who would go on to win close to 140 more games for various clubs.
In the course of a year, the organization managed to rid itself of a grand total of 671 future victories, replacing them with pitchers who would win 140
for St. Louis. It is virtually impossible to count the pennants that were
kissed good-bye.

The strike of '72 proved devastating not only to our ballclub but to my
personal future. My discussions with Mr. Busch concerning the beer distributorship had continued along over the years, and I had become fairly
secure about the prospects. Owing to the permanent financial hunger I
had developed in the projects, my wife's penchant for spending, and the
basic needs of my daughters, I was extremely motivated to make and save
money and confident that the distributorship would more than adequately
meet my needs after I stopped playing baseball. But the strike changed all
of that. Although he never said a harsh word about my active involvement
in it, and in fact our relationship remained cordial until the day he died,
during the course of the strike Mr. Busch stopped talking to me about the
distributorship and never mentioned it again. I've revisited the subject
now and then with his successors at the brewery, and it has never been
completely closed, but a hell of a lot of Budweiser has gone down the
hatch in the meantime.

# CHAPTER XI

I knew only a couple of things about Jesse Haines. He was the guy who got the blister in 1926, prompting the Cardinals to bring Grover Cleveland Alexander—drunk or not, depending on which version of the story you believe—out of the bullpen to strike out Tony Lazzeri and save the World Series. And, as a Hall of Famer who spent virtually his whole career with St. Louis, he had won 210 games, which was more than any other pitcher in the history of the franchise.

His name came up in 1972 as I approached his club record. Against my wishes, I took the slow approach. Having finished 1971 with 206 wins, I needed only five more to pass Haines (and six strikeouts to supplant Warren Spahn as the National League's career leader in that department). A good month or so should have put Haines behind me, and in fact I wasn't pitching as badly as I often did at the outset of the season—my ERA was around 2.00—but after all of April (which was abbreviated because of the strike) and most of May, I was 0–5. Having already gone into too much detail about the Cardinals' inability to score runs when I pitched, I won't belabor the point here. At any rate, after finally picking up my first victory of the season on May 25 against the Pirates (in the process stopping their nine-game winning streak), conditions improved. I clicked off four in a row to tie Haines in a game at San Diego on June 9, but then, the little unpleasantness with our offense having finally been cleared up, *weather* conditions intervened. Rain washed out consecutive attempts at my 211th win, false starts in which I didn't give up a run in four innings and two. June 21 finally brought a good night at Busch Memorial, and it proved to be a very good night. We scored ten runs in the first three innings and I hit a three-run homer in the seventh in a 14–3 rout of the Padres. Ironically, the home-plate umpire that night was Stan Landes, who had also called my first victory for the Cardinals in 1959.

After I had broken his record, I found out something else about Jesse Haines. Word had it that he was a hardened racist, which was not unusual for a man of his generation but was out of place in the Cardinal clubhouse, which was where he would be when former Cardinals mingled with the active ones during a club reunion that summer. Figuring that Haines and I would be the subject of numerous photographs, I couldn't resist the temptation to dress up in the most colorful African dashiki I could find, complete with beads, sandals, and the works. To his credit, Haines didn't flinch as the photographers fired away.

While Haines, at the age of seventy-nine, no doubt enjoyed his brief return to the spotlight, he was not the former Cardinal pitcher most prominent in the news of 1972. That would have been Steve Carlton, who, in his first year away from St. Louis, was having an incredible season in Philadelphia. The last-place Phillies were an extremely bad ballclub, managing only fifty-nine wins on the season, a number greatly inflated by the fact that Carlton accounted for twenty-seven of them. On no other occasion in modern baseball has a pitcher won so many games for a team that won so few, as attested by the statistic that Carlton (27–10) posted a winning percentage of .730, whereas on the days he didn't pitch the Phillies (32–87) won at a .269 clip. Although disgusted that Carlton's victories were not ours, as they should have been, I derived some consolation from the knowledge that his performance did not escape the notice of Mr. Busch.

Wise, who suffered unfairly from comparisons with Carlton's unique season, held up his part of the bargain by producing sixteen victories for us in '72; even with twenty-seven from Carlton we would not have challenged the Pirates. However, the sixteen games that Torrez won for Montreal and the fourteen that Briles pulled down for Pittsburgh would have closed the gap considerably. With those guys on the staff, my eleven-game winning streak—the final six coming on the other side of number 211—might have meant something in the pennant race. As it was, I could concern myself with nothing more than personal goals, the chief one, as usual, being twenty victories. Despite a 2.46 earned run average (Carlton led the league at 1.97), I finished up a win short at 19–11. Gratification that year had to come from a different source—namely, the fact that my creaky thirty-six-year-old body had enough life left in it to out-homer or tie all but two of our regulars (Simmons and Torre) with five. Our *whole team* hit only seventy home runs all season.

Having managed to rid the club of pitching and power, the front office meanwhile turned its sights to the defense, trading Maxvill to Oakland at the end of August for a couple of minor leaguers who never played for us. Although Schoendienst didn't make the final call on trades, when I heard that we were shopping Maxvill I pleaded with him not to do it. His response was that we needed more offense, to which I said, "Red, don't trade Maxie! We only score one or two runs a game—let's put somebody at shortstop who can catch the ball!" Unless we could get Dick Allen back and teach him to play shortstop, there was nobody around who could field the position and improve our offense at the same time. Sure enough, early the next season, after one of Maxvill's several replacements had booted another ground ball, Red was stomping around the dugout one night screaming, "We need a goddamn shortstop!" I said, "Red, we *had* a good shortstop. You traded him."

With Maxvill gone, only Brock and I remained from the team that had won the National League pennant just four years before. The league was different, the fields were different, the rules were different, and most of all the names and faces were different. In the space of a single presidential term, we had moved into an all-new era that was a world removed from the one in which Cepeda had danced on the money trunk and Denny McLain and I had squared off in the World Series.

The sense of change was intensified for me by the fact that my home life was also in a state of transition. Charline and I had drifted apart. She was an independent woman with her own ambitions, and it was becoming apparent that my professional success was not advancing her agenda. There were occasions when she was able to capitalize on our public status—in 1970 she wrote a book called *A Wife's Guide To Baseball*—and it provided her with introductions to such friends as Susie Buffett (wife of Omaha financier Warren Buffett, the head of Salomon Brothers) and Camille Cosby (wife of Bill), with whom she often traveled and partied, but the more she ventured on her own the less attached she became to me.

As a ballplayer who was away half the year, I preferred to putter around the house in my free time and consequently was less sociable than Charline, but I also enjoyed the company of people who had distinguished themselves in other fields. I'd first met Cosby at Enrico's in San Francisco, where some of the Cardinals often went after ballgames and occasionally found him playing dominoes. (Jonathan Winters also hung out there and frequently entertained us in the company of our announcer, Jack Buck, with whom he had once worked at a radio station.) It was an interesting lesson in human dynamics to be around a celebrity like Cosby. There was the time, for instance, when we were attending a party at his house and Cosby was behind the bar mixing drinks. The thing of it was that Cosby didn't drink and didn't know anything about mixing drinks, but for the hell of it he was throwing all kinds of crap into the glasses and handing them out to the guests, most of whom were saying, "Wow, this is really great stuff!" All the while Cosby was behind the bar gagging.

Buffett, too, provided me with an indelible party memory. He was visiting at our house one night when, for no apparent reason, he suddenly asked me, "How much do you pay for your American Express card?" I said ten dollars. He said, "If it went up to twelve, would you still take it?" I said I probably would. I didn't think anything more of it until I read sometime later that he had bought American Express and raised the price of membership from ten dollars to twelve, then turned around and sold it for a huge profit.

Our association with the Buffetts was more sociable than business-oriented, although in 1972 Buffett's capital helped Rodney Wead and me and several others from the black community start up the Community

Bank of Nebraska, for which I was a director and vice president. After a meeting at my house, Buffett and a few of his associates agreed to put up half of the five hundred thousand dollars required by the FDIC to open the bank. Then, as we had done with the radio station, we went knocking on doors to raise the other quarter-million in increments as small as two hundred dollars. Operating at first out of a trailer in a commercial pocket of Omaha's principal black district, the bank did reasonably well; but when we attempted to open a satellite branch in West Omaha, the banking commission informed us that another bank was not needed in that section of town. Within two years, however, a large established bank opened at the same location we had applied for. It was an educational experience, at best, and one that made me determined to stay in baseball for as long as I could.

My future in the game had become an issue at age thirty-seven. It was getting more difficult every year to condition myself—especially mentally—through the winter and then drag my body down to spring training knowing damn well that something, if not everything, would soon start to hurt again. The prospect of reporting to the club in 1973, however, sounded much better when I heard that the Cardinals had reacquired Tim McCarver from Montreal, where he spent half a season after more than two in Philadelphia.

Simmons had become a big-time hitter and McCarver was no longer an everyday catcher—he played a lot of first base for us in '73—but it was good just to get back some of the Cardinal spirit from the sixties. Having McCarver around gave me someone to laugh and bitch with at the everyday diversions—as when the club outfitted each player on the team with a blazer that had a little redbird mounted on a yellow patch over the pocket. We had to wear those things on the plane, and it made us look like some kind of goddamn glee club.

McCarver also commiserated with me about the shadow that followed me around in 1973, an impressionable and free-spirited young pitcher named Scipio Spinks. We had purchased Spinks by trading Jerry Reuss, and on the basis of talent I had no argument with the deal. There were times in 1972 when it appeared that he would be a star someday soon if only he would concentrate more on pitching and less on clowning (among other bits, he carried around a stuffed ape to which the St. Louis media took quite a fancy). But his career was ruined when he tried to run over Johnny Bench at home plate and tore up his knee. He hung around trying to come back in 1973, but the sizzle was gone from his fastball. His personality, however, was undaunted. I admired Spinks's energy and appreciated the fact that he apparently thought he could become a better pitcher by hanging around me.

> *Scipio Spinks loved Gibson. He modeled everything he did after Bob and was constantly seeking his approval. He apparently regarded Bob as something of a father figure, and Gibson tolerated him patiently—most of the time. There was one unforgettable moment, however, when Scipio had gotten into some kind of mischief late on a Saturday night in St. Louis and about six o'clock Sunday morning found his way to Bob's door at the apartment building where they both lived. He then started pounding on it, yelling, "Bob! Bob! You in there?" Poor Gibson could barely keep his eyes open that day at the ballpark. He spent the whole game leaning back against the dugout wall moaning, "Scipio! Scipio!"*
> —TIM MCCARVER

We certainly could have used Spinks at his best in 1973, when we made a run at the division title despite a wretched start. It was an unusual season from beginning to end, and the one, perhaps more than any other, that I would like to have over. I'd like to have April over, anyway. Maxvill's heir apparent, an oversized shortstop named Ray Busse (whom some in the organization likened to Marty Marion, a graceful former Cardinal star who had been able to put his height to great advantage), made eleven errors in the first twenty-five games of the season, at the end of which our record was 5–20 and our first-place deficit was already in double digits. But Busse wasn't the only one at fault, by any means. I certainly didn't help the cause, going winless for the month. In fifteen years, I'd never been on a Cardinal ballclub that played quite so badly.

The situation improved when Red switched to a stocky rookie shortstop, Mike Tyson, who had been playing second base while Ted Sizemore recovered from an injury. It helped, too, that I picked up the slack a little bit. Brock and Simmons were playing at all-star levels (my days on the National League squad ended with 1972), and despite our chronic lack of power—it didn't seem to help at all that the fences at Busch Memorial were moved in ten feet for the '73 season—we somehow managed to get back into contention. Part of the reason was that none of the teams in the division showed much enthusiasm for the pennant race.

Things started to happen fast for us just before the all-star break, when we took over first place from the Cubs. Later in July I moved past Jim Bunning into second place behind Walter Johnson on the career strikeout list (several of my younger contemporaries, including Carlton, Seaver, Jenkins, and finally Nolan Ryan, would move ahead of me before they were through), and a short while later set a major-league record by starting my 260th consecutive game without a relief appearance (a number that eventually reached 303). I failed, however, to observe the latter occasion with any sort of appropriate theatre. We were playing the Giants in San Francisco and before the game Torre, noting that (1) the record would be established with my first pitch and (2) Bobby Bonds would be leading off for San Francisco, advised me in his inimitable way to "just make sure we don't have to go over the fence to get that fuckin' ball." Naturally, Bonds homered on the first pitch and I never saw the baseball again. As it left the park, I looked over at Torre and he was turned in the other direction, making sure to keep his eyes away from mine.

By early August we seemed to be in control of the race, leading the second-place Cubs by five games when I made my first start of the month on August 4 in New York. At the time, the Mets, along with the Pirates and Expos and even Chicago, were caught in a knot of teams tangled around .500. We appeared to be the only club *capable* of winning the division, but it turned out that our hold on first place was tenuous—as fragile, in a way, as the cartilage in my right knee. Early in the game that night, the knee gave out as I scrambled back to first base to avoid a double play after Sizemore's line drive, which I thought was headed for left field, was caught by the third baseman. I assumed—or hoped—that the knee was just twisted and told the medics to take back the stretcher they brought out for me. But on my first warm-up pitch the next inning, I collapsed the moment my weight shifted to my right leg. The cartilage in the knee, weakened from wear and tear and driving hard off the mound over the years, had finally ripped. They brought the stretcher out again, but I leaned on Sizemore and our trainer, Gene Gieselmann, and hobbled off the field confident that the team would get the job done without me as it had in 1967.

Following the surgery, there was a lot of skepticism in the media concerning whether I would pitch again. There were also serious questions—and, as the season wound down, more pertinent ones, in my estimation—about whether the Cardinals would be able to hold the lead. We lost twenty-nine out of our next forty-seven games after I was hurt, and in the meantime the Mets took advantage of our slide to move into first place with a very mediocre record. There were only a few days left in the season when I finally came off the disabled list. We were two games under .500 but only two behind New York, and with the club still harboring a slim chance of catching the Mets I had one start in which to make a mark on the race and at the same time find out if my knee was sound enough to keep me in baseball. The opportunity came on the Saturday before the last game of the season. Although I couldn't push off consistently hard on my right leg for an entire game, the night resulted in a 5–1 victory over Carlton and the Phillies that gave me a final record of 12–10. The next day we completed the season at .500, but the Mets took care of the Cubs over the weekend to hold us off by a game and a half.

Over the years, Bob Broeg has written countless times in the *Post-Dispatch* about the pennant that slipped out of the Cardinals' grasp on the night I hurt my knee. Our near-miss was especially agonizing for me and Brock, who, having been through the cycle with the ballclub, would have savored the accomplishment of climbing back to the top with a whole new cast—and, to boot, doing it the hard way by coming from far behind. To some, a division title in 1973 might have seemed like a cheap one considering that it could have been attained with only eighty-three wins, but on the other hand I can't disagree with the numerous stories that summer, local and national, commending the team—and Red Schoendienst, who deserved his share of the credit—for our turnaround. It would have been easy for the guys to chuck the season back in May, when we were fifteen games under .500, and it made me feel damn good to see some of the old Cardinal mettle coming through. Our run at the pennant gained a little esteem when the Mets beat the heavily favored Reds in the playoffs and then took Oakland to seven games in the World Series.

The '73 season proved that the Cardinals could contend again, and we actually had a better team when we returned to camp in 1974. For that reason and others, I would have given anything to be twenty-eight that summer instead of thirty-eight. If I had been twenty-eight, my knee would have responded much better because I no doubt would have worked harder at rehabilitating it; I would have been hungrier and had more energy; and I wouldn't have had the complications at home that I had in 1974. By then, divorce proceedings were under way between Charline and me. That deprived me of both spirit and time, much more of which I had to devote to raising Renee and Annette.

When we started playing for keeps in 1974, I had to face the fact that I wasn't the same pitcher anymore. I could still summon up the strength and stuff to strike out a good hitter when I needed to, but I couldn't sustain the pace required to pitch consistently well. My knee simply would not allow me. And when a pitcher's leg is weak, it brings out the problems in his shoulder and elbow and everywhere else. At the age of thirty-eight, my ninety-five-mile-an-hour fastball made only rare cameo appearances.

> *One of the young guys on our club—I won't mention his name— hit a fly ball to left field off Gibson in 1974 and came back to the bench throwing his helmet and cussing, saying things to the effect of how Gibson wasn't so tough and he should have taken the old man out of the park. I didn't say anything, but it was all I could do to hold my tongue. Inside I was thinking, "Son, a couple of years ago hitters like you were lucky to get a loud foul off of Mr. Gibson."* —HANK AARON

Maybe the most frustrating part about my physical decline was the fact that the ballclub scored runs in '74. We had acquired Reggie Smith (along with pitcher Ken Tatum, whose ill-advised remarks about Dave Ricketts's skin color had made him unwelcome in our clubhouse) from the Red Sox for Rick Wise and Bernie Carbo, and his presence—Smith was both talented and tough—improved our lineup in virtually every respect; a rookie outfielder named Bake McBride showed incredible speed and the ability to turn it into base hits; Ted Simmons had taken his offense up a notch by supplying power that we badly needed; and Lou Brock, at age thirty-five, was stealing bases at a rate that made heads spin. Torre and Sizemore were pros, and our third baseman, Ken Reitz, sucked up every ground ball within reach. In better days, I believe I could have won twenty games for that club before school started and then set my sights on twenty-five.

I managed to start as many games as anybody on the staff but was no longer a legitimate ace. We didn't have one. Lynn McGlothen, a young righthander obtained from Boston for a similar pitcher, Reggie Cleveland, was our biggest winner, but we sorely missed the kind of pitching leadership I wished like hell I could still provide. We would have blown away the division that year if I had been twenty-eight.

Of course, if I had been twenty-eight, I wouldn't have registered my three-thousandth strikeout that year. I was only the second pitcher in history to reach three thousand, behind Walter Johnson, and the batter who put me over the top was Cesar Geronimo of the Reds on July 17. It wasn't a grand occasion, however. I was taken out in the ninth for a pinch hitter and we lost the game 6–4 in twelve innings. Dizzy Dean died the same day.

As the summer wore on I kept wishfully thinking that at any moment I would break out with a winning streak, as I'd done so many times in the past, but every time I put a couple of good games together my knee would swell up. It might have been advisable to miss a start now and then, but we were battling Pittsburgh for first place and our staff was not deep enough to pick up the slack. Consequently, if I couldn't reduce the swelling with heat treatments, our team physician, Dr. Stan London, would drain the knee—something I did *not* look forward to—and I'd get back out there.

*I would walk into the trainer's room and they'd be sticking this huge needle into Gibson's knee to remove some of the fluid from it. The fluid was so thick it was frightening. His elbow was also swollen and stiff to the point that he could barely straighten it out. I re-*

*member talking to Tim McCarver about it. McCarver used to*
*commiserate with Gibson about his pain, and Gibson would tell*
*him, "Yeah, so what? I still have to pitch."*
                                              —REGGIE SMITH

As painful as it was to keep pitching and to keep myself in condition to
pitch, it was worth the ordeal in 1974 just to watch Lou Brock run the
bases. He had lost some of his speed—at that time, Bake McBride was
much faster—but Brock's knowledge of pitchers was so thorough that he
was able to steal 118 bases on cunning. He and our entire outfield—Smith
and McBride being the others—batted over .300 that year, and behind
their lead we stayed abreast of the Pirates into September. Early in the
month we endured twenty-five innings to beat the Mets and then won our
next five games to take over first place. After that, we went back and forth
with Pittsburgh and when the final weekend of the season arrived, we
were on the Pirates' heels, desperately needing a big series in Montreal to
pull out the pennant.

I got the ball Sunday for the last game, which we needed to win while
Pittsburgh was losing, and carried a 2–1 lead into the bottom of the
eighth. Everybody in the ballpark knew I was tired, and when the Expos
put a man on base with a strong left-handed hitter, Mike Jorgensen, at the
plate, Red came out to talk things over with me. The Mad Hungarian,
lefthander Al Hrabosky, was ready in the bullpen, and the percentage
move was to bring him in. I'm sure Red knew that, and I wouldn't have
blamed him for doing it. But I'd been pitching well that night and for some
time, and everybody in the park knew also that it was my ballgame to win
or lose. I told Red that, and he respected it. At the same time, I was aware
that there was a stiff wind blowing out to right field and Jorgensen was
very capable of putting the ball in the air. But that didn't matter. In my
head I was still twenty-eight, and I didn't think he could beat me.

Shit.

In January, I announced that 1975 would be my last season.

I took a small pay cut to come back for one last turn, but what the hell,

I didn't expect a raise after going 11–13 and giving up the home run that lost the pennant. The fact is, I probably should have hung it up after the Montreal game—dying with my boots on, more or less—but I needed baseball for just a little while longer. It was my therapy after the divorce.

Our daughters were staying with me in Omaha, which wasn't an easy thing to work out when I was gone half the year playing ball. Fortunately, though, I'd met a young woman named Wendy Nelson, who volunteered to look after them when I was away. The girls were teenagers and Wendy was too close to their age to act like a mother, but it helped enormously just to have her there. In the meantime, I got home whenever I could. When the club was in St. Louis, I'd catch the last plane to Omaha every night and fly back there so Annette and Renee could at least see me in the morning before they went to school.

The way things were going early that year, often as not I was eager to get the hell out of town after the ballgame. There was the April night, for instance, when Rusty Staub, playing for the Mets, hit a grand slam—that should have been some kind of sign—and Tom Seaver beat me 7–1. There was the game in San Diego when I pitched a four-hitter and lost 1–0 on a run that came across on my goddamn throwing error. Victory seemed to want no part of me.

I had been through periods like that at the beginnings of many seasons, however, and they had never lasted. Even in 1974, my worst season since becoming a regular starter, I'd pitched strongly for most of the second half. For that reason, I strongly disagreed when Red took me out of the rotation around the 1975 all-star break, putting a stop to my major-league record of consecutive starts. It wasn't as if we had a staff of Cy Youngs-in-waiting ready to step in.

I didn't conceal my anger at being sent to the bullpen, but I suspect now that some of it actually stemmed from my frustrations at home. There was a lot of pressure in suddenly being the primary parent for two teenage girls, and a degree of devastation over the shattering of a family life that had been nearly twenty years in the making. It was no secret on the ballclub that I was going through tough times. Even Gussie Busch called me often to check in and ask if everything was all right. McCarver, Torre, and Reggie Smith were also good company when I needed some.

*I knew he was troubled by all that was going on at home. When he cared to discuss it, I'd listen. He was obviously hurt. It can't be emphasized enough that when Gibson was coming up through the ranks, he faced all sorts of obstacles, and through all of that, he completely dedicated himself to building a meaningful life, a comfortable life, for his family. They had money because of his extra efforts as a player. They had mobility. To see it all fall apart was a crusher for Bob. And to make it worse, at that stage of his career he was suffering from all sorts of injuries.*

*He knew the damage he was doing to himself by pitching in that condition. But I believe that pitching was his escape—his way of dealing with the personal things that were so painful. When his body didn't respond and then the club put him in the bullpen, it was an embarrassment to Bob. He was off his rhythm, he seldom pitched; I sometimes wondered how he did it. But still, he had moments. There was one game toward the end where he came in against Houston and pitched an inning in relief. He reared back that night and struck out the side on ten pitches, every one of them mammoth heat. I was awed.*

—REGGIE SMITH

My affinity for Reggie Smith was a natural because we were very much alike, both of us maintaining an exterior toughness that really wasn't what we were about. Smith was a very bright, thoughtful guy who was ready to fight if somebody looked at him wrong. I called him Spike because he reminded me of those spike-collared bulldogs on Saturday morning cartoons. Because he was somewhat of a bully, a lot of the guys on the ballclub gave him a wide berth, including Red. One day in San Francisco, when we were scheduled to play a Sunday doubleheader, Reggie missed the bus to the ballpark and still wasn't there an hour before the game, so Red, knowing I was friendly with Reggie, asked me to run back to the hotel and check on him. I took a cab, knocked on his door for about five minutes, and finally roused him out of bed. He looked terrible, his eyes half-closed and his hair all over the place. I said, "Come on, man, you're late." He said, "No, I can't make it. I'm not feeling too good." Saturday night was the reason he wasn't feeling so good, so I pushed him into the shower and got him to the ballpark just in time for the game to start. Red already had him in the lineup, and Reggie went out and hit three home runs that day.

It was nearly three weeks after being banished to the bullpen that I actually pitched out of it. On July 28 I picked up my first relief victory in eleven years (the last one being the final game of 1964, when we clinched the pennant by beating the Mets), inheriting a 6–4 lead in the fourth and, after permitting two baserunners to score, holding the Phillies without another run until Simmons's homer in the seventh handed me career win number 251. It proved to be my last.

I was used on an irregular basis the rest of the season. We weren't much of a factor in the pennant race—the Pirates were once again in charge of it—and about the only thing that kept me interested in the schedule was the supper club that Gene Gieselmann and a few other players and I had formed to get us through road trips. It was time, anyway, to turn my attention to things other than baseball, considering that very soon I would have to get along without it altogether. By the summer, when school was out, I especially looked forward to the weeks when Wendy could bring the girls to St. Louis.

Practically my whole family was in town on Labor Day when the Cardinals honored me at Busch Stadium. I was a nervous wreck, and was even more concerned for my mother, who was asked to stand before the microphone and address fifty thousand people. She had never piped up in a crowd bigger than the congregation at church, but when her turn came she strode confidently to the mike, adjusted it, and spoke without a hitch for two minutes, along the way thanking Mr. Busch "for being so nice to my baby." I only wish I had been so eloquent. When we were finished, Busch pulled up in his gift for the occasion, a deluxe motor home, and drove me, my mother, and my daughters one time around the ballpark. As we were enjoying the ride, he said, "I bet you never had a chauffeur like this before."

Two days later I was back on the mound in relief against the Cubs in a close game that we had to win (as far out of first place as we were, we had to win *all* of them) to entertain any pretense of remaining in the pennant race. I'd been pitching well over the previous week or so—striking out the side against Houston and throwing several scoreless innings against the Pirates—and was not especially concerned when Chicago filled the bases and I faced a left-handed hitter named Pete LaCock, who was best known for being the son of game-show host Peter Marshall. LaCock, a part-time first baseman, had rarely hit anything more than a soft foul off me in the past, and when he pulled a fastball over the right-field fence for a grand slam, I had not only suffered my tenth loss in thirteen decisions but reached my absolute limit in humiliation. I said to myself, "That's it. I'm out of here." When Red came out for the ball, I handed it to him, walked off the mound, and never pitched again.

We were to spend the last ten days of the season on the road, three of them in New York, where my life had been threatened on the previous visit. I saw no reason to go. The team was out of the race and I obviously wasn't in its plans for either the present or the future. So I shook some hands, boxed up my things, and stopped in to see Bing Devine.

I'm not sure what I was expecting out of the meeting with Devine except to say good-bye to the man who was more or less my link to the organization. I considered Devine a friend and respected his baseball judgment in spite of the several trades that were so hard to justify—some of which, I understood, were urged upon him from above. I suppose I went to his office as a courtesy and a formality, although I also needed a place to sit down with my feelings. I was never one to let my emotions get the upper hand—especially at the ballpark—but that day I was completely lost in them. I was concluding a career that had started when I was about seven years old and it felt like the last day of high school, when I had no idea what I would be doing with the rest of my life. It was scary. I knew, also, that I would miss the competition and the clubhouse and the national anthem.

Bing didn't pick up on any of that, which is probably my fault for putting on such a façade for all those years. It simply didn't occur to him that I would have a thousand sentiments swirling around inside. The thing on his mind was the ballclub, and he thought maybe I could give him some insights about it—what had gone wrong with it and what could be done to make it better; who could play and who couldn't; who knew how to win and who didn't. I was flattered to be consulted in that way and I was grateful, although not surprised, when Devine got around to offering me a job with the organization. He didn't define the job, but that didn't matter because I really wasn't interested at the moment. I was too confused to make any career decisions. So I thanked Bing for asking and told him not now because I was tired and needed some time off. I can't know for certain whether the job would have actually come through—he would have had to clear it with the higher-ups—but I've often thought how different my life would have been if I had said yes that day. If I'd known then what I know now, I would have certainly said yes. At the time, though, I couldn't imagine—how could I?—that the Cardinals would never call me again.

After wrapping things up with Bing, I loaded my stuff into the motor home and drove it back to Omaha, where Wendy and the girls were waiting. Wendy still kept an apartment not far away, but by that time she had moved all her belongings into the house to be with Renee and Annette. When I got home for good she told me she would move back into the apartment if I wanted her to, but I said I didn't want her to. She was the only good thing going in my life at the time. I had no idea what I'd be doing from then on, but it seemed to me that the best place to start doing it was next to her.

# CHAPTER XII

I figured that, in time, I would gravitate back toward baseball. Baseball was what I knew, but time was what I needed. That was where the motor home came in.

When the 1975 season was over, Gene Gieselmann and his wife, Rita, met Wendy and me in Omaha for a long trip west in August Busch's spacious and much-appreciated Gibson Day gift. We drove to Colorado (Renee was attending college there as a freshman, and we had a chance to visit her), Salt Lake City, Reno, and the California coast, where we camped and hiked and got pulled over by a state trooper. It probably caught the patrolman's attention that there was a black man in our foursome, a matter that tends to arouse the curiosity of the likes of state troopers—especially in a vehicle as expensive as a motor home. Gieselmann, who was driving when the guy started following us, became increasingly nervous the longer the patrol car remained in our rearview mirror, but I had been through that sort of thing before and told him to just keep going. After about twenty miles, the trooper pulled us over on the pretense that we had only one license plate (which had been given to me by the city of Omaha). I advised him that only one plate was required in Nebraska, but for the hell of it he kept us sitting there for a while before finally letting us back on the road and following us for another five or ten miles. I told Gene and Rita and Wendy that they had just gotten a small taste—very small—of what much of the country was like for black people.

A day or two later we were camping at Big Sur when a woman's screams woke us up at about six in the morning. Her son—he must have been about seven or eight years old—was hanging from a tree branch about two hundred feet over a cliff. If he had let go of that branch, it would have been all over for him. The father was in a state of panic and unable to do much about the situation, so Gene and I tried to climb up the cliff to get the kid. It was too steep, which meant we had to locate a trail above him and work our way down. I slid part of the way on the seat of my pants, ripping them, but finally we reached a point where we could help the boy. We put a slip knot in a rope we had taken from the motor home and told the kid to tie himself to the tree he was clinging to, using one hand at a time. While he was doing that, the father was screaming and crying so much that finally I said, "Man, you gotta get out of here." By then, we had tied the other end of the rope to a tree on higher ground, and slowly the boy climbed along the rope to where we could grab him. When we finally laid our hands on him—through his chest, you could feel the kid's heart pounding—I was practically crying myself. The father, as it turned out, was an artist, and after the ordeal was over he gave Gene and me pictures he had painted. An hour or so later, we were sitting back drinking coffee in the motor home when we heard the mother let out another scream. The kid had wandered off and gotten lost again.

When we arrived back in Omaha, I didn't have a lot to do. I was still on the boards of the bank and radio station and put in time at both places, but it wasn't my kind of work. Since there was really no hurry to find a new career—baseball had paid me handsomely (for those days) despite the fact that I always negotiated my own contract—I basically took it easy for a while, building things around the house, catching up on my hobbies, and trying to get *out* of shape, for a change.

On New Year's Eve, Wendy and I saw the Gieselmanns again in St. Louis, where a party of six or seven of us piled into a long Cadillac owned by a friend named Jimmy Mantilla. Jimmy carried a chauffeur's cap in the car and I was wearing it when we pulled up at an exclusive restaurant in west St. Louis for dinner. Everybody else in our group happened to be white, and as we walked to the entrance, I approached the doorman—still wearing my chauffeur's cap, of course—and asked if it would be all right if I went inside and ate with the others. He said, "Wait here a minute," and after conferring with somebody in the restaurant, he came out, patted me on the back, and said, "Have a good time."

That sort of thing represents what I refer to as "institutional" racism, which consists, to a large extent, of mild, no-offense-intended incidents that serve to perpetuate the race and class gap. I've often had a few laughs at the offhanded bigotry that is all around, but there have also been plenty of times when I was not so amused by it—like the day Brock and I were standing around the lobby of the team hotel in Pittsburgh and a woman walked up to Lou, handed him her keys, and told him to put her car in the garage. It was only *later* that we laughed that time. Many hotel guests have asked me to carry their luggage to their rooms. In hotel elevators, people have frequently stepped through the doors and announced their floor numbers to me. It happened in New York one time when I was in a bad mood—resulting, no doubt, from either a squandered ballgame or a death threat (which occurred only in New York)—and after the man said, "Twenty-second floor," I replied, "For all I care, Mister, you can take the whole damn hotel." I wouldn't be surprised if he'd notified the manager about an elevator operator with a bad attitude.

At the ballpark, it was probably a good thing that I played in the games and didn't have to watch them from the stands with my kids. They endured all sorts of racial taunts and comments and incidents. Once in St. Louis, Renee bought a hamburger from the concession stand only to discover that the meat was rotten. She took it back to get another one, but the attendant who had sold it to her said, "Get out of here. You've probably eaten a lot worse than that." When Renee returned to her mother and told her what had happened, Charline, who was never one to put up with that kind of crap, carried the hamburger back to the stand and threw it at the woman. I might have forced it down her throat.

The worst kind of bigotry in my experience, though—the cruelest and most damnable—is the subtle variety that impairs a person's ability to earn a living. It is the kind I have encountered not only in baseball but also in the pursuit of business opportunities that I have been forced to explore as alternatives to a position in baseball. Those incidents have not been restricted, by any means, to the public and private obstacles my partners and I ran into while trying to establish the minority-owned bank and radio station in Omaha. On the contrary, I have found repeatedly that many segments of the established white business community—in Omaha, anyway—are consistently unwilling or reluctant (the effect is virtually the same) to deal with any sort of black-operated enterprise. In the 1980s, for instance, I was involved in the founding of a modernized local yellow-page service called Ask-Me, which was going great guns until people found out that the friend of mine who was running it, Clarence Jones, was black. (About 90 percent of our salesmen happened to be white, which had caused our clients to assume that the management was white.) The service was so successful at first that out-of-town companies were coming in to study and copy our system. Along the way, we'd had overtures from businessmen and companies interested in buying it from us, but all of that changed with the knowledge that Ask-Me was not operated by white men. Gradually, our sales slowed to the point that the venture was no longer profitable.

Another time, I was all set to purchase a vacant building in the fashionable Old Market area of downtown Omaha—a converted warehouse district—and turn it into a jazz club. I offered the owner the price he had advertised, but was told that the building had been taken off the market. A short while later, it sold to a white buyer for roughly the same amount and was opened as an art studio. A similar thing happened when I tried to buy an old house in a section of town near the projects where I grew up that was being gentrified. I offered the asking price and was informed that the house was no longer for sale and would be condemned. Within weeks it was sold to a friend of the owner, who turned it into a nice five- or six-flat apartment building, just as I had intended to do.

In general, I find Omaha to be a decent place to live and raise a family (actually, I live now in an adjacent suburb named Bellevue), but I can't explain many of the peculiar things that have happened to me here in the past twenty-five years. On one hand, the city has given me a key and held days in my honor. On the other, until very recently I'd never been asked to sign autographs at a weekend show in my hometown.

While I suspect that considerations of race have limited my opportunities in an overwhelmingly white-oriented place like Omaha, it's possible—perhaps even likely—that in the baseball community my difficulties have had more to do with my reputation. My run-ins with various civic and men's clubs in St. Louis and elsewhere, for instance, have probably persuaded the Cardinals that I would not be a public relations asset. (I still haven't learned. In 1992 I was at a big function in Evansville, Indiana, which I knew was a Republican stronghold, and when somebody asked me who would win a baseball game between Bush and Clinton—this was during the campaign—I said Bush seemed to be a better ballplayer but I'm voting for Clinton anyway. There was dead silence except for one guy clapping alone in the back row.) Tact was never a preoccupation of mine with either the public or the press, unless absolutely necessary. The press, in turn, has advanced my image as an uncooperative, downright unfriendly sort of guy. Joe Falls, a sports columnist from Detroit, referred to me long after I had ceased playing as "the former ogre of the St. Louis Cardinals." I prefer to think of my demeanor—with the press and everybody else—as frank. I was never one for small talk and phony pleasantries. If a reporter asked me a stupid question (an extremely rare development, of course), I might respond by asking him, "Does it rain harder at night or in the summer?" I honestly wasn't trying to embarrass the guy; I just wanted to cut through the crap and move ahead to the things that mattered.

> *Gibson didn't suffer fools too well. I had ups and downs with him myself, although I considered us friends. Late in his career I confronted him on that because I felt he had put me off for little reason. It was on a Sunday, on a road trip, and I said to him, "Gib, it's funny—all these years together, and you've never said a kind word to me." When he heard me say that, he was really, genuinely upset. He thought he had offended somebody that, it seemed to me, he cared for. It told me something about him.*
> —BOB BROEG

A St. Louis newspaper writer recently expressed the opinion that if I had been more agreeable with the press—more like Lou Brock, I think he said—I would probably be working for the Cardinals and on top of that would be the toast of St. Louis. I'd like to point out two flaws in that statement. The first is that if I had been a sweet guy, an easygoing, friendly, chatty kind of fellow, I wouldn't have been the pitcher that I was. I can't even imagine what kind of pitcher I would have been with that sort of personality. The other fallacy with the statement is that Lou Brock is a lot more like Lou Brock than I am, and he doesn't have a job with the Cardinals either. There was a time, years ago, when the Cardinals wanted somebody to instruct their young players in baserunning skills, and instead of asking Brock, who was already with the team and was the man who revolutionized baseball with his baserunning, they hired a former football player named Sonny Randle. I will not say that racial considerations have motivated the Cardinals—the people I dealt with in the organization as a player were always good and fair to me—but I find it strangely coincidental that, of the players from our distinctive St. Louis teams of the sixties, those who have had the most trouble finding employment in baseball are me and Brock and Flood. Bill White, who became president of the National League after a successful career as a broadcaster for the Yankees, would seem to be an exception to that observation, but Bill would be the first to tell you that, despite what the owners said, being black certainly didn't hurt his chances of being appointed. I was thrilled for Bill and for the game when he was appointed, but I know and he knows that the real symbols of baseball's racial hiring performance are the dozens and dozens of black former players who have turned gray waiting at the reception desk. Even as the highest-ranking black official in professional sports, White has been frustrated by his inability to push through change and otherwise get things done. When he was telling me this over drinks one night and explaining why he felt compelled to resign his position, I said, "Why don't you just stay in it for the money?" He replied that he couldn't do that. I said, "Hell, I can. Give the job to me." In reality, though, I couldn't work under these conditions any more than Bill could.

I would include myself among the ranks of the former players who have been rebuffed by baseball, although my case is far from the most severe. I've had a few jobs in the game, both in coaching and in broadcasting, but the fact is that I have been out of it for a decade now, and not of my own choosing. I've had interviews, written letters, followed leads, and generally made myself available to the Cardinals and other clubs, all to no avail. The more time passes, the more doors close.

My first baseball offer after I quit playing came in the late seventies from my former Venezuelan Winter League teammate Joe Altobelli, who was then managing the San Francisco Giants. We met in Chicago and he asked me to be the Giants' pitching coach. Altobelli also said he had done some research and knew everything there was to know about me, which scared me because, hell, *I* didn't know everything there was to know about me. Besides, the timing wasn't quite right because I was preoccupied at the time with a restaurant I was starting up in Omaha, which had superseded the Community Bank and station KOWH as my primary business concern.

When I ultimately accepted a coaching job with Joe Torre and the Mets in 1981 (I carried the unprecedented title of "attitude coach," which was Torre's concoction), I had to resign from the board of the bank because the FDIC frowns upon directors who cannot attend meetings on a regular basis. I remained an investor in the bank but by that time had divested myself of any interest in the radio station. As the principal investor in KOWH, I had been operating at a personal liability that was eventually too much to handle—particularly in light of the fact that I was spending considerable time and money on the restaurant. In addition, my divorce had left me close to broke. Despite all of that, the black community was very upset over my decision in 1978 to sell the station (to Jeff Smulyan, owner of the Seattle Mariners) and went so far as to picket my restaurant. Due to the inherent demographics involved, the KOWH audience was simply not educated to the realities of business. Some of the listeners even complained when they heard advertising on the air—which, rest assured, didn't happen often. The whole episode baffled me. I couldn't understand how the community expected me to keep carrying a deficit that I couldn't cover—to remain exposed to the point that if the station went under, I went under with it. I'm sure the adverse publicity hurt the restaurant at a time when I was trying to get it started, but fortunately Gibson's Spirits and Sustenance seemed to have a life of its own.

It was located on North Thirtieth Street in Omaha, less than a mile from the projects and next to the Creighton University campus. Naturally, Gibson's catered to college students and faculty, but I was intent upon carving out a reputation citywide. For that reason, I had my hands in every facet of the operation, starting with the design and construction of the building. I'd originally hired an architect, but when I was dissatisfied with his plans I tossed them out and created my own. When those were approved, I spent a few more months driving in nails.

We served hamburgers and steaks and the usual fare, but I wanted to leave my mark on the menu as well as the building. I've always been proud of my chili and offered it at the restaurant much too cheaply, the purpose being not to make money on it but to have it recognized as the best chili in town. I had the same ambition for our hamburgers, which were handmade. The reviews, thankfully, were very good.

I worked ten or twelve hours a day at Gibson's and lost twenty-five pounds in the process. It was worth the effort, though, because running the restaurant was the thing that got me started on the second half of my life. Not long after it opened, Wendy and I got married and moved into the house in Bellevue where we still live. A few years later our son, Chris, was born. Nothing gives a man a new start like becoming a father at the age of forty-eight. (Actually, I was skeptical about that at first, fearing that I wouldn't have the energy and inclination to play with him as a father should. As it has turned out, Chris—who is so rough-and-tumble that at the age of eight he sent Wendy to the hospital with a jammed neck when they wrestled on the couch—has kept me in pretty good shape.)

The restaurant was also an education for me—my introduction, more or less, to a world without equipment managers and traveling secretaries and with only a few reporters. Among the things I found out about myself was that, contrary to the image of me portrayed by the press (which ballplayers tend to subconsciously believe even if they know better), I could get along with people. Some even liked me. I enjoyed throwing parties for our employees and surprising them with small favors, such as arranging for one of my waitresses to have her hair done by a hairdresser for the first time in her life. Frequently, I brought home the children of our waitresses and cooks and baby-sat them while the parents worked, sometimes keeping them the entire weekend. The staff became exceptionally close as a result, and it pleased me that the young people who worked at Gibson's considered me a counselor and confidant in sort of the same way that the kids in my neighborhood had regarded Josh.

By the time I joined Torre's staff with the Mets, however, I was unable to run the restaurant on a day-to-day basis and lost my handle on it. I had become so personally responsible for the place that I couldn't tolerate it when I discovered that some of my new managers were cutting corners and compromising our standards. Once, when I returned from a trip, I opened the freezer to find that one of the guys I'd just hired had taken it upon himself to order several hundred pounds of premade frozen hamburgers that he could just toss onto the grill. I went nuts when I saw that. I called the sales people and ordered them to come back and pick up their goddamn frozen hamburgers. Gibson's stayed in business for nearly ten years, but I had to reluctantly close it down in part because city regulations would not permit us to expand our parking and in part because it was becoming increasingly difficult to maintain the kind of establishment I wanted without being there. In the end, baseball was simply more important to me.

To fill the void created when I got out of the restaurant business, I undertook a few civic enterprises around Omaha, including some community projects with Rodney Wead. Another local endeavor I found myself briefly involved with was the proposed construction of a multisport stadium near the projects. The local Catholic church had approached me on the premise that it wanted to build the stadium and name it for Josh, which was only appropriate in light of the overwhelming influence he'd exerted on youth sports in that neighborhood. I went to several meetings and assisted the effort in ways that I could, only to find out that I was being counted on to raise all the money for the endowment. As I saw it, the church had used Josh's name in order to capitalize on me and the black community. When I understood what was going on—that *we*, not the church, would actually be building the stadium—I excused myself from the project, which of course never came off.

I was offended at being misled and taken advantage of in the manner that I was, but on the other hand I would have liked very much to leave a monument to Josh. He died in 1982, and at the time he did, our relationship was not indicative of what we had meant to each other over the years. Having become strained when I attained success as a major-leaguer, it never really improved. When I was inducted into the Hall of Fame in 1981, the great moment was accompanied by two regrets: that I neglected to recognize August Busch in the course of my impromptu speech, and that Josh was not there. He refused to attend on the terms that I thought were appropriate—that I would foot the bill for my sisters to get to Cooperstown but my brothers would be on their own. The Gibsons are a stubborn breed, and sometimes we pay the price. In a way, I'm still paying for that one.

My election to the Hall of Fame had come on the first ballot, a distinction about which I was uncertain going in due to my cool relationship with the press. I was the only modern player elected that year, outpolling what I considered to be a hell of a group—in order of votes: Don Drysdale, Gil Hodges, Harmon Killebrew, Hoyt Wilhelm, Juan Marichal, Nellie Fox, Red Schoendienst, Jim Bunning, Maury Wills, Richie Ashburn, Roger Maris, Harvey Kuenn, Elston Howard, and Orlando Cepeda. Five of them (Drysdale, Killebrew, Wilhelm, Marichal, and Schoendienst) eventually made it in, and I can attest to the qualifications of Bunning, Wills, Ashburn, Maris, and of course Cepeda.

I was the eleventh player to be elected in the first year of eligibility and the sixth pitcher, following Walter Johnson, Christy Mathewson, Bob Feller, Warren Spahn, and Sandy Koufax. Although I've never been a student of baseball history (part of the reason being that, prior to my time, most of baseball history excluded blacks), I knew enough to be flattered by the company I was joining. The whole business was literally beyond my most daring dreams as an undersized kid in the Logan Fontenelle projects. And as if the induction was not enough, Omaha marked the occasion with another Bob Gibson Day.

When I arrived at Cooperstown's venerable Otesaga Hotel, I had a telegram awaiting (one of many, actually, but the most memorable of them) from my friend and boss with the Mets, Joe Torre. "Congratulations," it said, "on being the first attitude coach elected to the Hall of Fame." Notwithstanding my carefully cultivated cynicism and a few smart-asses like Torre, I checked in determined to make the Hall of Fame weekend one of the happiest times of my life. Josh's absence and my faux pas with Mr. Busch compromised that ambition quite a bit, but otherwise I was undaunted—even when fans lined up outside the snow fences to boo baseball for the player strike that had split the 1981 season (actually, a settlement had been reached by that time and the second half of the schedule was to begin in a matter of days).

When my day in the sun arrived, I proudly received baseball's highest honor along with two players elected by the Veterans Committee, former Cardinal first baseman Johnny Mize and Negro League pioneer and pitcher Rube Foster. After Mize and Foster's son spoke, Bowie Kuhn, the embattled (by the strike, among other things) commissioner, introduced me as "the most competitive athlete I have ever seen in sports," which I appreciated. That was the theme I intended to emphasize in my own remarks, delivered without the benefit of notes.

Entering the Hall of Fame, I said nervously, was certainly a thrill but "there's nothing like winning the last game of the World Series." By that, I meant not to diminish the occasion—as I had managed so often to do in the process of receiving awards and honors—but to call attention to competition as the thing that drove and defined me. "I want to leave you with this one thought," I concluded. "A writer asked me a few days ago how I'd want to be remembered. I said I want to be remembered as a competitor who gave a hundred percent every time I went out onto the field. Sometimes I wasn't too good, but nobody could accuse me of cheating them out of what they paid to see."

I was still pumped up afterwards when the Cardinals' announcer, Jack Buck, called me aside to inform me, grimly, that I had failed to make note of Gussie Busch in the audience. My reaction was, "Oh, shit." I had also left Bing Devine out of my acknowledgments, which was another terrible oversight, but I knew immediately that my big mistake was offending Mr. Busch. Actually, as I understood it, he was more hurt than offended. I certainly understood why—he had gone out of his way many times to show his concern for me—and as soon as I got back to Omaha I rushed off a letter of apology to Mr. Busch, explaining that the omission was a result of my nervousness and perhaps unfortunate decision not to use notes. I also apologized publicly through the press. I have reason to believe, though, that my efforts at damage control, sincere as they were, proved to be inadequate.

It was after the 1981 season—my Hall of Fame summer and the one I spent on the staff of the Mets— that I had my first serious talks with the Cardinals since retiring as a player. My discussions were not with St. Louis directly, but rather with the Cardinals' Triple-A affiliate, the Louisville Redbirds, whose owner, A. Ray Smith, wanted me to be his manager. I'd been introduced to Smith at a banquet in 1980 and we'd had a long, cordial conversation. He had expressed an interest in hiring me and I had expressed a mutual interest, but the moment was not right for either of us. The situation would change a year later, by which time I'd put in a season with Torre and the Mets.

When Torre contacted me about a job in 1981, the Mets already had a pitching coach, a popular veteran named Rube Walker. Joe thought my hard-assed approach to the game would be an asset to the ballclub whether or not I was fussing with some rookie's pickoff move, so he came up with the position of "attitude coach." Nobody had ever heard of an attitude coach, and at the press conference announcing my hiring a New York writer asked me what it was. I replied, "Fuck you. That's an attitude coach."

My role with the Mets was something of a curiosity around the league. I was interviewed by writers in many cities the first time the Mets stopped there in the '81 season. Without having the pressure and mental preparation of pitching to deal with, I was more relaxed and sociable toward the media—with at least one exception. That was when we were in Philadelphia and I happened to notice a writer named Stan Hochman in the crowd. Many years before, I had often bantered with Hochman about the merits of Dick (or Richie, as he was known then) Allen. As you might imagine, I was Allen's defender and Hochman was his critic, but I always thought our arguments were friendly and had no real problems with Hochman until about 1971, when Bill White sent me clippings of articles in which Hochman had brutally criticized the book written by my wife, Charline. The next time I saw him, I told Hochman that I would never give him another interview. A year later, a cluster of writers cornered me one evening in Philadelphia to talk about the no-hitter I'd pitched the week before in Pittsburgh, and as I was answering their questions I spotted Hochman in the back of the group. "I'll be glad to talk to you guys," I said, "but one of you knows that I promised I would never talk to him again. And so I won't continue until you [I was looking straight at Hochman by this time] leave." He left, and that was that—until 1981, when I was coaching for the Mets and he came up to me and asked me a question about Pete Rose. When I paused, he looked at me and said, "Ten years is a long time to carry that thing around, isn't it?" I said, "I told you that you wouldn't ever interview me again, and you won't." Forgiveness about a thing like that is not my strong suit, but my word is pretty damn good.

The Mets were in a state of transition when I joined them, having just been sold to Fred Wilpon and Nelson Doubleday at the highest price ever paid for a baseball franchise. Frank Cashen was named general manager, and with all the administrative changes it seemed that Torre did not have the full support of the front office. Our jobs were complicated by the fact that Cashen advised Torre and me to concern ourselves less with the pennant races (there was one in each half of the split season) and more with the future of the club—this, despite the fact that we were well within reach of first place during the second half, ultimately finishing only 5½ games behind Montreal. Cashen's order was particularly confusing to me, since I was there to teach *winning*. As it turned out, my role became largely one of a counselor for the likes of our two talented relief pitchers, Neil Allen and Jeff Reardon, both of whom were having difficulty dealing with their identities on the team as well as their working relationship with each other (in a nutshell, Reardon thought he was deserving of Allen's role as closer). But while Joe and I were trying to build the basis of a ballclub, others in the organization were angling for their own futures. When the maneuvering was over on the last day of the season, Torre had been fired and all of the coaches sent off with him.

Five days later, Ted Turner hired Joe to manage the Atlanta Braves. Torre and I were in touch and I knew that a job with the Braves was an option for me, but I was intrigued by the prospect being presented by A. Ray Smith in Louisville.

I had never considered myself the manager type because it was not my nature to kibbitz with the press and answer dumb questions as to why I had made a particular move at a particular time. But I liked Smith, who impressed me as a very dynamic man, and the idea of returning to the Cardinal organization sounded awfully good. We agreed that I would manage the Louisville team in 1982, subject to the approval of the St. Louis front office. Smith told me he would contact St. Louis and then get back to me. A week later, he called to tell me that the Cardinals had denied the approval. I never heard a reason why.

When the job with the Cardinals fell apart, the one with the Braves came through, thanks again to Joe Torre. George Steinbrenner also offered me a position with the Yankees as a minor-league pitching instructor, and I was tempted by the fact that the Yankee general manager was Bill Bergesch, who had signed me to my first Cardinal contract, but I had become loyal to Joe. This time, he hired me as a pitching coach, although he also brought Rube Walker with him. We divided up the duties to everybody's satisfaction—mine included being a lieutenant, more or less, to Torre—and went about the task of rebuilding a team that hadn't remotely challenged for a pennant since 1969, when Hank Aaron and Orlando Cepeda played for the Braves.

When we got to know the Atlanta players, it became obvious that they could hit and run and throw but were sorely lacking a sense of competitiveness—a malady that tends to set in when a club spends season after season in the second division. Ted Turner treated them so well—there was a country-club atmosphere on the team—that losing didn't seem to bother the Braves. The players seemed to think that everything was hunky-dory as long as they kept breathing. With the pitchers, the indifference toward winning showed up in the fact that so few of them would pitch with pain. My job was to point out the difference between pain, which can be pitched with, and injury, which can't.

The Braves proved, by and large, to be a willing group. They were provided with leadership from Chris Chambliss and Phil Niekro and power from Dale Murphy and Bob Horner. As the season progressed, even the young pitchers gradually seemed to catch on. On a particular occasion, when one of our inexperienced guys hit a wild streak and suddenly started throwing strikes after I visited the mound, the reporters asked me afterwards what advice I'd given him. "Not much," I said. "I just tried to get him to loosen up and relax. I told him that if there weren't fifteen thousand people watching, I'd hit him in the head."

One of my better pupils in Atlanta—or maybe I should say a typical one—was Bob Walk, for whom I had some words of wisdom early in the season. I told him that when he was facing singles hitters, he should throw the ball hard and outside and let them hit it as far as they could. Most of the time, they'd send high easy flies to the outfield. I went on to say that if he didn't worry about striking out the smaller guys and let them hit fly balls, he would save his strength for when he needed it against the big guys. He kind of listened and grunted, like most of the pitchers did. Then, late in the season, he came to me one day and said, "You know, Bob, I figured something out. If I just throw my good hard stuff outside to the little guys, they'll hit fly balls to the outfield." I looked at him and said, "That's good, Bob. That's real smart."

There were times in 1982, when I realized how much the players had changed in the short time since I had retired and how inattentive they had become to the ways of winning, I actually thought that I could still go out and pitch effectively at the age of forty-six. My arm was up to it, and I really believed that if my legs permitted, I could hold off most of the teams in the league for five or six innings. I often pitched batting practice to the Braves, and in doing so I saw nothing that revised my opinion.

> *Brett Butler was with us when we came over to Atlanta, and I recall when we were on the road in Houston one time and I wanted some of the guys to get some good batting practice, simulating game conditions. Brett hadn't played much, and he wanted it. I asked Bob to pitch for us. I don't know how long he threw to But-*

*ler, but Brett didn't get a ball out of the cage against Gibson. It wasn't fair. We probably should have had someone else throwing BP at Brett for ten minutes or so to get him loose before he had to face Bob, but we put him right in the cage and I mean he was lit-*erally *in the cage. He couldn't get the ball out of there. Afterwards, he approached Gibson and said, "Were you trying to show me up?" Bob told him that he was just trying to give him game con-ditions, but Brett still thought he was being shown up. Bob was that good.*        —JOE TORRE

I enjoyed throwing to the hitters because it felt a little bit like pitching, for one thing, but also for the workout. An athlete, even an aching, retired one, never loses the urge to push and challenge his body. It felt good to grunt and sweat. One hot day, I was out there so long, sweating so much, that I drank a hell of a lot of water without going to the bathroom. After a couple of hours like that, I bet one of our outfielders, Terry Harper, that I could pee a pound. Of course he didn't believe me. So we went into the clubhouse and I got on the scale. It said 210. Then I stood over the urinal for a while and came out and weighed again. The scale said 208½. Harper couldn't believe it. "Goddamn!" he screamed. "Gibson peed a pound! Gibson peed a pound!" For a few minutes, I was a hero again.

That summer, though, the Atlanta clubhouse was full of heroes. Practically overnight, the chronically mediocre Braves had turned things around and put themselves in position to win the National League West. Dale Murphy's 109 RBIs had a lot to do with it, as did Niekro's 17–4 record, but I can't let it go at that without giving credit to Torre, whose prospects had not been especially promising when he took the job. I did my part by pacing up and down the dugout and yelling at the players, much like I'd done in St. Louis on the days I wasn't pitching. When we hustled and played well, I was everybody's biggest fan, and when we didn't, I would say, "You guys are losers. Give me a Dodger (or a Cub or Pirate) uniform, because I'm going to the other side where they know how to win!" Now and then I came up with the other team's uniform from the clubhouse and took the bit a step further.

The race went down to the last weekend of the season with our guys holding a precarious lead over the Dodgers and Giants, who were playing each other. We were down the coast in San Diego, and by Sunday all we had to do was win one more game to take the division.

> *Bob and I were sitting around in the stadium on the morning before the last game at San Diego because we normally didn't take batting practice on Sundays. We were talking about the game ahead of us—one game for all the marbles—and I said to Bob, "You know, if I could have just one wish, I'd wish I could give you the ball today. I'd take my chances if you had the ball and went out there right now." I was dead serious. Well, about five minutes later Ted Turner walked in and I told him exactly what I'd said to Bob. When he heard that, Ted got all excited. He said, "Can we do it? Is it possible?" He was ready to sign Bob to a one-game contract right on the spot. I told him it wasn't legal, but he said, "Aw, come on, there's gotta be a way." If we could have gotten away with it, I absolutely would have started Gibson that day. He was still throwing close to ninety miles an hour, and he was still Bob Gibson. I didn't care how old he was: When you talk about a pitcher for one game, you're talking about Bob Gibson.*
> —Joe Torre

When Sunday was over we had won the pennant by one game, only to lose to the Cardinals, of all teams, in the divisional playoffs. October that year marked the first and only Cardinal world championship since 1967. In many ways, it hurt that I could not be a part of the St. Louis organization in its return to the top, but on the other hand I was enthused about what was happening in Atlanta and privileged to be working with a man and manager like Torre. Based on what we accomplished in 1982, we had reason to believe we would be back in the playoffs very soon.

It didn't work out in 1983, though, as the Dodgers beat us by three games. When it became apparent that we might not repeat as division champions, I began to see evidence of the same pattern that had developed in St. Louis in the late sixties, by which high expectations lead to a ballclub's undoing. There was rumbling in the press, dissatisfaction in the front office, and tension in the dugout.

Under that sort of pressure, people tend to do and say things they may later regret, which was the case when Dal Maxvill and I had a disagreement during one of the Braves' games. Maxvill had been a resourceful, independent-minded player with the Cardinals—a Cardinal kind of player—and when Torre got the Atlanta managing job he wanted Maxie in his corner as third-base coach. I had always gotten along fine with Maxvill, mainly because I respected his work ethic and loved his glove behind me at shortstop. However, being on the same coaching staff fostered different dynamics, inherently more political, and although there had never been any significant amount of friction between Maxie and me, it became apparent one day that we were not exactly on the same page. The situation boiled over when Claudell Washington, one of our outfielders, hit into a double play on which Maxvill thought he hadn't run hard enough to first base. The play ended the inning, and as Washington took his place in right field Maxie, in the dugout, called him a "jaking son of a bitch." That sent me over the edge because I believed it to be incorrect and because it was an opinion that should not have been shared with Claudell's teammates even if it were accurate. So I told Maxie that. I said, "Man, you fucked up! If there's anybody on this ballclub who hustles, it's Claudell." A little while later, Maxvill came over to me and said I shouldn't have stood him up in front of the players that way. I told him he shouldn't have criticized Claudell in front of the players that way. We left it at that, but as the game went on and I thought about it, I realized I owed Maxie an apology. I still thought he was dead wrong, but rather than making the same mistake he did, I should have waited and told him about it later instead of jumping him in the dugout. So an inning or so later I walked over and started to apologize. Maxie said, "Fuck you." I called him a cocksucker and at that point we went our separate ways.

By 1984, it seemed that nearly everybody in the organization was going separate ways. We finished in second place again, tied with Houston but a dozen games behind San Diego. Our decline was blamed in large part on the loss of Phil Niekro to free agency (and the Yankees), and the loss of

Niekro was blamed in large part on me. Although I had no decision-making power in the organization, I had been of the opinion that our talented young pitchers would be more of an asset to the ballclub than Niekro at age forty-five. I certainly believed in an organization's loyalty to its cornerstone players—Lord knows I'd been down that road with the Cardinals—but at some point, loyalty steps aside and good judgment takes over. It turned out that Niekro did have some good pitching left in him and he still could have been valuable to the Braves, but in his absence younger arms like Rick Mahler's and Pascual Perez's came along nicely and our team earned run average actually improved. I received some credit for the emergence of Perez and also that of reliever Donnie Moore, but the Niekro affair had made me an unpopular figure in town and in certain parts of the front office.

It was obvious that I was not long for Atlanta—and neither were Torre and most of his assistants—when Joe and I and two other coaches, Rube Walker and Joe Pignatano, arrived at the stadium from the golf course one day to find that Ted Turner had held a team meeting without us. From that moment on, it became a matter of finishing out the season and not missing any paydays. The general spirit of resignation on the team was probably best demonstrated when Steve Bedrosian, one of our top relief pitchers, asked if he could pass up the last road trip of the season because his dog was being operated on. Torre told him he was out of his fucking mind.

Even after the second time, I couldn't get accustomed to the experience of being fired and I had no interest in taking it well. It would be dishonest to say that I didn't enjoy watching the Braves fall to fifth place in 1985. They didn't finish any higher than that until 1991. I would occasionally bump into some of the Atlanta players whom I liked and knew I could agitate, such as Bruce Benedict, the catcher, and always took the opportunity to say things such as, "I saw where you guys won one in a row and it really pissed me off." It may have sounded vindictive, but it was.

Unable to keep my career alive like so many of the tobacco-spitters on the old-boy network, who seem to get hired every time they're fired, I haven't had a job in baseball since then. I've had jobs *around* baseball—specifically, in broadcasting—but I haven't been offered a job by a major-league team in more than ten years. I really thought my luck would change after Al Campanis made his ill-fated remarks on *Nightline* in 1987, saying that blacks "may not have the necessities" to serve in high-level baseball positions (and, as an example of the differences between the races, pointing to the fact that many blacks can't swim). As Ted Koppel was conducting the Campanis interview, Torre phoned me and said, "Bobby, turn on *Nightline* and watch Al Campanis fire himself." I wasn't offended by what Campanis said because I can swim pretty well. Actually, I suggested at the time that we ought to give him some sort of award for bringing a bad situation to light. He simply articulated a school of thought that had been operating within baseball circles for generations. The only difference this time was that the press and public were brought into the loop and suddenly it became an important issue.

The Campanis stir made a difference for many former black players, but when my status remained unchanged I had to wonder what was going on. No doubt there have been personal considerations working against me—my past, my reputation, my relationships, etc.—but there is also the matter of baseball's bias against superstars (I hate to use that term in reference to myself but need to for the purposes of this discussion) as coaches and managers. I've always been perplexed by the theory that former superstars can't work with average players because things came easy for them or because they were not students of the game. That's a blatant myth, in my estimation. How could a man like Willie Mays or Mickey Mantle *not* benefit a ballclub on the field or in the front office? To reach the level of a superstar, a player has to have an understanding of the game and its craft at the expert level; excellence is not an accident. In addition, young players look up to men who have accomplished great things. Most important, superstars are winners and winning is contagious. I really believe that coaches coach attitude more than anything else. If you examine great players, you'll find something in each of their psyches that makes them great, and that sort of thing—that attitude, that aura—rubs off. It seems to me that the people who say superstars can't be coaches and managers are the guys who were never worth a shit.

One of the clichés about great players as coaches is that they become impatient with lesser, ordinary players—as if Hall of Famers have a corner on impatience. That label attached itself to me when I coached with the Braves, and while it is true that I have little tolerance for those who aren't interested in competing at a higher level, my attitude has nothing to do with a player's level of skill.

> *It was reported in Atlanta that Bob had difficulty with guys if they weren't prepared to challenge people. Bob was a power pitcher, and his thinking is inherently to support that type of approach. But do you mean to tell me that a man as smart as Bob Gibson wouldn't adjust if the situation called for it? I'm telling you, he would adjust. He belongs in baseball—working—and it's a shame he isn't. It's a blemish on baseball that he isn't.*
> —BING DEVINE,
> *former Cardinal general manager*

I've had my share of opportunities in the broadcasting field, where Hall of Famers get a better shake, but have never really found a niche. The year after I retired as a player, I secured my first national job as a color commentator for ABC on its short-lived Monday night baseball telecast. I worked alongside former Detroit Tiger Norm Cash and play-by-play announcer Al Michaels, and for the most part the reviews—of both the telecast and me—were favorable. For my purposes, however, all of that came undone on the night in 1976 when John Candelaria pitched a no-hitter for the Pirates at Three Rivers Stadium. Having done the same thing in the same place four years earlier, I was asked on the spot to interview Candelaria, an assignment for which I was unprepared. I stayed with ABC for one more season after that regrettable night, but then the gig was up.

In 1978, I worked for a year with Len Berman on an HBO series about baseball and then did some basketball commentary for WTBS while I coached in Atlanta. When I was fired by the Braves, I contacted KMOX radio in St. Louis, which aired the Cardinal broadcasts, about the possibility of a full-time position. What developed instead was a talk show I did out of my house in Omaha with Dan Dierdorf of the football Cardinals (and later *Monday Night Football*), who was at the studio in St. Louis. It went over very well for all concerned, and the next spring I was hired by KMOX to conduct a preview show before every game and a call-in show afterward. The new job started with spring training in St. Petersburg, where KMOX rented a house from which I did the nightly talk show. After each show I would take a long walk, reflecting and asking myself questions about where my life was headed. I seemed to sense that my separation from baseball might be long-term.

The KMOX job was not unpleasant, however. I especially enjoyed the rain delays, when I would slip over to the booth and swap stories with Shannon and whatever former ballplayers were handy. The night with Don Drysdale stands out in my mind, each of us accusing the other of being the nastiest pitcher to come down the pike. The St. Louis audience seemed to appreciate our reminiscences, and my talk shows were also highly rated (although they were not my favorite thing; I wasn't enchanted with the zillion callers who always wanted to trade two of the Cardinals' reserve infielders for Don Mattingly). I stayed with the St. Louis broadcasting crew for five years, airing some of my best shows from Mike Shannon's restaurant in the shadow of Busch Stadium. The last season, 1989, I announced on both radio and cable TV, but then, needing to pick up the pace, I accepted an offer to do color commentary for baseball games on ESPN in 1990. I would have renewed the agreement for 1991 except that the station wanted me to be on call for four games a week, which would have meant about six days a week away from my family. That was too much. The ESPN experience was generally a good one (I got a kick out of all the complaining that goes on there; compared to those guys, I'm Ernie Banks), but it left me with the opinion that my best arrangement as a broadcaster would be to do color commentary for one team, which would enable Wendy and Chris to stay with me, wherever it would be, for half the summer. I applied for the color job with the Colorado Rockies when they started up in 1993 but was not granted an interview.

Meanwhile, the scenario I foresaw on those long walks in St. Petersburg has come to pass. I haven't done a lot of knocking on doors around the major leagues, but since foiling my managing job with A. Ray Smith, the Cardinals have rejected me three more times over the years. On one occasion, I spoke about a position with Whitey Herzog, who was both the manager and general manager of the club, but he never got back to me with an answer. (It was reported that Whitey had offered me a job and I'd turned it down, but that wasn't the case.) Then, when the Cardinals plucked Dal Maxvill out of the third-base coach's box in Atlanta and made him the general manager, I let Maxie know I'd be happy to take anything the organization had to offer, even scouting. He told me the team didn't have any openings in the scouting department. Ten days later he hired Rube Walker as a scout.

There is no shortage of speculation as to why things haven't worked out between me and the ballclub I played so long for. The most familiar explanation is that I'm hard to get along with. In that context, I recall one Cardinal executive inquiring if I had changed my attitude since I quit playing (although I don't recall many Cardinal executives questioning my attitude when I was winning twenty games nearly every year). Another common criticism is that I never say the right thing, which is the sort of observation that seems to apply mainly to black people. Whites who speak out are outspoken; blacks who do the same thing are uppity and have a serious attitude problem.

Although it is not among the more popular theories concerning my estrangement with St. Louis, I suppose the August Busch incident at Cooperstown might also offer a clue to the riddle. And I suppose my squabble with Maxvill in Atlanta could factor in. (I'm aware that the story has made the rounds of the Cardinal offices. When I interviewed with Fred Kuhlmann, the Cardinals' chief operating officer, about a job on Torre's staff, he asked me directly, "How do you get along with Maxvill?" I said, "Fine, as far as I know.") There may be one person in the organization standing in my way; there may be several. There may be sound, objective reasons why the Cardinals don't want me around; there may be misguided, personal motives. I just don't know.

> *I really believe there are people in baseball, former teammates of Gibson, who resented his stardom, his fame. You have to realize that Bob Gibson was one of the first blacks to command the type of press coverage that would eventually boom in recent years. Suddenly at World Series time, we were swarmed with reporters and the electronic media, and all of a sudden, Gibson's teammates*

*were seeing Gibson front and center. In my mind, those team-*
*mates who were brought to the title room by Gibson and now are*
*in positions of power in baseball resented Gibson for his very tal-*
*ent. I honestly believe that some of the guys who are in positions of*
*power were determined to leave Gibson out if the tables were ever*
*turned. In baseball's politics, the tables certainly are turned.*
—CURT FLOOD

I'm not too proud to say that my relationship with the Cardinals bothers me on at least two counts. One is that I love baseball. (I guess baseball gets into your blood. Strange as it sounds, twice a week or so I still dream that I'm playing the game. In the dreams, it's always before a game, on the bus or in the clubhouse, and I'm supposed to pitch that day. Sometimes I'm in my Cardinal uniform. But I never get around to actually throwing the ball.)

The other reason is more practical. I was never a young man when I wasn't a Cardinal. When I made my career choice, it was to join the St. Louis baseball organization; and now, having followed that choice, I am without a career. To support my family and retain my self-respect, I need a career. I need to work. When I'm not working, I'm not satisfied. I'm restless, unfulfilled, even nervous. As a pitcher, I experienced a hell of a lot of pressure and thrived on it, but even then—even in the heat of the pennant race, and in the ninth inning of the seventh game of the World Series—I never felt stress that was anything like the stress I feel now trying to earn a living for my family. It's an anxiety that doesn't ever really go away, and it's compounded by the fact that it doesn't make any apparent sense.

On that score, I appreciated the item that Murray Chass of *The New York Times* printed in his baseball column in 1993. "After languishing among the unemployed for a few years," Chass wrote, "Dallas Green and Davey Johnson were named managers earlier this season. Bob Gibson, on the other hand, is in his ninth year as an unemployed baseball person.

'Gibson, who last week was honorary captain of the National League All-Star team, was asked why no one has hired him since his four-year tenure as a pitching coach with the Mets and the Atlanta Braves. He was the wrong person to ask, he suggested. Only the people who haven't hired him would know the answer.

" 'Obviously, there aren't enough jobs,' the Hall of Fame pitcher said. 'As soon as one is available, I'm sure I'll get one.'

"Baseball deserves the sarcasm. There aren't enough jobs available to hire every former player who wants to stay in the game, but as poor as the quality of pitching has become, this is one former pitcher who could add knowledge and attitude to any staff."

The only major-league job I was considered for in recent seasons originated with Bill White in his role as president of the National League. White was interested in hiring me before the 1992 season to oversee the National League umpires, but of course he needed input from the owners before making such an appointment. When he conferred with Fred Kuhlmann of the Cardinals, Kuhlmann told him to hold off because the Cardinals were staging a big bash that summer to commemorate their one-hundredth anniversary and they had something in mind for me. As it turned out, the centennial was a very nice affair, but I didn't do shit for it. I mean, I was there, along with dozens of other players, but all I did was say a few words to the crowd at Busch Stadium.

I reminisced a little about the sixties, and then I said, "You know, baseball has changed so much from the days we played that I'm fast becoming a stranger to the game."

# CHAPTER XIII

We came damn close to starting a new baseball league in 1990. It would have been called the Baseball League, and it would have been made possible by virtue of the problems major-league baseball was having with free agency.

The group behind the Baseball League was organized by Richard Moss, who had been assistant director of the major-league players' union when Marvin Miller was in charge of it. Moss correctly anticipated that the collusion cases being heard at the time (in which the owners were charged with conspiring to manipulate the marketplace) would result in many big-name free agents being liberated from their contracts and set loose to make another deal. We figured that if the Baseball League could get its stuff together by the time those players became available, we would have a large talent pool with which to build our foundation. To that end, the Baseball League had franchises lined up in Denver, Miami, Charlotte, Vancouver, and Portland, along with traditional major-league cities like Los Angeles and New York.

Donald Trump was to head up the New York franchise, which would more or less be the flagship of the new league. The plan called for Trump to sign pitcher Ben McDonald out of LSU, acing the major leagues out of the player who was considered the best prospect in the upcoming draft. McDonald, like all of the Baseball League players, would commit to a long-term contract (although I believe long-term contracts are harmful to baseball, they were necessary for the stability of an upstart league). We would make big money available to him and the top free agents but would avert the free-agency problems that plagued major-league baseball by instituting a salary cap for all franchises and revenue sharing to help out the smaller ones.

As the agenda for the new league came together, it seemed for a time that I might be named commissioner. It was apparent at the meetings, though, that my presence was only incidental; the owners paid almost no attention whatsoever to me or my ideas. The implications of race certainly came to mind, and I thought, "Oh, shit. Here we go again. Are we still fighting this battle?" That disappointment notwithstanding, the prospects of the new league were exciting and I wanted to be part of it. Ultimately, the role settled upon for me was second in command, in charge of on-field activities, player development, and minor-league administration. That was fine.

We were close to a deal with McDonald when circumstances out of our control collaborated to blow us out of the water. CBS-TV, which had just lost its contract with the National Basketball Association, was desperate to broadcast baseball and paid an unexpected windfall of $1.06 billion for the rights. The result was that the major-league owners suddenly had a mountain of capital available to sign whoever they wanted to sign. With that grim reality staring them in the face, the owners of the Baseball league had no choice but to throw in their cards. The moment had passed.

It was a pity, really—not just for me but for the game of baseball and its fans. As I viewed it, free agency had briefly opened the window for a new league but the real reason we had a chance was that people missed the game they had grown up with and loved. Major-league baseball was—and is—no longer that game.

What it lacks these days is the competitiveness that baseball used to be all about. Small, subtle changes have piled up to the point that the game has been basically redefined. To wit, the changes that were implemented after the pitchers' season of 1968—i.e., the lowered mound, the revised strike zone, and the umpires' crackdown on brushback pitches—have since been accompanied by additional developments and trends that have greatly expanded their influence. I have no problem with ballplayers making all the money they can make and don't really bemoan the fact that I missed out on the really big bucks, but I recognize, on the other hand, that runaway salaries have drastically altered the game we once had.

By looking closely at just one issue—pitching inside—it can be easily perceived how financial considerations have dominated the scene. Owners are against inside pitches because they threaten to nick their million-dollar investments. The whim of the owners of course trickles down to the umpires, whose warnings to pitchers lead the batters to believe that they are well protected at the plate. Nowadays, the umpires can eject a pitcher for throwing at a batter even *without* warning him first. All of this not only gives the hitters a false sense of security—accidents happen—but makes them indignant and ready to fight if a pitch merely *sounds* too close. Some of the pitches that are starting fights these days are only three or four inches off the plate. A few years ago, Kevin Mitchell of the Giants charged the mound after Bruce Hurst of the Padres hit him *in the foot* with a pitch that first *bounced in the dirt*. What the hell?

Of course, that wouldn't have happened if Mitchell and Hurst had been represented by the same agent. The salary explosion has led directly to the proliferation of agents, any one of whom may have a dozen or more major-league clients. Some of the clients, in turn, become fast friends who wouldn't think of throwing fastballs in the vicinity of each other's gold-plated body parts. Dollar-driven motives have become so deep-seated in baseball that they have established a whole new consciousness. Pitchers, on the whole, are so reluctant now to brush hitters back—reluctant even to defend their teammates—that many hitters, on the rare occasions they are knocked down or pitched tight, feel their only recourse is to charge the mound. To avoid this, the pitchers keep the ball away from the hitters and the hitters take their whacks and the battle between them becomes less and less compelling as the cycle plays on and the years pass. (There are many other factors in this trend that I have not mentioned. For instance, aluminum bats, which are now used in all levels of amateur baseball, have deprived the pitcher of one more good reason to throw inside, that being the capacity to break off a batter's bat. The American League designated hitter rule has also played a part in the new order. Because the pitchers never come to the plate to face the music, the only way to get to retaliate against them for pitching inside is to take up the issue in person at the mound.)

In the sixties, pitching inside not only created much of the drama that made the games so interesting, but also helped foster some of baseball's best characters. Stan Williams of the Dodgers, for example, would have been a good but not a memorable pitcher if he hadn't been so damn creative about throwing at people. It's said (which doesn't make it true) that Williams kept a list of every pitcher who had ever hit him. It would have been a sizable list, because there was a lot of retaliating to do in Williams's case. After being traded late in his career, he was allegedly pitching batting practice for his new team during a spring training workout when he suddenly drilled one of the veteran pitchers, who slowly pieced himself together and then asked Williams what the hell he was doing. Williams explained, "You were the last one on my list."

It would seem to me that the developments of the past twenty years have made that sort of ballplayer an endangered species. Players under long, huge contracts are naturally not as hungry as those struggling to carve out a niche, and with few exceptions—the exceptions are generally the superstars—a comfortable player is not one who will do anything to get an edge and win a ballgame. I believe that this condition, so painfully prevalent in today's game, results not only from the dollar figures the players are making but from the security of long-term contracts. In all my seventeen years of pitching, I never had a contract for more than a season and never wanted one. I knew what it would do to me. The numbers show that a player with a long-term contract will, as a rule, do well in the first season or two of the contract, fade in the middle, and rally as he nears renegotiation or free agency. More devastating is the effect of a long contract on the player's willingness to stay in the lineup with bumps and bruises. In the first ten years of free agency, players with multiyear contracts spent 50 percent more time on the DL than those with one-year contracts. These days, there are more players on the disabled list in one month than there were in an entire season twenty years ago. With the advances in training techniques and equipment, it's hard to imagine that more players are actually getting hurt than before. Obviously, the change is within the ballplayer. It has a lot to do with his comfort level and also results in part from the advice he is getting from his agent, many of whom, perhaps to protect their own investments, tell their clients not to step onto the field at less than a hundred percent. Meanwhile the ballclub, fearing a possible lawsuit in this age of attorneys, goes along. Hell, there wasn't a day in my career when I was a hundred percent.

Money changes everything, of course, but its impact on baseball goes all the way to the bone. There is so much of it at stake that it has redirected the evolution of the ballplayer. In my day, a player's improvement was often judged according to his skill at such things as hitting behind the runner and throwing to the right base—by his maturity in the context of the team. But a ground out that moves a runner to third is a hard thing to take to the negotiating table. It's not something an agent can work with. An agent needs statistics. He needs base hits and home runs and RBIs. And so the tying run is on second base with no outs in the ninth inning and the batter, thinking only of a base hit, flies out to left field instead of moving the runner along with a ground ball to the second baseman. That's *bad* baseball, but it's modern baseball. Why is a guy going to slide hard into second base to break up a double play if (1) there is no statistic for it and (2) it might get him hurt, in which case he would be unable to rack up any statistics at all for a while?

The most admirable players today are the ones who can overcome the modern bullshit and play hard. Among pitchers, the one who has most impressed me in the past ten years is Dwight Gooden. Before his injuries slowed him down, Gooden had incredible velocity but, more to the point, he knew how to pitch and compete. I was amazed by how complete a pitcher he was at the age of nineteen. When I was nineteen, I was still playing the outfield and catching because I didn't know enough about pitching to do it very well. By and large, young pitchers today have a better feel for the artistry of pitching than my contemporaries and I did, but most of them are hopelessly deficient in the methods and the mindset required to win.

It is no coincidence that Roger Clemens, who has been the most consistently effective pitcher of the past decade, approaches the game in the hard-nosed tradition familiar to my era. He is intimidated by neither the batters nor the umpires, and that fearlessness has done as much for him as his fastball. I've admired Clemens for as long as I remember him, although on that score he has pointed up a possible flaw in my memory. When he won his first Cy Young award Clemens said, somewhat angrily, that he had worked out for Torre and me in Atlanta as a high schooler and that we had refused to sign him. I'll take his word that I watched him throw—I don't recall it—and if so I must not have been overwhelmed or else I'd have a better recollection of what happened. But whatever took place, I can guarantee that I didn't have a thing to do with whether or not we signed Roger Clemens or any other player. I wish I'd had that kind of power.

In the same manner that Clemens's competitiveness has set him apart from other pitchers of his day, I believe that Nolan Ryan's much-acclaimed feats in his mid-forties were due not only to his remarkable physical skills—he had those in even greater supply when he was in his twenties—but to the fact that modern batters simply don't see many pitchers like him. Ryan didn't screw around with the hitter, didn't defer to him, didn't back off. He took charge of the game by competing with his opponents man to man. When he was on the mound Ryan seemed to be carrying the flag for the old days, and as noteworthy to me as his amazing strikeout totals and longevity was the reaction to him from the fans. They revered Ryan to the extent that they made an icon out of him nearly twenty years past his prime. That tells me more about the fans, and about baseball, than it does about Nolan Ryan.

Ryan's enormous popularity seemed to be indicative of a larger theme that has been emerging in recent years. The fans want more and more of that old-time baseball. The incredible success of Camden Yards in Baltimore is another example of the same thing. Now, every city craves an old-fashioned-style ballpark. They can't all have one, of course, but many teams—the Cardinals, the Braves, the Phillies, the Reds, and the Giants in the National League alone—have taken note of the trend and turned back the clock with uniforms patterned after those the players wore thirty or forty years ago. I'm convinced there's more at work here than nostalgia. I think a whole lot of people long for baseball to be the way it was.

These days, it seems that any new way to revisit baseball's past is a good way. Fantasy camps are another. People spend large amounts of money and vacation time to be on the ball field with guys from the sixties. We are badly out of shape and in no way resemble the athletes we were, but the customers take that into account and are still extremely satisfied. In my opinion, that's because, consciously or not, they think of us as *ballplayers* and apparently always will. I could be wrong, but I don't think they would feel that way about the modern players.

I've participated in several fantasy camps and actually carved out a little reputation at them. Most of it is based on falsehood, of course. There are all kinds of stories going around about how I nailed some fat old guy or another in the back, but I wouldn't do that. I might *threaten* to do it, but I wouldn't do it. Perhaps my friend Curt Flood gave these tales a little assist when some would-be young stud at one of the camps kept popping off that I wasn't so tough and Curt drew a bull's-eye on his shirt, which shut the guy up. Another fellow, a bank president from Florida who is a regular at the Cardinal camps, always tries to put fear into the hearts of newcomers by telling them, "Just wait till Gibson gets here. Just wait." All I have to do is squint and somehow another story starts making the rounds.

I don't usually crank up my arm too much at the fantasy camps, but now and then I have to rise to the occasion of a challenge. A guest at one of the camps was Bob Avellini, the former Chicago Bears quarterback (at the time, he was still active), who prided himself on being a pretty good hitter. I told him he might be right but he couldn't hit me if I didn't want him to. He told me he could hit anybody. There was only one way to settle it. He stepped up to the plate and I said, "Fastball." Strike one. I said, "Fastball." Strike two. I said, "Slider." Strike three. A while later, Avellini came up to me and said, "You know, I could have hit any of those pitches if they hadn't been *moving* that way."

Like fantasy camps, the Equitable and Upper Deck Old-Timers series have capitalized on the public's enchantment with players from the past. I participate in the charity games only because they support a good cause, the BAT foundation, which raises money for former players who need it. (BAT stands for Baseball Assistance Team; I'm on its board of directors, along with Warren Spahn, Larry Doby, and others.) Before BAT was brought into the picture, I had quit playing in old-timers' games for the simple reason that they are not for pitchers. Everybody wants to see if the old hitters can still hit, and the pitchers' job, as a result, is basically to throw batting practice. I may be fifty-eight years old, but I still have a hard time with the concept of *allowing*—hell, *encouraging*—somebody to beat me. Although I make an exception now for the charity affairs, my general rule of thumb is that there will be no more gift pitches to anyone under eighty-five.

When the occasion demands that I lob the ball up there, I often live to regret it. In one of my most recent games I floated one to Ellis Valentine, who was not yet forty years old, and he reciprocated with a shot off the side of my head. I was taken to the hospital, but there was no serious injury. I wasn't angry at Valentine, who called me several times in the hospital to make sure I was all right, but I will say this: If the batter expects the pitcher to make him look good, in return he has to pull the ball away from the middle of the field.

Because of their nature, at old-timers' games I enjoy taking my cuts much more than pitching. Hitting is an easier thing than it used to be, anyway, because of the pitching restrictions and also the livelier ball. The honchos in the commissioner's and league offices can keep denying that the ball has been juiced up, but I was taking batting practice before an Equitable game at Busch Stadium a few years ago and deposited one just under the stadium club in the upper deck. There's no way in hell I could have done that with the 1968 ball.

Although it's not my choice, nowadays a guy could practically make a career out of being an old-timer. On the other hand, I don't really *have* a choice; so between charity games, fantasy camps, and card shows, I'm away from home about as much as I care to be, if not more. Christopher is ten now, and it's important for me to know what's happening with him at school and on his baseball team. (I'm pleased that he likes playing ball but I don't expect him to take after me. When I told him he ought to be a pitcher because they make a lot of money, he said, "Yeah, Dad, and you get knees like yours.") I have to say, with regrets to my daughters, that

I'm a better father now than I was when they were growing up. I have time to be. I have time, for instance, to take my son and Wendy on camping trips and long, lazy boat rides up the Missouri River to as far away as Sioux City, Iowa, where we eat dinner and turn around. I had time to build Chris a room.

Of course, I also built a room onto Joe Torre's house in Atlanta. I'm a chronic builder. I built our bar in the basement as well as our sunroom, playroom, and wine cellar. When I'm not pounding on the house, I'm probably tinkering in my shop off the patio, putting together, among other things, model cars and radio-controlled helicopters and speedboats. All the while, I keep one eye on the soap operas I got hooked on as a ballplayer. Most of the rest of the time, I fool around with Chris or watch ballgames (all kinds) or cook (there's usually a friend or relative or both—most of my friends know most of my relatives—sitting around the kitchen) or hang out in our finished basement, where I keep my stereo system (heavy on Ray Charles, Frank Sinatra, Nat King Cole, and Aretha Franklin), my baseball photos (in addition to those of most of the five presidents I've met), and, under lock and key, my trophies and autographed baseballs from Hall of Famers (with apologies to DiMaggio and Aaron and the rest, the one I treasure most is the ball that Cy Young signed in 1908, which was sent to me after I won the Cy Young award in 1968 by a woman I didn't know).

It's a life that has practically all I could want except a job in baseball. What I most want is to make things better for my son, but I can't be assured that he will have a fair chance until I have one and Lou Brock has one and Curt Flood has one and so do all the former black players who have said they will take any job available. The question of opportunity goes beyond baseball, of course, but baseball is the world I belong to— or *did* belong to—and deal with. What I specifically have to deal with is the fact that baseball seems to want nothing to do with me because (a) I'm a black man, (b) I have an attitude, or (c) I'm a black man with an attitude. I'll take a wild stab at (c). I object to the attitude part of it because my demeanor as a ballplayer was affected mainly for professional considerations, but the reputation it engendered seems to haunt me all along the way. In fact, my reputation—my rap, more or less—is the demon I have to somehow pin down. The goddamn irony of it all is that the very things that made me the pitcher I was twenty-five years ago—my intensity and total devotion to the job (the effects of which made me nasty in the eyes of outsiders)—might, in a twisted way, be what is keeping me out of the game today.

No matter what I try or where I go, I can't seem to escape my reputation. I was at a banquet a while back, standing against a post outside with a glass of wine, when some man, a stranger, strolled up with his wife and said, "Honey, I want to introduce you to the meanest man who ever played baseball." He didn't intend any offense and laughed because he thought it was cute, but I thought, shit, what a hell of a way to introduce somebody. I was *not* the meanest man who ever played baseball; I was just a pitcher who took his work very seriously. Why is that such a difficult concept?

For the most part, my son is removed from all of this. He attends a good public school in a good neighborhood (when I was growing up in Omaha, Bellevue was the sticks—the place where we bought firecrackers after a half-day bike ride) and, except for our periodic and purposeful trips to the old ghetto, has no contact with the prejudice I encounter or the kind of poverty I grew up with. He has a great mother who doesn't have to work (although she does anyway, once a week) and good friends, one of whom vacations with us.

When the four of us travel—Chris and his buddy Zach and Wendy and I—people generally assume Chris to be my son and Zach to be Wendy's. It's not much of an issue, however, except occasionally, such as the time recently when we were camping in Montana. The people camping next to us apparently came from a very underprivileged background in terms of racial enlightenment. Another way to describe them would be "rednecks." At one point, Chris and Zach were playing catch between the campsites when one of the rednecks said to Zach, "Don't let that ball hit me, you little son of a bitch." Wendy heard what was said and naturally spoke up. With that, a fat woman at the other tent shouted, "Shut up, bitch, or I'll wipe this campground with you." It doesn't take much imagination to figure out why our lovely neighbors, paragons of racial purity, hated us so much. Fortunately, I was off seeing a man about a horse at the time and

Wendy was sensible enough to let the situation cool down before she told me about it.

Incidents like that notwithstanding, I've encountered hate with less frequency in recent years, and when I do it's often of a variety more difficult to decipher than that expressed by our Montana friends. I've found hate, on the whole, to be a very mysterious thing. It baffles me, for instance, that baseball would feel so antagonistic toward me as to keep me out of its ranks when all I ever did was try to play it to the best of my ability. I don't *know* that hate is the problem, but that's usually when it is. Until I find out for sure, all I can do is ask questions. Why have the game and I become strangers? Why does it keep me at such a distance? Why can't I drink out of its water fountain?

Even if I get some answers in the years ahead, I don't think I'll ever understand hate or the people who perpetuate it—those in business and perhaps in baseball who do it subtly, or the less refined types like the rednecks at the campground and the woman in the hamburger stand and the guy whose wife wouldn't wait for an autograph. She came up to me in a restaurant, while I was having a nice dinner with my wife and three or four other couples, and handed me a piece of paper to sign. That happens often, and the custom is to keep the paper, sign it privately, and pass it along later, thereby avoiding a procession at tableside. It's a pretty good system, but after I told this particular woman that I would drop off the autograph when I finished eating, the enraged husband barged over, cursed me for being too good to write my name for his wife, tore up the paper, and threw it in my plate. I suffered the incident in silence for about five minutes before walking across the restaurant and giving the bastard a piece of my mind. I told him what I'd like to do to him and his wife, and added that if they had kids, I'd kick their asses, too.

Another time I was on an airplane when a man stopped at my seat and said, "You're Bob Gibson, aren't you?" I said yes. He said, "Go to hell," and kept walking. I didn't even have a chance to find out what team he worked for.

# FOR THE BEST IN PAPERBACKS, LOOK FOR THE

In every corner of the world, on every subject under the sun, Penguin represents quality and variety—the very best in publishing today.

For complete information about books available from Penguin—including Puffins, Penguin Classics, and Arkana—and how to order them, write to us at the appropriate address below. Please note that for copyright reasons the selection of books varies from country to country.

**In the United Kingdom:** Please write to *Dept. JC, Penguin Books Ltd, FREEPOST, West Drayton, Middlesex UB7 0BR.*

If you have any difficulty in obtaining a title, please send your order with the correct money, plus ten percent for postage and packaging, to *P.O. Box No. 11, West Drayton, Middlesex UB7 0BR*

**In the United States:** Please write to *Consumer Sales, Penguin USA, P.O. Box 999, Dept. 17109, Bergenfield, New Jersey 07621-0120.* VISA and MasterCard holders call 1-800-253-6476 to order all Penguin titles

**In Canada:** Please write to *Penguin Books Canada Ltd, 10 Alcorn Avenue, Suite 300, Toronto, Ontario M4V 3B2*

**In Australia:** Please write to *Penguin Books Australia Ltd, P.O. Box 257, Ringwood, Victoria 3134*

**In New Zealand:** Please write to *Penguin Books (NZ) Ltd, Private Bag 102902, North Shore Mail Centre, Auckland 10*

**In India:** Please write to *Penguin Books India Pvt Ltd, 706 Eros Apartments, 56 Nehru Place, New Delhi 110 019*

**In the Netherlands:** Please write to *Penguin Books Netherlands bv, Postbus 3507, NL-1001 AH Amsterdam*

**In Germany:** Please write to *Penguin Books Deutschland GmbH, Metzlerstrasse 26, 60594 Frankfurt am Main*

**In Spain:** Please write to *Penguin Books S. A., Bravo Murillo 19, 1° B, 28015 Madrid*

**In Italy:** Please write to *Penguin Italia s.r.l., Via Felice Casati 20, I-20124 Milano*

**In France:** Please write to *Penguin France S. A., 17 rue Lejeune, F–31000 Toulouse*

**In Japan:** Please write to *Penguin Books Japan, Ishikiribashi Building, 2–5–4, Suido, Bunkyo-ku, Tokyo 112*

**In Greece:** Please write to *Penguin Hellas Ltd, Dimocritou 3, GR–106 71 Athens*

**In South Africa:** Please write to *Longman Penguin Southern Africa (Pty) Ltd, Private Bag X08, Bertsham 2013*